Human Development and Disparities

Dedicated to my political ideal

Smt. Mamata Banerjee

— Dr Anupam Hazra

Human Development and Disparities

Issues and Concerns for Northeast India

Edited by

Anupam Hazra
Member of Parliament

RAWAT PUBLICATIONS
Jaipur • New Delhi • Bangalore • Guwahati • Kolkata

ISBN 978-81-316-0844-9

Published by
Prem Rawat for **Rawat Publications**
Satyam Apts, Sector 3, Jawahar Nagar, Jaipur 302 004 (India)
Phone: 0141 265 1748 / 7006 Fax: 0141 265 1748
E-mail: info@rawatbooks.com
Website: www.rawatbooks.com

New Delhi Office
4858/24, Ansari Road, Daryaganj, New Delhi 110 002
Phone: 011 2326 3290

Also at *Bangalore, Guwahati* and *Kolkata*

Typeset by Rawat Computers, Jaipur
Printed and bound in India

"...Dear Babi Maa... whatever I am today, just because of you. I am blessed to have you as my parents...!!!"

—Anu

"... My dearest brother (Nirupam) ... you have always been the source of inspiration for my every academic venture...!!!"

—Dada

Contents

Contributors

Anupam Hazra is currently a Member of Parliament of the Sixteenth Lok Sabha from Bolpur constituency, West Bengal and also an Assistant Professor, Department of Social Work, Visva Bharati University, West Bengal.

Purusottam Nayak, Professor, Department of Economics & Dean, School of Economics, Management and Information Sciences, NEHU, Meghalaya.

S.M.I.A. Zaidi, Professor and Head, Department of Educational Planning, National University of Educational Planning and Administration, NUEPA.

Jayanta B. Sarma, MBBS, is Consultant Microbiologist, Northumbria Healthcare NHS Trust.

Walter Fernandez, Director, North Eastern Social Research Centre, Guwahati.

Bidisha Mahanta, Assistant Professor, Department of Economics at Doomdooma College (Assam).

Harendra Sinha, Associate Professor and Head, Department of Political Science, Government J. Buana College, Lunglei, Mizoram.

Polly Vauquline, Assistant Professor, Department of Women's Studies, Gauhati University.

Rituparna Bhattacharyya, Trustee/In-Charge of Training and Development, Alliance for Community Capacity Building in North-East India (UK Registered Charity).

N. Bhupendro Singh, Assistant Professor, Department of Humanities and Social Sciences, NIT Silchar.

Introduction

ANUPAM HAZRA

In an era when countries across the globe are obsessed with development, the issue of ensuring sustainable development is drawing prime attention of the academicians, development experts, researchers and policy-makers. Northeast India – comprising seven states namely Assam, Arunachal Pradesh, Manipur, Mizoram, Tripura, Nagaland and Meghalaya – is recognised to be a geographically isolated region, densely administered, sparsely populated, and the least developed region as compared to other states of India. An overall scenario of the region in the post-globalisation period is not very impressive as in the case of other regions of the Indian union. This may be attributed to the prevailing scenario of human development in the region and attitude of the Central Government in tackling the emerging issues and challenges in the sphere of human development of the Northeastern states. The unattended issues and problems of the past are being accumulated, multi-layered and have become multifarious. Over and above, the mounting pressures of emerging challenges for rapid transformation need to be countered. The clock is ticking fast and situation in the region is very delicate which may explode anytime from now if not tackled carefully. This edited volume, with its ten comprehensive chapters makes a concerted effort to explore some key areas' concerns in the context of attaining the long cherished goal of ensuring sustainable growth in the Northeastern region of India.

In the introductory chapter, Nayak provides a brief account of findings of various human development reports and studies undertaken by individual researchers on the states of Northeast India. The findings reveal that achievement of Northeastern region is quite satisfactory in comparison to all-India average achievements in some dimensions of human development but it has failed miserably in bringing commensurate economic growth and equitable distribution. There exists widespread disparity of socio-economic achievements across different states and within, from urban to rural areas and between males and females. If the problems of poor economic growth, poverty, gender disparity and general health of the people are not properly addressed the region may fall into the trap of vicious quadrant instead of moving to a virtuous one. The way out from this trap is through achievement of a productive, balanced and sustainable economy with appropriate intervention in health sector and poverty alleviation programmes.

Zaidi discusses in detail about various aspects of the development of elementary education in the Northeastern region of the country. The discussion covers all the eight states coming under the Northeastern region, namely Arunachal Pradesh, Assam, Manipur, Meghalaya, Mizoram, Nagaland, Sikkim and Tripura. The paper highlights the latest elementary education scenario in these states by presenting data on various items related to elementary education and also examines the problems faced by these states in the development of elementary education. The paper extensively uses the District Information System of Education (DISE) data published by NUEPA, to show the progress made on various parameters and indicators related to elementary education in this region. Data on access, enrollment and efficiency of elementary education system has been analysed by presenting state-wise scenario of all the eight Northeastern states.

The review by Sarma outlines the state of healthcare infrastructure and availability of services including key health indices, and sheds light on universal health coverage in the seven Northeastern states vis-à-vis national scenario using 2005 (the year National Rural Health Mission (NRHM) was launched), as the base year. The concept universal health coverage and challenges that India faces are briefly discussed at the outset to describe the context. Based on the survey and critical appraisals, strategic approach required for speedy achievement of universal coverage is discussed focussing on the India's Northeast.

Studies indicate that India has deprived an estimated 60 million people of their sustenance in the period 1947–2000 in the name of national development. Some of them have been physically relocated and are known as displaced persons (DP). Others are deprived of their sustenance without physical relocation and are called project affected persons (PAP). The tribes that are a little over 8 per cent of the population account for around 40 per cent of the DP-PAPs. Many consider tribal deprivation necessary because their regions are resource-rich and those riches should be used for the whole country. But they ignore the impoverishment and marginalisation that deprivation causes and the legal status of their land that allows the State to displace them without rehabilitation or compensation and with no possibility of beginning life anew. Tribal proportion is higher in the Northeast. Also conflicts and disasters displace people. Fernandes, through his paper, has studied the impact and possible solutions to the impoverishment of the DP-PAPs especially tribal.

In the next chapter, Mahanta and Nayak have made a comprehensive attempt to analyse the status of gender inequality in Northeast India using various indicators based on secondary data. The study reveals that the Northeast is better off than the nation as a whole in terms of gender equality. However, inequality between women and men exists in the region in spite of the predominance of various ethnic groups who by and large do not believe in sex discrimination. The study reveals that women are relatively disempowered and have a somewhat lower status than that of men in the region. Gender gap exists in terms of access to education, employment and health. A large gender gap exists in political participation both at the levels of state and nation. Among the Northeastern states, Meghalaya, Manipur and Mizoram show relatively lesser degree of gender inequality in terms of work participation, literacy, infant mortality and sex ratio. The situation is, however, adverse in case of Tripura, Assam and Sikkim. The study concludes with an observation that access to education, employment and health are not the only enabling factors which may guarantee the achievement towards the goal, and this, largely depends on the mindset of the people.

Regionalism is a rather continuous phenomenon in Northeast India – This is due to the interaction of diverse psychological, historical, social, political and economic factors. The growing intensity of terrorism and militancy as means of pursuing narrowly conceived regional goals is indeed alarming and its immediate and effective handling is needed. At the same time, identification of the root cause of regionalism and its solution is also required. Out of the various factors of regionalism, economic disparity is one of the main reasons behind the regionalism in Northeast India. The backwardness is unequivocally manifested in every sector of the economy. It is argued that the policy initiatives followed, since Independence, by the Central Government have, by and large, failed to satisfy the needs and aspirations of the people of Northeast. The massive development initiatives undertaken by the Central Government so far benefitted only an elite section of the society and the marginal section of the society is deprived, oppressed and exploited leading to continuous demand for autonomy. In this context, Sinha's paper has made an attempt to identify the development initiatives undertaken by the Government of India for development and thereby help in countering regionalism in the Northeast and suggested some fresh initiatives for further development of the region.

The seven states of Northeast India though clubbed together in most of the references, comprises a mosaic of heterogeneous culture and diversified society. This diversity of customs and traditions accordingly construct the identity of the woman and thereby her position within the society. Her position reflects her status and the privileges she enjoys and at the same time the disadvantages and discrimination she confronts. Vauquline, in her paper has put a concerted effort to analyse the spatial pattern of these discriminations in the form of crimes against women, more so domestic violence, in the seven states of the region. The temporal growth of these atrocities since the last 10 years is be another aspect of the study (2002–11). The types, occurrences, causes and the solution put forth by the victims of domestic violence will be examined through gender perspective on the basis of their ethnic background. Sixty cases of domestic violence are consulted from the most crime prone area (crimes against women) of the region. Purposive random sampling method is applied for the collection of these data. In-depth interview, a form of feminist research methodology, is implied to get a comprehensive understanding of the incidences. Secondary data regarding records of crimes against women of Northeast India is collected from National Crimes Record Bureau. The study reveals a clear variation of the occurrences of crimes against women within the region and that her position differs on the basis of her ethnicity.

Amid a general feeling that the Northeast is a zone of conflicts where some efforts for peace are made, one needs to ask, Where do the tribal communities of the region stand today? Why do the conflicts arise? An answer to these questions requires an understanding of their past history and present situation in order to move towards the future. One sees in the past of the region, tribal traditions followed by change of religion, i.e. their Christianisation or Hinduisation, modern inputs like education and commercial forces, the political processes, laws and other components impacting their everyday life and the value system guiding them; the paper by Fernandes has aptly focussed on some of those issues.

Public spaces are those spaces where all citizens, irrespective of gender, caste, class, sexuality, disability or any other social identity have a right to access. Importantly, the public spaces are gendered and 'practiced places', where individuals use these spaces to fulfil their varied needs and aspirations of everyday life, while trying to maintain dignity, safety and self-respect. With increased urbanisation and neoliberal economic transformation, women's mobility through the public spaces of Northeast India has increased. However, a number of recent evidences suggest that towns and cities of Northeast India fail to safeguard its women and vulnerable population; and thereby, unable to create a general sense of belongingness – increased incidents of anti-social elements and street assaults against women restrict their mobility and freedom in public spaces. Based on a questionnaire survey and telephonic in-depth interviews, Bhattacharyya's paper seeks to address the gendered dimensions of fear, which affect women's access to public spaces including their mobility; how and where women feel (un)safe (in their usage of public space) or how they negotiate with these spaces in their everyday practices. The key findings of the study suggest that there is an urgent need for a safety audit to improve the safety and security of these spaces.

The forces of globalisation have opened the doors of many new opportunities as well as formidable challenges. In some ways or the other, the nation-states have been shaken by the forces. The effects of globalisation in the socio-politico and economic lives of the people of a nation have become visible at the onslaught of it. With all its promises on the overall qualitative improvement of life and social harmony, it can be seen as a saviour of universal peace and prosperity. However, it also has its own limitations. Keeping in view such dynamics, Dr Singh through his paper, discusses the promises and opportunities that it bestowed and also look into the formidable challenges that it brings along with reference to the Northeast part of India. It attempts to suggest ways in tackling the menace of the vicious cycle of insurgency and under-development; infra-structure and governance. This paper also attempts to suggest ways in reaping the fruit of globalisation by exploring the vast areas of opportu-nities and potentials of Northeast – in the form of eco-tourism, border trade and in the field of sports that the Northeast is capable of.

1

Human Development in Northeastern Region of India

Issues and Challenges

PURUSOTTAM NAYAK

UNDP for the first time took initiative in preparing human development report at the global level in 1990. Since then it has been a regular exercise to produce reports on an annual basis, of course, with emphasis on different themes. Similar exercises have also been undertaken by various countries, including India, with the help of UNDP. The National Human Development Report (NHDR) 2001 and India Human Development Report (IHDR) 2011 are the outcomes of the Central Government in this regard (GoI, 2002 and 2011). Subsequently, six out of eight Northeastern states joined the race in publishing human developments reports for their individual states at different points of time in the first decade of 21st century. Although for the other two states, namely Manipur and Mizoram, reports are yet to be published; some information, however, is available from the works of individual researchers. To have an idea about the region let us have a glance over these reports, research works of some individual authors and recent available data on development indicators of different states in the region.

The Region

The NHDR provides us information about the status and growth of human development in different states in the country, including various states in the Northeastern region of India. However, data for the Northeast are somewhat outdated. Though one of the reports was published in 2002 it could not provide data on human development for the Northeast including few other smaller states in the country beyond 1991. The report revealed that the region comprising the eight states of Arunachal Pradesh, Assam, Manipur, Meghalaya, Mizoram, Nagaland, Sikkim (the last to be included in the region) and Tripura, constitutes a land surface of 2,62,230 square kilometres where a population of 38.9 million belonging to different ethnic and cultural groups inhabits. Topographically the region is a mixture of hills and plains. While Arunachal Pradesh, Meghalaya, Mizoram, Nagaland and Sikkim are almost entirely hilly, about four-fifths of Assam is plain. Manipur and Tripura have both plain areas and hilly tracts. The hills account for about 70 per cent area and accommodate about 30 per cent of population of the region and the plains constituting the remaining 30 per cent of area hold about 70 per cent of its population. Wide variation in altitude coupled with abundance of rainfall has given rise to wide variations in climatic conditions within the region which in turn has endowed the region with rich bio-diversity. The richness of bio-diversity of the region is almost matched by its ethnic diversity. The region is a meeting place of large number of races, creeds, cultures and languages. The impingement of the diversity of physical and cultural environment is naturally found in the organisation of economic life of the people of the region.

According to the report, the Human Development Index (HDI) during 1981 in the region varied from the lowest figure of 0.242 in Arunachal Pradesh to the highest of 0.461 in Manipur as against national average of 0.302. Similarly in 1991, the lowest and highest figures were 0.328 (Arunachal Pradesh) and 0.548 (Mizoram) as against 0.389 at the national level. Some of the states in the region in this regard were much ahead of India. However, there was a yawning gap between urban and rural areas. The rural-urban disparity index varied from the lowest figure of 0.113 in Manipur to the highest of 0.234 in Tripura in 1981. The situation did not improve much in 1991. Instead it got deteriorated in Meghalaya. Contrary to popular perceptions, the status of women in the region was far from being on an equal footing with that of men. Particularly gender disparities were consistently very high in Tripura and Assam and varying widely from one state to another. It was lower in four states, namely, Manipur, Meghalaya, Nagaland and Sikkim in the year 1981 as compared to all India average situations. In 1991, however, five states such as Manipur, Meghalaya, Arunachal Pradesh, Mizoram and Nagaland went ahead of the country.

The UNDP (2003) in its human development report devoted for the first time an entire chapter to the region and reiterated the same findings as observed in NHDR. It reported that in the recent past the area in which the region seems to have had done better than the nation as a whole was the social sector and more particularly in the spread of literacy. Though the region somewhat lagged behind the country in terms of literacy during

1970s, by the beginning of the 21st century it surpassed the average national achievements in this regard. Individual states such as Mizoram, Tripura, Manipur and Nagaland marched ahead of the country average, Assam more or less kept pace with the national average, and starting from relative backwardness in 1971, by 2001 Meghalaya and Arunachal Pradesh closed gaps with the country average. Considering that Arunachal Pradesh had a literacy rate of only 11.30 per cent in 1971, the attainment to 54.34 per cent by 2001 constituted a huge progress in just three decades. Besides, female literacy in the region surpassed the corresponding female literacy rate in the country. The infant mortality rate came down well below the country average in all the states of the region barring Assam. While identifying yawning gap between urban and rural areas in human development, the report mentioned that educational, healthcare and other welfare services were heavily concentrated in the urban areas. Though the region achieved significant progress in literacy, it was 'marred' by rural-urban disparities, inter-district variations and a high dropout rates in schools. Barring Manipur, the dropout rate in schools exceeded 60 per cent. A striking feature of the health sector was that there was a wide inter-state disparity. For instance, while Mizoram had just a single nurse for every 22,000 persons, it was 5,353 persons in case of Assam. The incidence of rural poverty was far greater in the region. More than 39 per cent of the rural population was living below the poverty line. The report also busted some popular myths of higher status of women in the Northeast, particularly on their education and empowerment.

Table 1

HDI and GDI of Northeastern States and India in 2001

State/Country	*Index*			*HDI*		*GDI*	
	Education	*Health*	*Income*	*Value*	*Rank*	*Value*	*Rank*
Ar. Pradesh	0.55	0.68	0.23	0.49	8	0.48	7
Assam	0.62	0.76	0.13	0.50	7	0.49	6
Manipur	0.73	0.85	0.18	0.59	3.5	0.58	3
Meghalaya	0.62	0.72	0.23	0.52	6	0.51	5
Mizoram	0.87	0.83	0.30	0.67	1	0.67	1
Nagaland	0.67	0.76	0.29	0.57	5	N.A.	—
Sikkim	0.71	0.80	0.29	0.60	2	0.59	2
Tripura	0.73	0.79	0.25	0.59	3.5	0.56	4
India	0.64	0.78	0.28	0.56	—	0.54	—

Source: Tripura Human Development Report 2007

The latest information on estimated HDI available for all the individual Northeastern states is for the year 2001 in the *Human Development Report* published by the Tripura State Government (GoT, 2007). According to this report the performance of human development across states in the region varied significantly (Table 1). Mizoram and Arunachal Pradesh witnessed the highest and lowest HDI of 0.67 and 0.49, respectively as against the all India average of 0.56. Only three states of the North-East, namely, Arunachal Pradesh, Assam and Meghalaya lagged behind all India average whereas performance of other five northeastern states surpassed India. Similar situations prevailed in different components of human development such as in education, health and income indices. Mizoram not only got the first rank in terms of HDI but also first rank in GDI. Similarly performance of Arunachal Pradesh was worst among all the northeastern states both in HDI and GDI. It is to be noted that Meghalaya in spite of having a matrilineal society performed very poorly in terms of GDI and got fifth rank among all the North-Eastern states.

The latest report on human development is a departure from the earlier report(s) in terms of analysis on the basis of category of states, castes and social groups (Government of India, 2011). Comparisons have been made between Non-Special Category States and Special Category States, among different social groups such as SC, ST, OBC and Others and among major religious communities such as Hindus, Muslims, Christians and Sikhs. Assam figures as an individual Non-Special Category State whereas all other states of the Northeast which are Special Category States are clubbed together for the purpose of analysis. The report mentions that there exists a two-way relationship between economic growth and human capital formation. Investment in health and education can enhance human functioning, which can eventually alleviate income poverty and further economic growth. Similarly, resources generated through income poverty reduction and economic growth can be used to enhance human functionings which in turn gives a push to economic growth. The report reveals that HDI in India increased by 21 per cent from 1999–2000 to 2007–08. The major contributor to improvement in HDI during the period has been education which improved over 28 per cent. Achievements of the poorest states have been much faster than that of the average achievements of the nation leading to convergence across states in terms of HDI. Poor and educationally backward states, respectively have registered a significantly higher than average improvements in Income and Education indices. Although incidence of poverty has declined over time in the country it continues to remain high among SCs and STs. The SCs, STs and Muslims suffer the most on account of poor health status and illiteracy. One-third STs and around half of SCs reside in *pucca* houses compared to 66 per cent for all India. However, the Northeastern states in general have a higher proportion of households living in *kutcha* and semi-*pucca* houses. What is noteworthy is that the Northeastern states, excluding Assam, have done remarkably well in terms of human development outcomes. Over the period of eight years it has improved its all India rank from 9 to 6 with an improvement of HDI from 0.473 to 0.573 as against national averages from 0.387 to 0.467.

State Human Development Reports

During the last few years human development reports in the region have also been prepared for six individual states like Sikkim (GoS, 2001), Assam (GoA, 2003), Nagaland (GoN, 2004), Arunachal Pradesh (GoAP, 2005), Tripura (GoT, 2007) and Meghalaya (GoM, 2008) with the sponsorship of UNDP and the Planning Commission, Government of India, whereas for the other two states like Manipur and Mizoram, the reports are yet to be published.

Sikkim

Sikkim is the first state in the region to produce state human development report. According to the report it is a landlocked state being bounded on the north and Northeast by Tibet, on the east by Bhutan, on the west by Nepal and on the south by the Darjeeling district of West Bengal. It became the twenty-second state of the Indian Union in 1975 and recently it has been included as the eighth and last state in the Northeastern region of India with a population of 5.4 lakh according to 2001 Census. The state has a mixed performance in the area of development and growth. The per capita Net State Domestic Product (NSDP) in real terms in the state witnessed a substantial increase, i.e. from ₹ 1,571 in 1980–81 to ₹ 9,472 in 1995–96. Infant mortality rate dropped from 60 in 1991 to 51 in 1997. Literacy rates went up from 7 per cent in 1951 to almost 70 per cent in 2001. In 1998–99, as against the national average of 47 per cent, only 21 per cent of children below 3 years were malnourished – the lowest among all the Indian States and Union territories.

Table 2

HDI and GDI of Sikkim in 1998

District/State	*Index*			*HDI*		*GDI*	
	Education	*Health*	*Income*	*Value*	*Rank*	*Value*	*Rank*
North	0.607	0.512	0.282	0.467	4	0.467	4
East	0.694	0.730	0.310	0.578	1	0.567	2
West	0.589	0.687	0.271	0.576	2	0.518	3
South	0.613	0.692	0.282	0.529	3	0.571	1
Sikkim	0.641	0.663	0.292	0.532	—	0.528	—

Source: Sikkim Human Development Report, 2001.

Physical indicators of the quality of life suggested reasonable provisioning of many basic amenities in the state. According to the

National Family Health Survey-II, over 80 per cent of households had electricity as against 60 per cent in the country. Almost 85 per cent of households had drinking water as against 78 per cent in India. Close to 73 per cent of households had a toilet or latrine facility as against 36 per cent for the whole country. It had a HDI value of 0.532 as against all India average of 0.563 in 1998 (Table 2). Though the state recorded several significant gains in human development, particularly in terms of education and health indicators, it failed miserably in terms of per capita income indicator (0.292). North Sikkim remained as the worst performer with lowest rank both in HDI and GDI. In contrast to this, east Sikkim got the first rank in HDI whereas south Sikkim got first rank in GDI.

The proportion of population living below income poverty went up from 36 per cent in 1987–88 to 41 per cent in 1993–94. There was, however, a large disparity in the prevalence of income poverty between rural and urban areas. In 1993–94, for instance, only 8 per cent of the urban population lived below the poverty line as against 45 per cent in rural areas. In 1998–99, 61 per cent of women and 77 per cent of children below 3 years of age were reported to be suffering from anaemia. Progress on the industrial front had been constrained by many factors including lack of appropriate infrastructure and trained manpower. The benefits of growth and human development in the state had not been equitably distributed across districts. Although the economy had been dependent on agriculture, food production declined during the period from 1996–97 to 1997–98 and the technology used was often obsolete. The service sector, particularly health, education and eco-tourism has a huge potential to absorb the workforce of the state through employment generation.

Assam

At the time of Independence of the country, the entire Northeastern region consisted of only three administrative units of which two were princely states, namely Manipur and Tripura, and the rest of the region was undivided Assam province. In the post-Independence period, Arunachal Pradesh, Meghalaya, Mizoram, and Nagaland were carved out from Assam at different points of time. Presently, Assam is the biggest and most important state in the region having border with Arunachal Pradesh in the east, West Bengal, Meghalaya and Bangladesh in the west, Arunachal Pradesh and Bhutan in the north and Manipur, Meghalaya, Mizoram, Nagaland and Tripura in the south with a total population of 2.66 crore according 2001 Census of India. The economy of the state is mainly based on agricultural activities and exploration of oil. It produces a significant percentage of the total tea production in the globe and more than half of India's petroleum. A close examination of the report of Assam reveals that in spite of abundant natural resources, the state is lagging behind the rest of the country and the gap is increasing. Per capita income of the state during the Independence period was only marginally less than that of the average for the country. In 1998, per capita income for the country was over 1.8 times that of Assam. Industrial diversification and growth were constrained by the inadequacy and quality of complementary infrastructure, the geographical isolation of the region, and the lack of well developed markets.

There is also inter-district inequity. The per capita income of the district with the highest income is more than three times that of the district with the lowest per capita income. In 1994–95, seven districts accounted for nearly half of the State Domestic Product and the remaining 16 districts contributed to the other half. Kamrup district contributed almost one-fifth of the state's Gross Domestic Product (GDP) originating in the tertiary sector, and over a sixth of state's GDP in the secondary sector. At the other end of the scale, the North Cachar Hills district contributed only one per cent of the state's GDP in the secondary sector, and about 1.5 per cent in the primary and tertiary sectors.

The incidence of unemployment, measured as a per cent of the labour force, has been increasing, and is higher than that in the rest of the country. The primary sector continues to dominate the sectoral composition of workers although the share has been declining. The substantial increase has been in the tertiary sector. Throughout the state the rate of work participation for men is higher than that for women. The female work participation rate is higher in rural areas than in urban areas. While female marginal workers are almost negligible in urban areas, a sizeable proportion of women in the rural areas participate in work in a marginal capacity. The per cent of women workers in the primary sector actually increased during 1971–2001, indicating that more women are now entering the work force in the agriculture sector. Unemployment increased during 1983–2000, both in rural and urban areas. The unemployment percentage in urban area was extremely high, 9.8 per cent in 1999–2000, and as much as 20.5 per cent for women.

Assam has an extremely high proportion of its population living in poverty. Despite a decline in the proportion, more than a third of its people are below the poverty line. The per cent of poor in the state is the highest (36.03%) among the seven states of the Northeast. There is a rural-urban divide; two out of five people in rural areas are likely to be under the poverty line, while in urban Assam, the incidence is less than one in 10. Rural poverty was much higher (40.04%) than urban poverty (7.47%) in 1999–2000 and the incidence of rural poverty was higher than the all India figure of 27.09 per cent.

There are several positive features of the education sector, and its development over the last two decades. There has been impressive growth of the elementary education. This is reflected in the significant increase in the number of primary and middle schools, the number of teachers at the primary and middle levels, in enrollments and in improved school infrastructure. Enrollment in schools, measured by gross and net enrollment ratios has increased.

Assam has been moving towards the attainment of the goal of 'health for all'. The state government has emphasised not only the adequate provision of primary healthcare, but education and awareness of health issues, dissemination of information on prevention, hygiene and healthy practices, food security and nutrition, safe drinking water and good sanitation, maternal and child health and family welfare. People in the state now live longer than their parents did, and health profiles have improved. Yet, health indicators in the state reveal inequity – between districts, between income and other groupings. There is a rural-urban divide, and a gender gap reflected across almost all indicators. Life Expectancy at Birth (LEB) is below that of the country as a whole, and is one of the lowest amongst major Indian states. In the 1970s, men could expect to live longer than women. This has since been reversed; women can now expect to live longer than men. This is a trend that began to take place initially in urban areas, but is now true of rural areas as well. There is still a very significant gap between the LEB for rural and for urban areas. There is rural–urban gap and a gender gap here too; males have a better chance of surviving beyond forty years of age.

Table 3

HDI and GDI of Assam in 2001

District/State	*HDI*				
	Education Index	*Health Index*	*Income Index*	*HDI*	*Rank*
Jorhat (Best)	0.722	0.644	0.564	0.650	1
Dhubri (Worst)	0.454	0.086	0.102	0.214	23
Assam	0.595	0.343	0.286	0.407	—

	GDI		
	Performance	*GDI Value*	*GDI Rank*
N.C. Hills	Best district	0.877	1
Karimganj	Worst district	0.012	23
Assam	—	0.537	—

Source: Assam Human Development Report, 2003.

As regards human development, HDI value was as low as 0.407 in the state as against the lowest value of 0.214 in Dhubri and highest value of 0.650 in Jorhat (Table 3). Thus, there was a widespread variation in the performance of human development across districts in the state. Out of 23 districts in the state 16 of them were having below the average performance of the state. While the state witnessed educational index as high as 0.595, it performed poorly in income (0.286) and health (0.343) fronts. Performance in terms of GDI also varied widely across districts. The best district was N.C. Hills having a GDI value as high as 0.877 as against the worst performance in Karimganj where the corresponding figure was as low as 0.012.

Nagaland

According to the state human development report, Nagaland emerged as a state out of the Naga Hills district of Assam and North-East Frontier Agency (NEFA) province in 1963. It is a land of diverse tribes, systems of governance, cultures, and variety. The state has been confronting insurgency on a continuous basis, committing much of its scarce resources to administrative and related expenditures.

The NSDP of Nagaland showed an increase from ₹ 10,547 lakh in 1980–81 to ₹ 57,898 lakh in 1990–91 (at constant 1980–81 prices) and further to ₹ 2,23,042 lakh in 2000–01 (at constant 1993–94 prices). The per capita income also increased from ₹ 1,361 in 1980–81 to ₹ 5,520 in 1990–91. During 2000–01, per capita income was ₹ 11,473 (at constant 1993–94 prices) as against ₹ 10,306 for the country as a whole.

There has been a phenomenal increase in the levels of literacy in the state. Literacy rate which was 20.4 per cent in 1961 increased to 67.11 per cent in 2001. However, against a national increase of 21.39 per cent during the period from 1991 to 2001, the state witnessed an increase of only 8.86 per cent. A positive aspect of the state is the increase in the female literacy, which was 13 per cent in 1961 but steadily increased to 39.9 per cent in 1981 and further to 61.92 per cent in 2001. Women literacy rate and the enrollment rates for girls in the state were higher than the national average.

Despite various challenges the indicators for health in the state are impressive. The positive achievements are improving sex ratios, absence of female foeticides and low maternal mortality rate. There are almost no cases of malnourishment among women and children. The life expectancy at birth were calculated at 73.4 years, way above the national average of 62.3 years, and much closer to the figures in developed countries. Infant mortality rate at 42.2 per 1,000 was also much better than the national average of 68 per 1,000 live births. Similarly, under-five mortality rate, per 1,000 live births, was 63.8 as against the national figure of 96. In terms of maternal mortality rate, the state's figure of less than 1 per 1,000 live births, against the national average of 5.4, was much closer to the figures in developed countries. However, the total fertility rate at 3.77 has been a cause for concern.

The HDI of the state was estimated to be as high as 0.623 as compared to 0.472 for the country as a whole in 2001 (Table 4). The state's good performance and ranking can be best understood by looking at the constituents of the indices and the factors that influence them including literacy, health status and income levels. According to per capita indicator it was almost at par with the national average. Literacy rate in the state was higher by 1.8 per cent over the national average of 65.2 per cent. However, it witnessed wide variations in terms of HDI across districts. HDI was estimated to be highest in Dimapur (0.733) as against the lowest figure of 0.450 in Mon district. Mon district was the worst performer both in HDI and GDI. While Dimapur was the best performer in HDI, Kohima was the best performer in GDI.

Table 4

HDI and GDI of Nagaland in 2001

District/State	*HDI*	*Rank*	*GDI*	*Rank*
Dimapur	0.733	1	0.472	1
Mokokchung	0.705	2	0.460	3
Wokha	0.699	3	0.448	5
Kohima	0.674	4	0.580	1
Phek	0.652	5	0.450	4
Zunheboto	0.611	6	0.414	6
Tuensang	0.512	7	0.299	7
Mon	0.450	8	0.220	8
Nagaland	0.623	—	0.420	—

Source: Nagaland Human Development Report 2004

Arunachal Pradesh

Arunachal Pradesh is one of the remotely located border states of the region. The state, according to its human development report, had a primitive economy with a low level of development and meagre infrastructural facilities at the time of Independence of the country; however, the people living in the state did have enormous traditional skills which have been passed down through the generations. During the beginning of 1970s, the per capita income was 63.38 per cent of the per capita national income and by the end of that decade it was increased to 75 per cent. During the 1980s, the state moved faster than that of the country as a whole. By the beginning of the 1990s, it surpassed the national average and from 1991–92 to 1995–96, it continued to remain higher. After 1995–96, however, the growth of income slowed down. In 1999–2000, it stood at 84.64 per cent of the national average. An examination of the relative per capita Net District Domestic Product (NDDP) showed substantial variation across districts. The per capita income of Lower Subansiri was less than half of the richest district, Dibang Valley.

A poverty estimate made by the Directorate of Rural Development of the state showed that 54 per cent of families in rural Arunachal Pradesh were poor in 1992–93 which increased to 78 per cent in 1997–98. The estimates also showed a high degree of inter-district variation in both the periods. In 1997–98, East Kameng had the lowest incidence of poverty (49%) while Upper Subansiri recorded a poverty ratio as high as 97 per cent.

In the beginning of the 20th century, the state did not have a single school. The first school was established in Pasighat in 1918, and the second in 1922 at Dambuk. At the time of Independence, there were only three schools in the entire state and that too only up to the primary level. In 1951, as many as 67 lower primary (LP) schools were set up including one middle school. The big spurt in the expansion of schools was during 1981–91 after which the growth has been more gradual. The literacy rate increased from 25.55 per cent in 1981 to 54.34 per cent in 2001. In spite of a steady increase in literacy, it remained low as compared to the national average of 64.80 per cent. The rate varied from the highest of 34.94 per cent in Lohit district to as low as 9.39 per cent in East Kameng district. In East Kameng and Upper Subansiri districts, the female literacy rates were as low as 3.52 and 6.48 per cent, respectively. During 1991–2001, enrollment in middle and secondary schools doubled, and in the primary schools it went up by a little over 50 per cent.

Though health status of the people in the state improved it was not able to keep pace with the spread of literacy or the growth of income. There were no estimates available for life expectancy during 1950–51. It was estimated to be 54.05 years in 2000 which was not only 9.25 years less than the national average but also being one of the lowest in the country and 4.56 years less than that of the neighbouring state Assam. People who lived in districts situated in the upper hill ranges had lower life expectancies than those who lived in districts located in the plains and plateaus. The state had an infant mortality rate (IMR) of 77 per 1,000 live births as against 14 in Kerala and 75 in Assam. Though IMR did not vary between sexes, considerable inter-district variation existed. Kurung Kumey had the highest IMR of 133 as against the lowest of 53 in Lower Dibang Valley.

The HDI for the state for the year 2001 was estimated to be 0.515 and the education index, health index and income index were respectively 0.566, 0.484 and 0.495 (Table 5). Considerable variations in the levels of human development were observed across districts. East Siang district had the first rank with an HDI of 0.660 as against the lowest of 0.362 in East Kameng. East Siang was not only the best performer in HDI but also in

GDI. Similarly, East Kameng was the worst performer both in HDI and GDI. Variations across districts were more acute in terms of income index followed by education and health index. The GDI for the state was estimated to be as high as 0.529. GDI rankings of various districts in the state followed a similar ranking pattern as HDI implying the fact that the districts having relatively better HDI did better in GDI and the districts with relatively lower HDI values had higher gender inequity.

Table 5

HDI and GDI of Arunachal Pradesh in 2001

District/State	*Performance*	*HDI*	*Rank*	*District/State*	*Performance*	*GDI*	*Rank*
East Siang	Best district	0.660	1	East Siang	Best district	0.654	1
East Kameng	Worst district	0.362	13	East Kameng	Worst district	0.400	13
Ar. Pradesh	—	0.515	—	Ar. Pradesh	—	0.529	—

Source: Arunachal Pradesh Human Development Report, 2006.

Tripura

Human development report of Tripura observes that it is a land-locked state of three million populations of which 31 per cent are tribal people. Overcoming the odds inherited by the state caused by the Partition of the country on the eve of freedom, the people of the state experienced significant progress in the social, economic and political spheres. The state made substantial progress in the expansion of literacy and schooling in the 1990s. In 2001, it witnessed a literacy rate of 73 per cent as against 65 per cent in the region and 63 per cent in India. Among the Northeast states, Tripura ranked second after Mizoram, and its rank improved during 1991–2001.

Estimates showed that in 2001, life expectancy at birth for males and females in the state was 71 years and 74 years, respectively. In terms of life expectancy, attainments in the state were higher than the national average, which was 61 for males and 62.5 for females. There was, however, inter-district variations. Women in West District lived five years longer than women in Dhalai; men in West District lived four years longer than men in Dhalai. Infant mortality rate in the state was as high as 52 as against 30 in Manipur and 57 in India in 2005–06. IMR instead of declining increased from 44 in 1998–99 to 52 in 2005–06. District-level estimates indicated that Dhalai had the highest IMR followed by South, North and West Districts. IMR for girls in Dhalai district even was lower than the all-India IMR.

In 2001–02, the per capita income of the state was ₹ 18,759. In terms of access to resources, the average person in Tripura had fewer resources than the average person in India. The growth record of incomes, however, has been remarkable. The compound annual growth rate of NSDP was 5.2 per cent in the 1980s and 6.7 per cent in the 1990s. In fact, in several years, the annual rate of growth of SDP exceeded 10 per cent. Moreover, when India had a growth rate of NSDP of 5.5 per cent during 1993–94 to 2002–03 it was 8.3 per cent in Tripura. All the districts showed a good performance in terms of growth rates, although with variations, being lowest in Dhalai (6.1%) and highest in North District (7.9%).

The estimated HDI for the state was 0.59 in 2001 and following the classification used by the UNDP, the achievements correspond to the 'medium' level (Table 6). While education and health indices were as high as 0.73 and 0.79 respectively, income index was too low at 0.25 implying a very poor performance in per capita income. The estimated value of GDI was 0.56. The ranks of the districts in terms of GDI and its components were similar to the ranking of districts with respect to HDI other than in terms of the 'equally distributed income index'. West District, which ranked first in terms of the income index, ranked second in terms of the equally distributed income index. The noteworthy feature of these estimates is that the HDI and GDI for the state were higher than the corresponding values for India. Among the Northeast States, Tripura shared third rank with respect to the HDI and fourth rank with respect to the GDI. The state ranked second with respect to the education index and fourth with respect to the health and income indices.

Table 6

HDI and GDI of Tripura in 2001

District/State/Country	*Education Index*	*Health Index*	*Income Index*	*HDI*	*GDI*
West District	0.77	0.82	0.26	0.62	0.58
South District	0.70	0.76	0.24	0.57	0.55
Dhalai	0.61	0.74	0.19	0.51	0.50
North District	0.73	0.80	0.25	0.59	0.56
Tripura	0.73	0.79	0.25	0.59	0.56
India	0.64	0.78	0.28	0.56	0.54

Source: Tripura Human Development Report, 2007.

Meghalaya

The latest human development report among all the Northeastern states is that of Meghalaya. According to the report, Meghalaya emerged as a full-fledged state within Indian Union on 21 January 1970. The state is bounded by the Brahmaputra valley of Assam in the north and northwest, the Cachar area of Assam in the east, and Bangladesh in the south and southwest. The report, while examining certain key components of human development in the state, highlighted the achievements and described what else needed to be done to consolidate the gains. While outlining the geographic location, topography and the areas of strength and weaknesses of the state, it presented some of the unique socio-economic features of the state. It also highlighted the problems of development of the state as perceived by the indigenous people living in the state. The report mentioned population of the state to be predominantly tribal; 81 per cent of its people living in rural areas were dependent on agriculture for their livelihood. In spite of having rich natural resources the state had not been able to provide stimulus for its growth and development. The state has a long way to go in respect of basic services to improve its health status, level of education and overall economy. In 2005, the state ranked 26th in HDI, 21st in the index of social and economic infrastructure, 16th in per capita consumption of electricity, 25th in road density, 21st in per capita income, 30th in per capita utilisation of credit, 27th in literacy rate and 28th in infant mortality rate among all the states and union territories in the country.

Table 7

HDI of Meghalaya in 2001

District/State	*IMR*	*Literacy*	*Per Capita NSDP (₹)*	*HDI*	*GDI*	*HDI/GDI Rank*
East Khasi Hills	34.51	76.98	24,793	0.676	0.640	1
West Garo Hills	18.13	51.03	13,782	0.571	0.550	2
Ri Bhoi	60.63	66.07	14,752	0.496	0.478	3
South Garo Hills	102.01	55.82	23,321	0.484	0.477	4
Jaintia Hills	77.34	53.00	20,405	0.469	0.437	5
East Garo Hills	86.17	65.64	9,926	0.405	0.392	6
West Khasi Hills	90.60	61.70	12,047	0.396	0.321	7
Meghalaya	52.28	63.31	17,595	0.550	0.534	—

Source: Meghalaya Human Development Report, 2008.

In terms of HDI, Meghalaya performed poorly (Table 7). From a rank of 21st in 1981, its position deteriorated to 24th in 1991 and further to 26th in 2005. The state had a HDI value of 0.585 as against a value of 0.858 in Himachal Pradesh. Instead of witnessing a declining urban infant mortality rate, it increased from 44 in 2003 to 46 in 2007. It also witnessed a declining gross enrollment ratio from 92.19 per cent in 1999–2000 to 87.75 per cent in 2004–05. Though health and educational status of women were no better than their counterparts in the rest of the country, because of their higher work participation rate, the state witnessed a better index of GDI showing women being better off in the state. While

West Garo Hills performed poorly in HDI, West Khasi Hills performed poorly in GDI. The report further observed that there was a widespread disparity of human development and gender development among different districts in the state.

In terms of health indicators the state had been lagging behind. Different health programmes such as full immunisation of children, antenatal care for pregnant mothers, etc. had miserably failed. The literacy rates were marginally lower in the state as compared to all India average. But the gender gap in the state was not prominent unlike other states in the country because of her matrilineal character. According to a household survey conducted by the state government in 2002 about 50 per cent of the people were poor.

Findings of Individual Authors

Study undertaken by Singh (2010) throws some light on the status and trend of socio-economic development of the state of Manipur. Geographically Manipur is characterised into two distinct physical regions – an outlying area of rugged hills and narrow valleys, and the inner area of flat plain, with all associated land forms. The state is bounded by Nagaland to the north, Mizoram to the south, Assam to the west and Myanmar to the east. It covers an area of 22,347 square kilometres. The Meiteis, who live primarily in the valley region of the state, form the majority ethnic group constituting 60 per cent of the total population but occupying only 10 per cent of the total land. The Muslims (Meitei-Pangal) also live in the valley; the Kukis, Nagas, Hmars and other smaller groups form about 40 per cent of the population but occupy the remaining 90 per cent of the total land of the state.

According to Singh the state had the highest HDI among all the North-eastern states and it occupied the 4th position in the all India ranking in 1981. Despite having substantially a low and erratic per capita income, the overall performance of the state was much better than most of the Indian states mainly due to its remarkable achievements in respect of literacy, enrollment, and life expectancy. Though, HDI of the state increased by 11.43 per cent during 1981–91, her all India rank dropped to 9th position, and in the region the state was 2nd to Mizoram. The state has the distinction of having the lowest infant mortality rate in the country. It declined from 32 in 1961 to 11 in 2006. Low infant mortality rate indicates better child care emanating from sound child care practices and awareness among mothers about hygiene and nutrition. Life expectancy at birth for the state was 68.64 for males and that of 72.42 for females in 1991, as against the corresponding figures of 62.3 and 63.9 at the national level during 2001–05. As per 2001 Census, the state ranked 15th in literacy rate. During the period from 1987–88 to 2004–05 with every one per cent increase in NSDP, the state witnessed an increase of employment by 0.67 per cent. Poverty ratio of the state declined by 65.37 per cent as against the decline of 49.94 at the national level during the period from 1973–74 to 2004–05. While urban poverty ratio declined by 91.06 per cent in the state in contrast to the decline by 57.66 per cent in rural areas. While national poverty ratio increased both in the rural and urban areas, there was no such reversal in the state of Manipur during the period from 1999–2000 to 2004–05.

Agarwal (2010), in his work, highlights some of the achievements and weaknesses of the state of Mizoram. Mizoram became the 23rd state of India in February 1987. The state is located in the remote Northeast corner of the country, sandwiched between international borders of Myanmar and Bangladesh. As a state it witnessed remarkable progress in terms of literacy rate, i.e. from 59.90 per cent in 1981 to 88.49 per cent in 2001 and was next only to Kerala having 90 per cent literacy. Gender-based differential in literacy was the lowest in the country at 90.7 per cent for males as against 86.7 per cent for females. Rural-urban disparities in terms of literacy rates were as high as 15.5 per cent. Enrollment rate for primary schools in the age group of 6–11 years was 119, while it was substantially lower around 80 for the age group of 11–14 years. While compared to other Northeastern states and all India average, the figure seems to be quite satisfactory. The figures on dropout rates, however, suggest a worrisome trend for some time. Along with high enrollment ratios, the state witnessed high dropout rates. In 1994–95, 63 per cent of students belonging to class I to V left studies before completing class V. In 2006–07, the dropout rates for the primary and secondary education were 3.93 and 10.54, respectively, while for high schools and higher secondary schools it remained at 23 and 70, respectively. Another noticeable feature is the high incidence of dropouts in rural areas as compared to urban areas. The reasons for dropout may be traced in engagement of children in household work and farms besides poverty, especially in rural areas. According to the report of National Family Health Survey-3 fertility rate was as high as 2.86 but has been declining over time due to women's education and a better standard of living. Besides attaining a high level of literacy it has performed better on the health front, too. Absence of manufacturing activities and shortage of skilled manpower has limited the scope of employment opportunities in the state. Another weakening force in the education system is the non-availability of qualified manpower and other supportive infrastructural facilities. The major concern is high growth rate of population due to high fertility rate. Private healthcare is gaining popularity, especially in urban areas, but the greater concern is the rural areas where more hospitals equipped with adequate infrastructural support are required. The state is in dire need of an appropriate delivery mechanism for a balanced development of human resources.

Current Status of the Region

The information presented and the analysis based on these in the previous paragraphs mostly refers to outdated data on various human development indicators. Till date attempts have not been made by any individual researcher, agency/organisation or government to construct HDI for any Northeastern state or for the country as a whole based on recently available data. This is mainly because of the fact that data on all the components of human development are not yet available. Keeping in view these limitations we have simply presented in this section some available recent data which can throw some light on the status of development in the region.

Table 8

Current Human Development Indicators of Northeastern States

State/Country	*Per Capita NSDP in 2010–11 (at 2004–05 constant prices)*	*Poverty in 2009–10*	*Literacy Rate in 2011*	*Literacy Gap between Male and Female*	*IMR in 2010*
Col. 1	*Col. 2*	*Col. 3*	*Col. 4*	*Col. 5*	*Col. 6*
Arunachal Pradesh	38,678	25.9	66.95	14.12	31
Assam	21,500	37.9	73.18	11.54	58
Manipur	23,298	47.1	79.85	12.71	15
Meghalaya	34,098	17.1	75.48	3.39	58
Mizoram	35,323	21.1	91.58	4.32	47
Nagaland	38,921	20.9	80.11	6.6	24
Sikkim	47,655	13.1	82.20	10.86	31
Tripura	35,732	17.4	87.75	9.03	29
India	35,917	29.8	74.04	16.68	47

Sources: (1) Col. 2, 3 and 6: Central Statistical Organization; (2) Col. 4 and 5: Census of India.

Per capita income data reveals that only three states in the region, namely Sikkim, Nagaland, and Arunachal Pradesh have surpassed the average per capita income of the country (Table 8). Although Tripura was lagging behind in this dimension for a long time it has made a tremendous progress and catching up with the country. The worst performer in this regard are Assam and Manipur whose per capita income are ₹ 21,500 and ₹ 23,298, respectively as against the all India average income of ₹ 35,917. Except Arunachal Pradesh and Assam, all other Northeastern states have performed better than the country as a whole. Similar type of situation and ranking prevailed as regards status of poverty in Northeastern states. There was a wide degree of variation of poor people across states.

According to 2009–10 estimates, Manipur had the highest magnitude of poverty followed by Assam. Sikkim witnessed lowest magnitude of poverty. While India, on an average, had 30 per cent of its people below poverty line the corresponding figures for the states of Manipur and Assam were as high as 47.1 and 37.9, respectively. All other states in the region were having poverty below the national average.

Mizoram has been retaining consistently its first position in terms of literacy in the region. While India achieved a literacy rate of only 74.04 per cent, Mizoram achieved literacy rate as high as 91.58 per cent. The performance of Northeastern states in the last decade has been observed to be better in reduction of gender gap in literacy rates. Among the states that have been able to reduce the literacy gap to a large extent are Meghalaya, Mizoram and Manipur. Although infant mortality rate is quite high (47) in the country achievements of some Northeastern states in this regard is quite satisfactory. Excepting Assam, Meghalaya and Mizoram all other states in the Northeast has been able to reduce infant mortality rate to a great extent. There exists, however, further scope to reduce infant mortality rate in the region.

Conclusion and Policy Implications

The findings reveal that achievement of Northeastern region has been quite satisfactory in comparison to all India average situations in some dimensions of human development for both the sexes. But the region has miserably failed in bringing commensurate economic growth because of very poor performance of mainly two states, namely Assam and Manipur of which Assam is the largest state in the region. There exists widespread disparity of poverty and socio-economic achievements across different states and within, from urban to rural areas and between male and female. If the problems of poor economic growth, poverty, gender disparities and general health of the people are not properly addressed, the region may fall into the trap of vicious quadrant instead of moving to a virtuous one. To overcome this on priority basis, the region has to adopt a two-pronged strategy of higher production and equitable distribution. To move on a path of higher and sustainable economic growth, the region must emphasize on productive activities instead of depending on central government for higher allocation of funds. Higher allocation of fund to the region has not been a problem in the last decade. Rather the region is facing at present the problem of utilisation of fund, and more so their proper utilisation. There exists a great scope of development in the area of horticulture, particularly production of fruits such as pine apple and orange, vegetables, mushrooms, culinary herbs and non-food crops such as flowers and processing of some of these items. Needbased scope for expansion of activities in the areas of fisheries and poultry farming do exists. Initiative should be taken to bring a change in the design and taste of the handloom and handicraft products of the region that can attract the customers outside the region and the country. Besides, marketing strategy for these products need to be devised with the help of experts to explore market of these products outside the region. There should be an approach of balanced economic development. Emphasis need to be made to reduce all forms of inequity that exists among different states, within the states and among different sections and social groups. Since the governments have failed to a large extent in the health sector, NGOs have a great role to play to provide a healthy life to the expectant mothers and the infants. Poverty reduction programme needs revamping through plugging of the holes in its execution process to ensure poor to be the real beneficiaries. These programmes have been successful in places where there has been political will to punish the officials who are found guilty in the implementation of the programme. In the absence of a strong political will in the region, the only way out to overcome the problem is to strengthen the hands of pressure groups that have the power to influence the mindset of the politician. Although some pressure groups are vigilant in the region and acting as watchdogs, they are concerned only with few issues, sometimes non-important and irrelevant issues. Therefore, every individual in the region has a role to play in her/his sphere to create awareness in the neighbourhoods to be vigilant against all such odds, inefficiency, illegal practices and injustice prevalent in the society.

References

Agarwal, A.K. (2010) 'Human Development in Mizoram: An Overview' in P. Nayak (ed.) *Growth and Human Development in North East India,* New Delhi: Oxford University Press. pp. 271–280.

Census of India. (2011) (http://www.educationforallinindia.com/chapter6-state-of-literacy-2011-census.pdf), accessed on 13 August 2012.

Central Statistical Organization. (2012) Online data on 'Per Capita Income' and 'Infant Mortality Rate' (http://www.indiastat.com/economy/8/stats.aspx), accessed on 13 August 2012.

Government of Arunachal Pradesh. (2006) *Arunachal Pradesh Human Development Report 2006,* Department of Planning, Itanagar, Arunachal Pradesh.

Government of Assam. (2003) *Assam Human Development Report 2003,* Planning and Development Department, Dispur, Assam.

Government of India. (2011) *India Human Development Report 2011*, Planning Commission, and Institute of Applied Manpower Research, New Delhi.

Government of India. (2002) *National Human Development Report 2001*, Planning Commission, New Delhi.

Government of Meghalaya. (2008) *Meghalaya Human Development Report 2008*, Planning Department, Shillong, Meghalaya.

Government of Nagaland. (2004) *Nagaland State Human Development Report 2004*, Department of Planning and Coordination, Kohima, Nagaland.

Government of Sikkim. (2001) *Sikkim Human Development Report 2001*, Social Science Press, New Delhi.

Government of Tripura. (2007) *Tripura Human Development Report 2007*, Agartala, Tripura.

Singh, E. Bijoykumar. (2010) 'Human Development in Manipur' in P. Nayak (ed.) *Growth and Human Development in North East India*, New Delhi: Oxford University Press, pp. 257–270.

UNDP (2003) *Human Development Report 2003*, Oxford University Press, New York.

2

Development of Elementary Education in Northeast India

Trends, Issues and Challenges

S.M.I.A. ZAIDI

After gaining Independence the process of planned development started in India in 1950–51 when the First Five Year Plan was launched and implemented in the country. As a result of this concerted effort towards over all development of the country, progress has been made in all sectors of economy and education is no exception to it. It has been envisaged from the beginning that over all development of the country can be achieved by developing the education sector and that is the reason that focus has been on the development of education in India. As a result country has made tremendous progress in the field of education during last six decades after Independence. However, it may be noted that the focus in the field of education right from the beginning has been more on elementary education.

Though the country, as per the directive under Article 45 of the Constitution, should have achieved the goal of providing free and compulsory education to all children up to 14 years of age by 1960, i.e. 10 years after the adoption of the Constitution but we are still striving to achieve this goal even after more than six decades of adoption of the Constitution. Provision made under Article 45 may be fulfilled only by achieving the goal of Universalisation of Elementary Education (UEE). The target date for achieving this goal has been shifted time and again but unfortunately still this goal has eluded the country.

Provision made under Article 45 of the Constitution has implication for the government because it has been the responsibility of the government to provide free and compulsory education to all children of the country. However, the term 'government' has been defined in the Constitution as Central Government, state governments and the local bodies. It is, therefore, clear that it is the joint responsibility of Central Government, state governments and local bodies to make all provisions for achieving the goal of UEE. It may further be noted that despite the fact that education is a concurrent subject under the Indian Constitution the development of school education has been more or less the responsibility of state governments and UT administrations and the role of Central Government has been marginal in this regard.

As mentioned above, the universalisation of elementary education is a constitutional directive and it has also been endorsed by various committees and commissions on education appointed by the government. Emphasis on achieving this goal has also been given in the National Policies on Education (NPE) 1968 as well as the NPE 1986. It may noted that the implication of such recommendation made in the NPEs and also endorsed in reports of various committees and commissions are not restricted to making only the provisions, i.e. opening of schools and providing all kinds of facilities in schools but also to ensure that all children participate in education till they successfully complete eight years of schooling.

In order to achieve the goal of UEE, apart from the recommendations made in the committees and commissions and endorsements in national policies on education, several projects and programmes were launched in various states of country in 1980s and 1990s. These include Andhra Pradesh Primary Education Project (APPEP), Bihar Education Project (BEP), Uttar Pradesh Basic Education Project (UPBEP), Lok Jumbish and Shiksha Karmi projects of Rajasthan and District Primary Education Programme (DPEP). In fact, DPEP was the first programme launched in the country that covered several states and it was through these projects and programmes only that the Central Government has started contributing towards achieving the goal of UEE.

It is interesting to note that none of the above mentioned projects and programmes cover any Northeastern states of the country barring Assam in which some districts were covered under DPEP. The latest in the series of these programmes implemented in the country is the Sarva Shiksha Abhiyan (SSA) programme that was launched in 2000–01 and its implementation started in 2001–02. It may be noted that this is the first programme that covers all the states and UTs of the country right from the beginning. However, in some Northeastern states the implementation of this programme started in 2002–03 and in few states as late as 2003–04 also.

A very important step taken by the Government of India, towards Universalisation of Elementary Education, recently is passing of 'Right of Children to Free and Compulsory Education Act 2009' which is popularly known as Right to Education (RTE) Act. This Act is extended to the whole country except the state of Jammu and Kashmir. It is therefore clear that this Act covers all the eight Northeastern states also.

This paper discusses in detail about various aspects of the development of elementary education in the Northeastern region of the country. It covers all the eight states coming under Northeastern region namely, Arunachal Pradesh, Assam, Manipur, Meghalaya, Mizoram, Nagaland, Sikkim and Tripura. The paper highlights the latest elementary education scenario in these states by presenting data on various items related to elementary education and also examines the problems faced by these states in the development of elementary education.

The Northeast Region

The Northeastern region of the country, as is clear from the name, is located in the Northeastern part of India. This region comprises eight states, namely Arunachal Pradesh, Assam, Manipur, Meghalaya, Mizoram, Nagaland, Sikkim and Tripura. Almost all these states are hill states except Assam which is not only the biggest state of the region but also has vast plane area. The whole region can be termed as backward region in terms of economic development as there are hardly any big industries here barring some such units in Assam. However, it does not necessarily mean that all these states of this region are educationally backward also. Geographically, except Assam and Arunachal Pradesh all states are small states while demographically except Assam all states are quite small states in the Northeastern region.

Demographic Profile of Northeast Region

As per 2011 Census, among the 28 states of the country, Sikkim is demographically the smallest state. So this state representing only 0.05 per cent of the country's population is not only the smallest state of the region but is even smallest in the country. In fact the 2011 Census data shows that out of the five smallest states in the country four states are located in the Northeastern region and these are Sikkim, Mizoram, Nagaland and Manipur. Goa is the only one of the five smallest states that is located out of the Northeastern region.

Table 1 shows the demographic profile of the eight Northeastern states as well as the Northeastern region as per 2011 Census.

The table reveals that the Northeastern region of the country comprising eight states (out of 35 states and union territories) represent only about 3.56 per cent of the country's population. However, Assam is the biggest state that comprises 2.58 per cent of the country's population and this state alone represents about 72.25 of the population of Northeastern region. It means demographically about three-fourth of the

Northeastern region is only one state, i.e. Assam and rest one-fourth population of the region comprises other seven states.

Table 1

Population of Northeastern States of India (2011)

Name of the State	*Total Population*	*Male Population*	*Female Population*	*% of Country's Population*
Arunachal Pradesh	13,82,611	7,20,232	6,62,379	0.1142
Assam	3,11,69,272	1,59,54,927	1,52,14,345	2.5755
Manipur	27,21,756	13,69,764	13,51,992	0.2249
Meghalaya	29,64,007	14,92,668	14,71,339	0.2449
Mizoram	10,91,014	5,52,339	5,28,675	0.0902
Nagaland	19,80,602	10,25,707	9,54,895	0.1637
Sikkim	6,07,688	3,21,661	2,86,027	0.0502
Tripura	36,71,032	18,71,867	17,99,165	0.3033
Total Northeast	4,31,37,982	2,33,09,165	1,98,28,817	3.5646
India	1,21,01,93,422	62,37,24,248	58,64,69,174	100

Source: Census of India, 2011.

The table shows that in the Northeastern region one state (Sikkim) has less than 1 million population, three states, namely Arunachal Pradesh, Mizoram and Nagaland, have population between 1 and 2 million, two states (Manipur and Meghalaya) have population between 2 and 3 million while one state, i.e. Tripura, has population between 3 and 4 million. Assam, the biggest state of this region, has more than 31 million population. So, demographically Assam is the biggest and Sikkim is the smallest state of this region.

The Table 2 presents some demographic indicators of the eight states of the Northeastern region as per 2011 Census.

The Table 2 shows that the Northeastern region has about 7.98 per cent of the country's area while its population is only about 3.56 per cent of the country's population. In the Northeastern region geographically Arunachal Pradesh (83,743 square kilometre) is the biggest state followed by Assam (78,438 square kilometre). Sikkim (7,096 square kilometre) is the smallest state in Northeast followed by Tripura (10,486 square kilometre).

Being small in population and relatively big in terms of geographical area, the Northeastern region has quite a low density of population. As against 382 persons per square kilometre in the country, the Northeastern region has only 164 persons per square kilometre. But Assam (397) is the state where the population density is even more than the national average while in Tripura (350) also population density is relatively high. In three states namely Manipur (122), Meghalaya (132) and Nagaland (119), the density of population is between 100 and 135. In other two states namely Sikkim (86) and Mizoram (52), the population density is between 50 and 100. Arunachal Pradesh (17) has a population density which is not only lowest in this region but is also lowest in the country.

Table 2

Demographic Indicators of Northeastern States of India (2011)

Name of the State	*Area (sq kms)*	*Density of Population*	*Sex Ratio*	*Growth Rate of Population (2001–2011)*
Arunachal Pradesh	83,743	17	920	25.92
Assam	78,438	397	954	16.93
Manipur	22,327	122	967	18.65
Meghalaya	22,429	132	986	27.82
Mizoram	21,081	52	975	22.78
Nagaland	16,579	119	931	-0.47
Sikkim	7,096	86	889	12.36
Tripura	10,486	350	961	14.75
Total Northeast	2,62,179	164	950	—
India	32,87,240	382	940	17.64

Source: Census of India 2011

Data pertaining to sex-ratio shows that the position in Northeastern region is relatively better as here the sex-ratio (950) is slightly better than the national average of 940. In the Northeastern region sex-ratio is highest in Meghalaya (986) followed by Mizoram (975) and Manipur (967). However, in three states, namely Sikkim (889), Arunachal Pradesh (920) and Nagaland (931), the sex-ratio is lower than the national average of 940 and that of Northeastern region (950).

The decadal growth rate of population in the states of Northeastern region shows a very typical trend. It is interesting to note that in Nagaland the population has declined between 2001 and 2011 and this is the only state in the region that shows negative growth rate of population (–0.47). Meghalaya (27.82) has the highest growth rate of population followed by Arunachal Pradesh (25.92) and Mizoram (22.78). Sikkim (12.36), Tripura (14.75) and Assam (16.93) have lower growth rate of population than the national average of 17.64.

Literacy Scenario of Northeast Region

Literacy is considered as one the most basic indicators of educational development of any area. It is, therefore, appropriate to look at the literacy figures of the various states of the Northeastern region and compare these with national scenario. Table 3 presents the literacy rates of the North-eastern states as per 2011 Census.

Table 3

Literacy Rates of Northeastern Region (2011)

Name of the State	*Total Literacy*	*Male Literacy*	*Female Literacy*	*Increase in Total Literacy (2001 to 2011)*
Arunachal Pradesh	67.0	73.7	59.6	+12.7
Assam	73.2	78.8	67.3	+10.0
Manipur	79.8	86.5	73.2	+9.3
Meghalaya	75.5	77.2	73.8	+13.0
Mizoram	91.6	93.7	89.4	+2.8
Nagaland	80.1	83.3	76.7	+13.5
Sikkim	82.2	87.3	76.4	+13.6
Tripura	87.8	92.2	83.1	+14.6
India	74.04	82.14	65.46	+9.0

Source: Census of India, 2011.

Table 3 reveals that except Arunachal Pradesh and Assam, all the other six states of Northeastern region have better literacy rates than the national average of 74.04 per cent as per 2011 census. In the total literacy, as observed in the table, Mizoram (91.6%) has the highest literacy while Arunachal Pradesh (67%) has the lowest literacy in the region. Out of the eight states, one state (Mizoram) has more than 90 per cent literacy and three states have more than 80 per cent literacy and these states are Tripura (87.8%), Sikkim (82.2%) and Nagaland (80.1%). Another two states, namely Manipur (79.8%) and Meghalaya (75.5%) have literacy rate between 75 and 80 per cent.

The figures of male literacy show that except Arunachal Pradesh (73.7%), Meghalaya (77.2%) and Assam (78.8%), remaining five states of Northeastern region have higher literacy rates than the national average (82.14%). The table shows that two states, namely Mizoram (93.7%) and Tripura (92.2%), have more than 90 per cent male literacy. Another three states have male literacy between 80 and 90 per cent and these states are Sikkim (87.3%), Manipur (86.5%) and Nagaland (83.3%). Only three states, namely Arunachal Pradesh, Assam and Meghalaya, have male literacy below 80 per cent and also below the national average.

The position of female literacy in Northeastern states is relatively better as all the states except Arunachal Pradesh have better female literacy than that national average of 65.46 per cent. In two states of Northeastern region the female literacy is more than 80 per cent and these are Mizoram (89.4%) and Tripura (83.1%). In two states, namely Nagaland (76.7%) and

Sikkim (76.4%) the female literacy is between 75 and 80 per cent. Manipur (73.2%) and Meghalaya (73.8%) have female literacy between 70 and 75 per cent. Assam has less than 70 per cent female literacy while Arunachal Pradesh has less than 60 per cent female literacy.

The figures presented in the table show that these states have made very good progress in literacy in 10 years, i.e. between 2001 and 2011. Mizoram is the state where the progress in literacy was slowest as the literacy here has increased by 2.8 per cent points only. The reason being the literacy rate of this state was very high even in 2001 (i.e. 88.8%) and so there was not much scope for this state to increase its literacy figures. In rest of the seven states, the net increase in literacy is more than the national average of 9 per cent points between 2001 and 2011. In this regard Manipur (9.3% points) shows the lowest increase followed by Assam (10% points) while Tripura (14.6% points) shows the highest increase in literacy. In rest of the four states, the increase in literacy is between 10 and 14 per cent points and these states are Arunachal Pradesh (12.7% points), Meghalaya (13% points), Nagaland (13.5% points) and Sikkim (13.6% points).

By looking at the literacy figures presented in Table 3 we can conclude that except Arunachal Pradesh and Assam the Northeastern states are educationally advanced states of the country as far as the literacy scenario in India is concerned. Further, almost all the North-eastern states have made very good progress in increasing the literacy rates between 2001 and 2011.

Elementary Education Scenario in Northeast

As discussed in previous passages, the literacy rates of the Northeastern states are quite impressive except Arunachal Pradesh and Assam. It may be mentioned here that the most important source of spreading literacy in any area is the availability of elementary schools and the participation in and completion of elementary education by the relevant age group population. It can, therefore, be perceived that in the Northeastern states the provision of schooling facilities and participation in elementary education may be better. However, this paper attempts to present the real picture of availability of elementary schooling facilities in these North-eastern states.

Access to Elementary Education

Access to the elementary education can be seen by looking at the number of schools imparting primary and upper primary education available in the Northeastern states. Table 4 presents number of schools imparting elementary education in the Northeastern states and also the percentage of government, private aided and unaided schools in these states.

Table 4

Number of Schools Imparting Elementary Education in Northeastern States (2010–11)

Name of the State	*Total Number of Schools*	*Percentage of Govt. Schools*	*Percentage of Private Aided Schools*	*Percentage of Private Unaided Schools*	*Percentage of Total Schools in the Country*
Arunachal Pradesh	4,441	92.32	1.64	5.99	0.326
Assam	64,653	68.63	11.04	3.63	4.746
Manipur	3,878	61.94	14.78	20.24	0.285
Meghalaya	12,414	61.19	27.83	10.68	0.911
Mizoram	2,904	80.41	2.27	16.80	0.213
Nagaland	2,826	74.35	0.00	25.65	0.207
Sikkim	1,201	74.52	3.00	22.48	0.088
Tripura	4,386	96.15	1.09	2.76	0.322
India	13,62,324	78.15	5.20	14.22	—

Source: NUEPA (2012) Flash Statistics DISE 2010–11

Totals may not add to 100 because of missing values and rounding of figures
$ Assam has more than 10,000 Venture (unrecognised) schools which are not included here

Table 4 shows that total number of schools imparting elementary schools in the country were 13,62,324 in 2010–11. In the Northeastern region highest number of schools are found in Assam (64,653) followed by Meghalaya (12,414). It may be mentioned here that in Assam, as has been reported in the DISE 2010–11 report, there are 10,654 venture schools which are unrecognised schools running in the state and these schools have not been included in the number of schools mentioned in the table. Two states, namely Arunachal Pradesh (4,441) and Tripura (4,386), have more than 4,000 schools each while Mizoram (2,904) and Nagaland (2,836) have less than 3,000 schools each. Sikkim being the smallest state in the region has the lowest number of schools (1,201).

As mentioned above the responsibility of providing elementary education mainly lies with the government. It can, therefore, be expected that the share of government schools may be quite huge in the schools functioning in any state. Table 4 shows that in the whole country the percentage of government schools is 78.15 which reveal that more than three-fourth elementary schools in the country are government schools. But in the Northeastern region Tripura has more than 95 per cent and Arunachal Pradesh has more than 90 per cent government schools while Mizoram has more than 80 per cent government schools. About three-fourth elementary schools in Nagaland and Sikkim are managed by the government while in Assam there are about 68.63 per cent government schools. In Manipur and Meghalaya, hardly 60 per cent schools are managed by the government.

Private aided schools are only about 5.20 per cent in the country while among the Northeastern states, these schools are relatively the highest in Meghalaya as in this state 27.83 per cent schools are aided schools which is followed by Manipur (14.78%) and Assam (11.04%). In rest of the Northeast states, private aided schools are less than 3 per cent with the exception of Nagaland where there is not even a single aided school.

Table 4 reveals that about 14.22 per cent elementary schools in the country are the private unaided schools. In the Northeastern region, in Assam and Tripura private unaided schools are less than 5 per cent each while in Arunachal Pradesh these schools are about 6 per cent. In Meghalaya private unaided schools are 10.68 per cent and in Mizoram these are 16.80 per cent which is more than the national figure of 14.22 per cent. It can be noted that in three Northeastern states, more than 20 per cent schools are private unaided schools and these states are Manipur (20.24%), Sikkim (22.48%) and Nagaland (25.65%).

It can be inferred from the above analysis and discussion that the Tripura Government is the best performing while Manipur Government is the worst performing state government in making provision of elementary schooling facilities as these states have the highest and the lowest percentage of government schools, respectively and lowest and highest percentage of private unaided schools, respectively.

In order to examine the availability of elementary schooling facilities in the Northeastern region it may be proper to see the population percentage of these states and compare it with their share in elementary schools. Table 5 presents the population percentage and the number of elementary schools and the share of elementary schools for the North-eastern states.

Table 5 reveals that in all the Northeastern states the share of the elementary schools is more than the share of their population in the country. It is clear that in Arunachal Pradesh the percentage of schools is about thrice the percentage of population, while in Meghalaya the percentage of schools is nearly four times that of percentage of population. Assam has only 2.57 per cent population of the country while it has about 4.75 per cent elementary schools of the country. In Mizoram, only 0.09 per cent population of the country lives while this state has about 0.21 per cent elementary schools. It can, therefore, be inferred that access to elementary education facilities in the Northeastern states is better than many other states of the country. Further, the elementary educational facilities are better in Northeastern region than the other regions of India.

Table 5

Percentage of Population and Elementary Schools in the Northeastern Region

Name of the State	*Population (2011)*	*% of Country's Population (2011)*	*Number of Elementary Schools (2010–11)*	*Percentage of Total Schools in the Country (2010–11)*
Arunachal Pradesh	13,82,611	0.1142	4,441	0.326
Assam	3,11,69,272	2.5755	64,653	4.746
Manipur	27,21,756	0.2249	3,878	0.285
Meghalaya	29,64,007	0.2449	12,414	0.911
Mizoram	10,91,014	0.0902	2,904	0.213
Nagaland	19,80,602	0.1637	2,826	0.207
Sikkim	6,07,688	0.0502	1,201	0.088
Tripura	36,71,032	0.3033	4,386	0.322
India	1,21,01,93,422	—	13,62,324	—

Source: Census of India 2011 and DISE 2010–11

Table 6 presents data on some indicators showing access to elementary education in the Northeastern states of the country.

Table 6

Access to Primary and Upper Primary Education in Northeastern States (2010–11)

Name of the State	*Primary Schools/ Sections per 1,000 child Population (6–11 years)*	*Upper Primary Schools/ Sections per 1,000 child Population (11–14 years)*	*Primary Schools/ Sections per 10 sq km area*	*Upper Primary Schools/ Sections per 10 sq km area*	*Ratio of Primary to Upper Primary Schools*
Arunachal Pradesh	44	16	0.52	0.14	3.59
Assam	16	10	6.15	2.41	2.55
Manipur	19	10	1.65	0.67	2.46
Meghalaya	43	22	4.12	1.56	2.64
Mizoram	23	23	0.91	0.66	1.38
Nagaland	13	8	1.42	0.67	2.12
Sikkim	24	12	1.68	0.62	2.72
Tripura	15	9	4.11	1.82	2.05
India	10	8	3.45	1.63	2.12

Source: NUEPA (2012) Flash Statistics DISE 2010-11

Data presented in Table 6 show that in the country there are 10 primary schools per 1,000 child population of relevant age group 6–11 years. But the situation in Northeastern states is better as all the eight

Northeastern states have more than 10 primary schools per 1,000 children in 6–11 age group. In fact in states like Arunachal Pradesh and Meghalaya, there are as many as 44 and 43 primary schools, respectively, per 1,000 relevant child population. There are two states where primary schools per 1,000 child population are 24 and 23 and these states are Sikkim and Mizoram, respectively. Assam (16) and Manipur (19) have more than 15 primary schools each per 1,000 child population against only 10 schools in the country. Tripura (15) and Nagaland (13) have the lowest number of primary schools per 1,000 child population but even in these states the number is more than 10, i.e. the national average.

There are eight upper primary schools per 1,000 child population of 11–14 years age group in the country. In the Northeastern region, all states except Nagaland have more than eight upper primary schools per 1,000 relevant child population. Even in Nagaland also number of upper primary schools per 1,000 child population is the same as in the country, i.e. eight schools. Mizoram (23) and Meghalaya (22) have the highest number of upper primary schools per 1,000 relevant child population followed by Arunachal Pradesh (16) and Sikkim (12). Assam and Manipur each have 10 upper primary schools per 1,000 child population while in Tripura the number of upper primary schools per 1,000 child population is nine.

From the above analysis it can be concluded that the access to primary and upper primary schools in the Northeastern region is better than the access provided in the other regions of the country and all the Northeastern states have more primary and upper primary schools per 1,000 relevant child population than the number of such schools in the country.

Table 6 shows that in India there are about 3.45 primary schools per 10 square kilometre area. However, in the Northeastern region, only three states, namely Assam (6.15), Meghalaya (4.12) and Tripura (4.11) have more primary schools per 10 square kilometre area than the national average. Manipur (1.65), Nagaland (1.42) and Sikkim (1.68) have less than two primary schools each per 10 square kilometre area. The position is worse in Mizoram (0.91) and Arunachal Pradesh (0.52) where per 10 square kilometre area, there is not even one primary school. It can be noted that in Arunachal Pradesh there is only one primary school per 20 square kilometre area which is probably because of very low density population in the state.

As far as availability of upper primary schools is concerned there are 1.63 schools per 10 square kilometre area in the country. In the Northeastern region only Assam (2.41) and Tripura (1.82) have slightly more number of upper primary schools per 10 square kilometre area while Meghalaya (1.56) has also more than one upper primary school per 10 square kilometre area. In other four states, there is less than one upper primary school per 10 square kilometre area. These states are Manipur (0.67), Nagaland (0.67), Mizoram (0.66) and Sikkim (0.62). The situation is worst in Arunachal Pradesh where there are only 0.14 upper primary schools per 10 square kilometre area. It shows that in Arunachal Pradesh, there are only about 3 upper primary schools per 200 square kilometre area and this may be due to the very low population density in the state which is lowest in the country.

From the above discussion it can be inferred that in Assam and Tripura primary and upper primary schools per 10 square kilometre area are more than the national average while in Meghalaya these are more or less at par with the national average. In other five Northeastern states there are relatively quite less number of primary and upper primary schools per 10 square kilometre area than the national average.

Access to upper primary schools can be seen by looking at the ratio of primary and upper primary school in a specific area. It is desired that there may be one upper primary school for every two primary, schools which means the ratio may be 1:2. Data presented in the table show that in India one upper primary school is available for every 2.12 primary schools. In the Northeastern region, except Mizoram (1.38), Tripura (2.05) and Nagaland (2.12), the access to upper primary education is worse than the national average. In Assam (2.55), Manipur (2.46), Meghalaya (2.64) and Sikkim (2.72) each upper primary school has to cover more than 2.4 primary schools. Arunachal Pradesh has one upper primary for every 3.59 primary schools which shows that in this state the ratio of primary and upper primary schools is 1:3.6.

It can be inferred from the above discussion that in the Northeastern states though per 1,000 relevant child population number of primary and upper primary schools are more as compared to states of the other regions but in Northeastern region children have to cover relatively more distance to attend the primary and upper schools. It can also be inferred from this discussion that the elementary schools in the Northeastern region are relatively small in enrollment size.

Facilities in Schools of Northeast Region

The access to elementary education does not only mean the availability of primary and upper primary schools but it also includes provision of all kinds of facilities and infrastructure that are necessary for ensuring a proper teaching learning atmosphere in the school so that the teachers are able to teach properly and children are able to learn. It is, therefore, necessary that all the primary and upper primary schools have proper facilities and infrastructure available.

Table 7 presents data on schools approachable by all weather roads and average number of classrooms available in the elementary schools of the Northeastern region.

Table 7

Schools Approachable by Road and Average no. of Classrooms in Elementary Schools of Northeast (2010–11)

Name of the State	*% of Schools Approachable by all Weather Roads*	*Average no. of Classrooms in Primary Schools*	*Average no. of Classrooms in Upper Primary Schools*	*Average Student Classroom Ratio Primary Schools*
Arunachal Pradesh	61.38	2.5	4.0	14
Assam	91.71	2.4	3.1	29
Manipur	94.12	3.6	6.0	17
Meghalaya	67.56	2.6	3.0	17
Mizoram	N.A.	4.3	4.6	16
Nagaland	82.73	5.6	7.1	15
Sikkim	100	4.8	7.5	10
Tripura	82.03	3.8	5.6	15
India	93.19	3.2	4.6	31

Source: NUEPA (2012) Flash Statistics DISE 2010–11

Table 7 reveals that about 93 per cent primary and upper primary schools in the country are approachable by all weather roads which means the accessibility to these 93 per cent schools is easy while the remaining seven per cent schools may not be easily accessible. In the Northeastern region it is quite heartening to note that in Sikkim all schools are approachable by all weather roads while in Assam (91.71%) and Manipur (94.12%) more than 90 per cent schools are approachable. In another two states, namely Nagaland (82.73%) and Tripura (82.03%), more than 80 per cent primary and upper primary schools are approachable by all weather roads. In Meghalaya, about two-third primary and upper primary schools are approachable by roads while the position is worst in Arunachal Pradesh where only about 61.38 per cent schools are approachable by road.

Availability of building is necessary for all the schools but provision of enough number of classrooms is also important in the schools. Ideally there should be one classroom per class which means that in primary schools for having five classes (i.e. I–V) there should be five classrooms. The data presented in Table 7 shows that average number of classrooms in primary schools is only 3.2 in the country. In the Northeastern region except Arunachal Pradesh (2.5), Assam (2. 4) and Meghalaya (2.6) all other states have more classrooms per primary school than the national figure of

3.2 classrooms. In this regard Nagaland has best facilities of classrooms (5.6) followed by Sikkim (4.8) and Mizoram (4.3). Tripura (3.8) and Manipur (3.6) have more than 3.5 classrooms per primary school.

At upper primary level, average number of classrooms in upper primary schools is 4.6 in the country. In the Northeastern region as many as five out of eight states have more classrooms per upper primary school than 4.6 which is the national average. The highest number of classrooms per upper primary school is available in Sikkim (7.5) followed by Nagaland (7.1), Manipur (6.0) and Tripura (5.6). Average number of classrooms in upper primary schools in the Northeast region is the lowest in Meghalaya (3.0) and Assam (3.1).

In primary schools, as the data show, average students per classroom is 31 in the country while in all the Northeastern states, except Assam where it is 29, the student classroom ratio is quite low. In four states the student classroom ratio ranges between 10 and 15 and these states are Sikkim (10), Arunachal Pradesh (14), Nagaland (15) and Tripura (15). In Mizoram there are 16 students per classroom while in Manipur and Meghalaya the average students per classroom are 17 each.

It can be inferred from the above discussion that in Arunachal Pradesh, Assam and Meghalaya provision of classrooms in the primary and upper primary schools is not satisfactory while in other five states the provision of classrooms is relatively better than the other regions of the country.

Classrooms in Government and Private Schools

It is generally perceived that facilities in private schools are better when compared to the government schools. In order to investigate on this issue, Table 8 presents data on average number of classrooms available in the government schools and in private schools as also data on average student classroom ratio in all elementary schools in the Northeastern region.

Table 8 shows that average number of classrooms in government schools is 3.8 while in private schools the number is as high as eight classrooms. Similar is the position of the Northeastern states also where in all the eight states average classrooms in private schools is more than that of government schools. In Northeastern region, average number of classrooms in government schools in Arunachal Pradesh (3.6), Assam (3.1) and Meghalaya (2.6) is less than the national average of 3.8 classrooms. Sikkim (7.3) has the highest number of classrooms per government school followed by Nagaland (5.5) and Tripura (5.3). In the private schools, average classrooms per school is very low in Meghalaya (3.5) and Assam (4.2) while average classrooms in private schools is the highest in Nagaland (11.9) followed by Tripura (11.5).

Table 8

Average Number of Classrooms and Average Student Classroom Ratio in Government and Private Schools of Northeast (2010–11)

Name of the State	*Average no. of Classrooms in govt. Schools*	*Average no. of Classrooms in Private Schools*	*Average no. of Classrooms in All Schools*	*Average Student Classroom Ratio All Schools*
Arunachal Pradesh	3.6	9.3	4.0	19
Assam	3.1	4.2	3.2	29
Manipur	4.5	8.5	6.0	22
Meghalaya	2.6	3.5	3.0	18
Mizoram	4.0	6.9	4.6	18
Nagaland	5.5	11.9	7.1	20
Sikkim	7.3	7.8	7.5	14
Tripura	5.3	11.5	5.6	25
India	3.8	8.0	4.6	31

Source: NUEPA (2012) Flash Statistics DISE 2010–11.

Data on student classroom ratio shows that in the country there are about 31 students per classroom in the primary and upper primary schools. But in the Northeastern region, except Assam (29), the number is relatively quite low. It is the lowest in Sikkim where there are only 14 students per classroom while in Meghalaya and Mizoram there are 18 students per classroom. After Assam, the highest students per classroom are in Tripura (25) and Manipur (22).

It can be inferred from the above discussion that private schools are of quite bigger size than the government schools as average number of classrooms in private schools (8.0) is more than double that of government schools (3.8) and that is applicable to all the Northeastern states as well. Further, in Northeastern states average students per classrooms in the elementary schools is relatively low.

Basic Facilities in the Schools

Provision of basic facilities like drinking water, compound wall, playground, toilets, electricity, etc. are necessary for primary as well as upper primary schools. It is important to probe into this issue and that is why data on these items have been taken for analysis in this paper. Table 9 presents data on the availability of basic facilities in elementary schools of the Northeastern region.

Table 9 shows that 92.71 per cent elementary schools in the country have drinking water facility. It is, therefore, clear that more than 7 per cent schools in the country do not have even drinking water facility. But the situation is still worse in the Northeastern region as except Sikkim where

98.17 per cent schools have drinking water, in all other seven states drinking water facility is available in less than 90 per cent schools. In three states this facility is available in more than 80 per cent schools and these states are Manipur (89.20%), Mizoram (86.05%) and Tripura (82.38%). In Arunachal Pradesh (78.16%), Assam (76.12%) and Nagaland (75.09%) more than 75 per cent schools have drinking water facility. It is disappointing to note that in Meghalaya only 58.56 per cent schools have this facility which means that more than 40 per cent schools in this state have no drinking water facility.

Table 9

Percentage of Elementary Schools having various Basic Facilities in Northeast (2010–11)

Name of the State	*Drinking Water Facility*	*Boundary Walls*	*Functional common Toilet*	*Functional Boys' Toilet*	*Functional Girls' Toilet*
Arunachal Pradesh	78.16	29.99	65.73	83.82	69.78
Assam	76.12	24.76	69.34	81.54	74.04
Manipur	89.20	30.38	82.98	89.70	87.15
Meghalaya	58.56	18.87	68.73	75.56	70.84
Mizoram	86.05	58.26	87.65	92.25	84.26
Nagaland	75.09	75.34	52.22	69.54	57.14
Sikkim	98.17	29.31	94.73	95.96	96.03
Tripura	82.38	13.18	75.34	82.24	78.57
India	92.71	55.41	72.56	88.40	80.87

Source: NUEPA (2012) Flash Statistics DISE 2010–11

Boundary wall is available in only 55.41 per cent schools in the country, while in Northeastern states the position is even worse. Except Nagaland (75.34%) and Mizoram (58.26%) no other state has even 40 per cent schools having boundary wall. About 30 per cent schools in Arunachal Pradesh, Manipur and Sikkim have the boundary walls. Tripura (13.18%) is the Northeastern state where lowest percentage of schools have boundary walls followed by Meghalaya (18.87%).

Availability of toilets in schools is necessary but it is more important that the toilets available in the schools are in functional condition. Data given in Table 9 shows that only 72.56 per cent schools in the country have functional common toilets. In the Northeastern region, Sikkim (94.73%) has more than 90 per cent schools having functional common toilet while in other 3 states more than 75 per cent schools have functional common toilet and these states are Manipur (82.98%), Mizoram (87.65%) and Tripura (75.34%). In three other states (Arunachal Pradesh, Assam and Meghalaya), more than 65 per cent schools have functional common toilet while position in Nagaland is worst as in this state only 52.22 per cent schools have this facility.

Data presented in Table 9 show that 88.40 per cent schools in the country have functional toilets for boys. In the Northeastern region, the highest percentage of schools having functional boys' toilets are in Sikkim (95.96%) followed by Mizoram (92.25%). As many as four Northeastern states, namely Arunachal Pradesh (83.82%), Assam (81.54%), Manipur (89.70%) and Tripura (82.24%), have more than 80 per cent schools having functional toilets for boys. Nagaland having provision of functional boys' toilets in only 69.54 per cent schools is the most deprived state on this count.

Functional girls' toilets are available in 80.87 per cent schools of the country which shows that about one-fifth schools do not have this facility. In the Northeastern region, performance of Sikkim is the best where about 96 per cent schools have this facility. Further, in Manipur (87.15%) and Mizoram (84.26%), more than 80 per cent schools have functional girls' toilets while another three states have more than 70 schools having this facility. These states are Assam (74.04%), Meghalaya (70.84%) and Tripura (78.57%). Nagaland (57.14%) has the lowest percentage of schools having functional girls' toilets.

From the above discussion it can be inferred that as far as the availability of basic facilities in the elementary schools is concerned the performance of Sikkim and Manipur is quite impressive while other Northeastern states show relatively poor performance when compared with the other regions of the country.

Table 10 presents data on the percentage of elementary schools having basic facilities like ramps, electricity and playground.

Table 10

Percentage of Schools having Various Infrastructure Facilities (2010–11)

Name of the State	*Primary Schools having Ramp*	*All Schools having Ramp*	*Primary Schools having Electricity*	*All Schools having Electricity*	*All schools having Playground*
Arunachal Pradesh	2.57	3.67	9.04	20.72	29.97
Assam	43.15	37.91	5.09	11.50	53.02
Manipur	4.25	5.29	5.13	23.05	55.93
Meghalaya	15.92	16.48	7.85	14.02	36.07
Mizoram	44.31	40.56	32.67	42.49	32.13
Nagaland	32.05	26.72	14.66	34.96	47.28
Sikkim	3.67	5.50	44.04	60.03	63.78
Tripura	48.40	57.20	2.93	14.32	62.59
India	49.71	50.39	32.20	43.14	55.03

Source: NUEPA (2012) Flash Statistics DISE 2010–11

Table 10 shows that about half of the schools in India have the facility of ramps which includes about 49.71 per cent primary schools and 50.39 per cent total elementary schools. In the Northeastern region except Tripura, no state has 50 per cent schools having the facility of ramps. In Mizoram 44.31 per cent primary schools and 40.56 per cent total elementary schools have ramps while in Assam 43.15 per cent primary schools and 37.91 per cent total elementary schools have this facility. In Nagaland more than 25 per cent and in Meghalaya more than 15 per cent schools have ramps. In rest of the states, namely Arunachal Pradesh (3.67%), Manipur (5.29%) and Sikkim (5.50%), not even 10 per cent total elementary schools and not even 5 per cent primary schools have ramps.

Electricity connections are available in 32.20 per cent primary schools and 43.14 per cent elementary schools in the country. It is, therefore, clear that more than 55 per cent elementary schools of the country do not have electricity connections. In Northeastern region in five out of eight states, electricity connection is not available in more than 90 per cent primary schools and in more than 75 per cent elementary schools. These states are Arunachal Pradesh, Assam, Manipur, Meghalaya and Tripura. Performance of Sikkim is the best where about 44 per cent primary schools and about 60 per cent elementary schools have electricity connection and it is followed by Mizoram where the respective figures are 32.67 per cent and 42.49 per cent.

About 55 per cent elementary schools in the country have playground facility while in the Northeastern region in four out of eight states more than 50 per cent elementary schools have this facility and these states are Assam (53.02%), Manipur (55.93%), Sikkim (63.78%) and Tripura (62.59%). In the Northeastern region, Arunachal Pradesh (29.97%) has the lowest percentage of elementary schools having playground facility while Meghalaya (36.07%) and Mizoram (32.13%) have less than 40 per cent elementary schools having playgrounds.

Computer Facility in Schools

In this age of information and communication technology, primary and upper primary schools are also expected to have computers. However, the data shows that the picture is quite dismal in India in this regard and the provision of computers is hardly available in the schools. To focus on this issue, Table 11 gives data on the percentage of primary and upper primary schools having computers in the Northeastern region.

Data presented in this table shows that only about 7 per cent primary schools in the country have computers which means that computers are rarely available in the primary schools as 93 per cent schools do not have this facility at all. Though the picture is very disappointing in the country but the scenario in the Northeastern region is even worse. Sikkim is the best performing state where about 16 per cent primary schools have computers, while Mizoram has 8.20 per cent and Nagaland has 5.35 per cent primary schools having provision of computers. In other four states less than 3 per cent primary schools have computers and these states are Arunachal Pradesh (2.41%), Meghalaya (2.46%), Tripura (2.01%) and Manipur (1.64%). Assam (0.53%), the biggest state in the Northeast region, has less than 1 per cent primary schools that have computers.

Table 11

Percentage of Schools having Computers (2010–11)

Name of the State	*Primary Schools having Computer*	*Upper Primary Schools/ Sections having Computer*	*All Schools having Computer*	*Upper Primary Schools having Functional Computers*	*All Schools having C.A.L. Facility*
Arunachal Pradesh	2.41	50.29	15.58	63.73	18.91
Assam	0.53	16.22	5.12	73.29	8.17
Manipur	1.64	44.37	18.18	90.07	17.06
Meghalaya	2.46	18.87	7.10	82.75	7.69
Mizoram	8.20	39.24	23.04	88.94	11.09
Nagaland	5.35	76.24	33.12	89.74	38.39
Sikkim	15.86	84.70	40.97	87.80	26.94
Tripura	2.01	22.13	11.65	83.95	4.33
India	6.99	36.80	18.70	82.81	14.70

Source: NUEPA (2012) Flash Statistics DISE 2010–11

When compared to primary schools, the position is better in the upper primary schools as about 36.80 per cent upper primary schools of the country have computers, i.e. a little over one-third of the total upper primary schools. It is heartening to note that the provision of computers in upper primary schools in some Northeastern states is very good. In two states, namely Nagaland (76.24%) and Sikkim (84.70%), more than 75 per cent upper primary schools have computers while in another two states more than 40 per cent upper primary schools have computers and these states are Arunachal Pradesh (50.29%), Manipur (44.37%). Here also the performance of Assam (16.22%) is not good and it is equally bad in Meghalaya (18.47%) as in these two states, less than 20 per cent upper primary schools have computers.

Overall, only about 19 per cent elementary schools have computers in India. Position in Mizoram, Nagaland and Sikkim is relatively better as in these states more than 20 per cent, 30 per cent and 40 per cent elementary schools, respectively, have this facility. The performance of Assam and Meghalaya is the worst as in these two states less than 10 per cent elementary schools have computers.

Having computers is not enough; it is important that the computers available in the schools are in working order. Data shows that only about 83 per cent upper primary schools having computers have computers in working order. In the Northeastern region in six states more than 80 per cent upper primary schools have functional computers while in rest of the two states only 63.73 per cent (Arunachal Pradesh) and 73.29 per cent (Assam) upper primary schools have functional computers.

Facility of computer aided learning (CAL) is available in only 14.70 per cent elementary schools in the country. In two Northeastern states, more than 25 per cent elementary schools have this facility and these states are Nagaland (38.39%) and Sikkim (26.94%). In Arunachal Pradesh (18.91%), Manipur (17.06%) and Mizoram (11.09%) more than 10 per cent elementary schools have CAL facility. However, in Assam (8.17%), Meghalaya (7.69%) and Tripura (4.33%) less than 10 per cent elementary schools have CAL facility.

Availability of Teachers in Schools

In order to make the school functional the most important input to be provided in the school education system is the availability of enough number of teachers who are well qualified and properly trained. Table 12 presents data on the number of teachers available in the elementary schools of the Northeastern region.

Table 12

Number of Teachers per Elementary School in Northeast States (2010–11)

Name of the State	*Average no. of Teachers per Government School*	*Average no. of Teachers per Private aided School*	*Average no. of Teachers per Private unaided School*	*Average no. of Teachers per School (Total)*
Arunachal Pradesh	3.6	10.8	9.9	4.2
Assam	3.8	7.4	8.5	4.2
Manipur	5.9	3.0	12.9	7.0
Meghalaya	2.9	3.7	4.0	3.3
Mizoram	5.1	7.0	8.0	5.6
Nagaland	5.7	NA	11.4	7.2
Sikkim	9.1	11.3	7.1	8.7
Tripura	7.1	11.5	12.4	7.3
India	4.0	7.6	7.6	4.7

Source: NUEPA (2012) Flash Statistics DISE 2010–11

Table 12 shows that there are about 4.7 teachers per elementary school in the country. It is heartening to note that in five out of eight North-eastern states, number of teachers per elementary school is more than 5.

The average number teacher per elementary school is more than 7 in three states and these states are Sikkim (8.7), Tripura (7.3) and Nagaland (7.2). Further, there are 7 teachers per elementary school in Manipur and 5.6 teachers per elementary school in Mizoram. However, in three states number of teachers per elementary school is less than 4.7 which Is the national average. These states are Arunachal Pradesh (4.2), Assam (4.2) and Meghalaya (3.3). It can, therefore, be observed that in the North-eastern region average number of teachers per elementary school is the highest in Sikkim and lowest in Meghalaya.

As far as the availability of teachers in government schools is concerned average number of teachers per government school is 4 in the country while in the private aided as well as unaided schools it is as high as 7.6 teachers each. It is, therefore, quite clear that average number of teachers in private schools (both aided and unaided) is almost double that of the government schools. It can be inferred from this discussion that private schools are better equipped in terms of availability of teachers than the government schools.

The average number of teachers per elementary school in government schools in the Northeastern region ranges from as high as 9.1 in Sikkim and 7.1 in Tripura to as low as only 2.9 in Meghalaya and 3.6 in Arunachal Pradesh. In the private aided schools average number of teachers per elementary school in Northeastern region ranges from 11.5 in Tripura and 11.3 in Sikkim to only 3 teachers in Manipur and 3.7 teachers in Meghalaya. In the private unaided schools average number of teachers per elementary school in Northeastern region varies from 12.9 in Manipur, 12.4 in Tripura and 11.4 in Nagaland to only 4 teachers in Meghalaya.

It can, therefore, be concluded that in the Northeastern region, Sikkim and Tripura are the best performing states while Meghalaya is the worst performing state as far as the availability of teachers per elementary school is concerned and this is true for government schools, private aided schools as well as private unaided schools.

Pupil Teacher Ratio (PTR)

Availability of teachers in the elementary school can also be seen in terms of pupil-teacher ratio (PTR) which is an indicator for the availability of teachers in schools. Table 13 presents data on the pupil teacher ratio in elementary schools of the Northeastern states of the country.

In the elementary schools of the country, the pupil-teacher ratio is as comfortable as 30 only. Though in many bigger states the ratio is even more than 40 but in the Northeastern region in all the eight states it is below 30. The pupil teacher ratio in Sikkim (i.e. 12) is the lowest in the Northeastern states and it is the highest in Assam (21) while in the rest of six states the pupil-teacher ratio is between 14 and 20 in the elementary schools.

Table 13

Pupil-Teacher Ratio in Elementary Schools of Northeastern States (2010–11)

Name of the State	*Pupil Teacher Ratio in Govt. Schools*	*Pupil Teacher Ratio in Private aided Schools*	*Pupil Teacher Ratio in Private unaided Schools*	*Pupil Teacher Ratio in All Schools*
Arunachal Pradesh	18	20	17	18
Assam	25	14	16	21
Manipur	13	27	25	19
Meghalaya	15	18	17	16
Mizoram	13	16	19	14
Nagaland	16	NA	27	20
Sikkim	13	12	10	12
Tripura	19	34	22	19
India	31	31	29	30

Source: NUEPA (2012) Flash Statistics DISE 2010–11.

The table also shows that there is not much difference in the pupil-teacher ratio of government and private schools. The pupil teacher ratio is 31 in the government and private aided schools while it is 29 in the private unaided schools in the country. But in the Northeastern region in government schools the PTR varies from 13 in Manipur, Mizoram and Sikkim to as high as 25 in Assam. However, in the private aided schools the PTR ranges from 12 in Sikkim to as high as 34 in Tripura which is more than the national average of 31. In the private unaided schools, Sikkim has PTR of 10 which is the lowest in the Northeastern region while it is 27 in Nagaland which is the highest in this region.

It can be inferred from the above discussion on PTR that North-eastern states have very comfortable pupil-teacher ratio at elementary level of education and the situation of availability of teachers in the elementary schools in this region is better as compared to the other regions of the country. It is, therefore, clear that despite the fact that average number of teachers per school in some Northeastern states like Arunachal Pradesh, Assam and Meghalaya is below the national average because of low enrollment per school in this region the pupil-teacher in all the Northeastern states is relatively low and thus the availability of sufficient number of teachers does not seem to be an issue.

Percentage of Trained Teachers

At the primary and upper primary level, all teachers in the schools should ideally be pre-service trained. This is a necessary requirement to ensure that the quality of education imparted in the schools is satisfactory. Table 14 presents the percentage of regular teachers who had undergone pre-service training and are the trained teachers in the Northeastern region.

Table 14

Percentage of Trained Regular Teachers at Elementary Level in Northeastern States (2010–11)

Name of the State	*% of Trained Teachers in Government Schools*	*% of Trained Teachers in Private aided Schools*	*% of Trained Teachers in Private unaided Schools*	*% of Trained Teachers in All Schools*
Arunachal Pradesh	75.80	45.45	26.78	23.45
Assam	29.49	4.82	6.02	34.46
Manipur	84.57	54.85	20.93	35.29
Meghalaya	60.06	37.90	15.87	32.39
Mizoram	94.48	33.33	15.98	63.82
Nagaland	61.77	NA	20.38	29.89
Sikkim	61.58	55.58	55.33	57.54
Tripura	86.19	32.97	18.50	43.53
India	82.78	84.60	69.10	78.66

Source: NUEPA (2012) Flash Statistics DISE 2010–11.

Table 14 shows that about 78.66 per cent regular teachers teaching in the upper primary schools in the country are pre-service trained. But the situation in Northeastern states is alarming in this regard as not even one of the eight Northeastern states has even 65 per cent trained teachers. In fact, there are only two states, namely Mizoram (63.82%) and Sikkim (57.54%), where there are more than 50 per cent trained teachers. Another four states have more than 30 per cent trained teachers and these states are Assam (34.46%), Manipur (35.29%), Meghalaya (32.39%) and Tripura (43.53%). Nagaland (29.89%) has less than 30 per cent, while Arunachal Pradesh (23.45%) has less than 25 per cent trained teachers in elementary schools.

It is clear from the table that percentage of trained teachers in the country is better in the private aided and government schools as compared to private unaided schools. In private aided schools 84.60 per cent teachers are trained while in government schools it is 82.78 per cent but in private unaided schools the percentage of trained teachers is less than 70 per cent.

In the Government schools, the percentage of trained teachers in three Northeastern states is more than 82.78 per cent which is the national average and these states are Manipur (84.57%), Tripura (86.19%) and Mizoram (94.48%). In Arunachal Pradesh (75.80%) about three-fourth elementary teachers are trained. In another three states namely Meghalaya (60.06%), Nagaland (61.77%) and Sikkim (61.58%) more than 60 per cent elementary teachers are trained. Assam (29.49%) has the lowest percentage of trained teachers in the government schools in the Northeastern region.

The private unaided schools in the Northeastern region face maximum problem in getting trained teachers as the data shows that except Sikkim (55.33%) and Arunachal Pradesh (26.78%) no state has even 25 per cent trained teachers in the private unaided schools. In Assam (6.02%), the percentage of trained teachers in the private unaided schools is even less than 10 per cent.

From the above discussion it can be inferred that in the Northeastern region there is dearth of trained teachers in the elementary schools and the problem has been found in almost all the states. But the problem is more serious in the private unaided schools while government and private aided schools are relatively in a better position in this respect.

Participation in Elementary Education

Accessibility to educational provision does not necessarily mean that all children are participating in education also. It is, therefore, necessary to see the participation rates of children in elementary education in the Northeastern states. Enrollment ratio is an indicator to show the enrollment of relevant age group children in a specific level of education and the enrollment ratio can be either Gross or Net though Net Enrollment ratio is a better indicator to show the participation in education. It is, therefore, better to use the net enrollment ratio.

It may be mentioned here that reliable data on the net enrollment ratio is not available for the Northeastern states from any document. Though DISE provides state-wise data on Net Enrollment Ratio for the country but the data on the Northeastern states are not available in DISE also.

In order to show the participation of children in elementary education, Table 15 presents enrollment in primary grades (I–V) and upper primary grades (VI–VIII) for the Northeastern states and also the enrollment in these states as percentage of enrollment in the country.

Data presented in the table reveals that the percentage share of enrollment in elementary education of each and every Northeastern state is more than the percentage share of the respective state in the population of the country. It can, therefore, be inferred from these data that participation of children in elementary education in the Northeastern region is better than the other regions of the country.

The performance of girls in participation of elementary education can be seen by looking at the enrollment of girls vis-à-vis boys at the primary and upper primary level in the Northeastern states. Table 16 presents data on percentage of girls in primary and upper primary level enrollment and the gender parity index in enrollment at these levels for the Northeastern states.

Table 15

Enrollment at Primary (I–V) and Upper Primary (VI–VIII) Level in Northeastern States (2010–11)

Name of the State	*Enrollment in Primary (Grades I–V)*	*Enrollment in Upper Primary Grades VI–VIII*	*Enrollment in Primary as % to total Enrollment in the Country*	*Enrollment in Upper Primary as % to total Enrollment in the Country*	*% of Country's Population (2011)*
Arunachal Pradesh	2,44,488	87,577	0.1808	0.1514	0.1142
Assam	40,70,490	17,51,673	3.0105	3.0282	2.5755
Manipur	3,63,833	1,39,849	0.2691	0.2418	0.2249
Meghalaya	5,07,945	1,52,184	0.3757	0;.2631	0.2449
Mizoram	1,74,025	61,302	0.1287	0.1060	0.0902
Nagaland	2,87,726	1,23,657	0.2128	0.2138	0.1637
Sikkim	89,837	36,705	0.0664	0.0634	0.0502
Tripura	3,94,418	2,15,680	0.2917	0.3728	0.3033
India	13,52,07,057	5,78,44,942	100	100	100

Source: (i) NUEPA (2012) Flash Statistics DISE 2010–11, (ii) Census of India 2011.

Table 16

Percentage of Girls' Enrollment and Gender Parity Index in Enrollment (2010–11)

Name of the State	*% of Girls' Enrollment Primary (I–V)*	*% of Girls' Enrollment Upper Primary (VI–VIII)*	*G.P.I. in Primary Enrollment (I–V)*	*G.P.I. in Upper Primary Enrollment (VI–VIII)*
Arunachal Pradesh	48.62	48.80	0.95	0.95
Assam	49.50	51.41	0.98	1.06
Manipur	49.67	49.61	0.99	0.98
Meghalaya	50.41	52.94	1.02	1.12
Mizoram	47.53	47.88	0.91	0.92
Nagaland	49.07	49.43	0.96	0.98
Sikkim	48.45	54.28	0.94	1.19
Tripura	48.95	49.13	0.96	0.97
India	48.41	48.39	0.94	0.94

Source: NUEPA (2012) Flash Statistics DISE 2010–11.

Table 16 shows that the percentage of girls in primary level enrollment in all the eight Northeastern states, except Mizoram, is more than 48.41 which is the percentage of girls in the country. In Mizoram, girls' enrollment is only 47.53 per cent of the total enrollment at primary level. It is interesting to note that in Meghalaya (50.41%) enrollment of girls is more than that of boys, while in Assam, Manipur and Nagaland percentage of girls is more than 49 per cent in enrollment at primary level.

Performance of girls in participation at the upper primary level seems to be better than that at primary level in almost all the Northeastern states. Here also except Mizoram (47.88%), in all the Northeastern states, percentage of girls in enrollment is more than 48.39 which is the national average. However, in upper primary enrollment three states have more girls than boys and these are Assam (51.41%), Meghalaya (52.94%) and Sikkim (54.28%).

It can, therefore, be inferred from the above discussion that performance of girls in participation of elementary education in Northeastern states is quite good and gender disparities are hardly found in these states which is a major issue in elementary education in the other regions of the country.

Dropout at Elementary Level

The participation of children in elementary education cannot be seen only by taking into account the enrollment figures but it is equally important to see how many children continue in the system and are completing primary and elementary level of education without dropping out. It is therefore important to see the dropout pattern of children at elementary level in the Northeastern region. Table 17 presents dropout rates of children at primary and elementary level of education in the Northeastern states.

Table 17

Dropout Rates at Primary (I–V) and Elementary (I–VIII) Levels in Northeastern Region (2009–10)

Name of the State	*Dropout at Primary (I–V) Boys*	*Dropout at Primary (I–V) Girls*	*Dropout at Primary (I–V) Total*	*Dropout at Elementary (I–VIII) Boys*	*Dropout at Elementary (I–VIII) Girls*	*Dropout at Elementary (I–VIII) Total*
Arunachal Pradesh	43.14	39.23	41.35	48.49	45.13	46.96
Assam	38.99	32.67	35.89	59.94	62.55	61.21
Manipur	33.05	40.08	36.48	57.65	56.59	57.13
Meghalaya	60.52	54.51	57.60	74.25	70.33	72.29
Mizoram	44.68	47.46	46.03	56.37	53.70	55.10
Nagaland	40.10	39.78	39.95	—	—	—
Sikkim	24.57	11.98	18.58	50.98	38.15	44.67
Tripura	25.95	24.97	25.48	45.42	41.77	43.66
India	30.25	27.25	28.86	40.59	44.39	42.39

Source: GOI, MHRD, Statistics of School Education 2009–10.

Figures presented in the table shows that at primary level the dropout rate in India was 28.86 per cent which means that only about 71 per cent children enrolled in class I reach class V. In the Northeastern region, dropout at primary level is lowest in Sikkim (18.58%) followed by Tripura (25.48%). However, the position in other Northeastern states is bad as in rest of the 6 states dropout rates are even higher than 35 per cent. Similar is the position of boys and girls dropout rates at primary level. Dropout rates are highest in Meghalaya where more than 57 per cent children dropout of the schools before reaching class V and boys' dropout rate is more than 60 per cent in this state.

If we look at the dropout at elementary level to know what percentage of children enrolled in class I actually reach class VIII, data presented in Table 17 show that dropout rate in the country at elementary level is 42.39 per cent. The performance of the Northeastern states is even worse as all the eight states have dropout rates more than this national figure of 42.39 per cent. Even in Sikkim and Tripura, where performance is better at primary level, dropout rates are more than 43 per cent. The performance of Meghalaya is the worst in the Northeastern region as here dropout rate at elementary education is more than 72 per cent which is 74.25 per cent for boys and 70.33 per cent for girls.

From the above discussion, it can be concluded that performance of Northeastern region is worse than the other regions of the country as dropout rates in almost all states of this region at primary as well elementary level is relatively high and it shows that the efficiency of primary and upper primary schools of the Northeastern region is relatively poor than the other regions of the country.

Overall Performance of Northeastern States in Elementary Education

The overall performance of a state can be seen by taking into account the performance of the state on various indicators related to access, infra-structure, teachers, and outcomes of the elementary education system. The Educational Development Index (EDI) has been developed by NUEPA using the DISE data and states have been ranked on the basis of these indexes. Taking into account various indicators, Composite Educational Development Index has been computed for the states of the country and all the 35 states and union territories have also been ranked on the basis of this index.

Table 18 presents composite educational development index of the Northeastern states and also shows their ranks in the country for primary, upper primary and elementary level of education.

In Table 18, lower EDI score shows the lower performance of the state and lower the rank of the state, higher is its performance. In the country, the performance of Puducherry is the best as its rank is 1 in the country while its EDI is the highest at primary, upper primary as well elementary level of education. The worst performance in the country is found in Bihar for upper primary and elementary level and Assam is the worst performing state for primary education (NUEPA, 2012).

Table 18

Composite Educational Development Index (EDI) at Primary, Upper Primary and Elementary Level (2010–11)

Name of the State	*EDI Primary*	*EDI Rank Primary*	*EDI Upper Primary*	*EDI Rank Upper Primary*	*EDI Elementary*	*EDI Rank Elementary*
Arunachal Pradesh	0.573	31	0.624	26	0.598	31
Assam	0.504	35	0.607	27	0.555	33
Manipur	0.556	32	0.684	22	0.620	25
Meghalaya	0.601	28	0.598	31	0.600	30
Mizoram	0.694	17	0.760	15	0.727	16
Nagaland	0.659	20	0.688	21	0.674	20
Sikkim	0.764	5	0.825	6	0.795	7
Tripura	0.597	29	0.671	23	0.636	23
India	—	—	—	—	—	—

Source: NUEPA (2012) Flash Statistics DISE 2010–11.

Table 18 reveals that in the Northeastern region in primary education, Sikkim is the best performing state as its rank is 6 in the country while Assam is the worst performing state in the country whose rank is last (35). Apart from Assam the performance of four states, namely Arunachal Pradesh (31), Manipur (32), Meghalaya (28) and Tripura (29) is quite bad as these states are ranked among eight lowest performing states in the country.

At the upper primary level in the Northeastern region again Sikkim is the best performing (ranked, 6) and Meghalaya (ranked, 31) is the worst performing state. Assam (ranked, 26) and Arunachal Pradesh (ranked, 27) are ranked among the eight worst performing states in the country as far as upper primary education is concerned.

At the elementary level the rank of Sikkim is 7 in the country and this state is ranked the highest in the Northeastern region. However, three states of this region namely; Meghalaya (ranked, 30), Assam (ranked, 31) and Arunachal Pradesh (ranked, 33) are the states ranked among the six worst performing states in the country.

Keeping in view the above analysis and discussion, it can be concluded that overall performance of the Northeastern region is poor as far as elementary education is concerned with the exception of Sikkim whose performance has been found to be among the top-10 best performing states of the country. Further even Mizoram has not performed badly as its rank in the country is 16 out of 35 states and union territories.

Problems of Elementary Education in Northeast

The Northeastern states have their own specific problems related to elementary education and many such problems have already been mentioned above that are related to availability of schools, basic facilities and infrastructure in schools, availability of qualified and trained teachers, etc. However, in order to identify the grossroots level problems, a discussion was conducted by the author with participants of the Northeastern states in a workshop organised by NUEPA in the last week of October 2012 at Gangtok, Sikkim in which officials working in the elementary education sector also participated. Except Manipur all the other seven states took part in the said discussion and highlighted the problems of elementary education in their respective states. Problems thus identified for the seven states of the Northeastern region are as given below.

Arunachal Pradesh is among the most backward states of the country and no doubt it is educationally the most backward state in the Northeastern region. Being a backward state people are poor and poverty as well as lack of awareness of people about the importance of education are the factors responsible for low level of participation in elementary education. Low female literacy in the state is a reason for low enrollment of girls' students in the schools.

In this state there is lack of academic support to the schools and teachers as the SCERT is new and not well equipped and also there is lack of training institutions and lack of qualified persons to provide academic support. The District Institutes of Education and Training (DIETs) are not available in all districts and those available have shortage of staff and are poorly equipped. Even the monitoring personnel are not fully conversant with the class room processes to support teachers in promoting learning.

The biggest problem faced in this state is the large percentage of untrained teachers which adversely affects the quality of elementary education. Teacher absenteeism and lack of professional aptitude of teachers is also a factor because of which teachers are not able to assess the learning achievements of the pupils. Since there is hardly any facility for capacity building in the state the lack of capacity of the headmasters to manage the schools properly aggravates the problem and as a result it hampers the scope of proper teaching learning process in the schools.

An important problem in the state is that the teachers' deployment policy has not been rationalised and that is why there is lack of teachers in the schools located in the interior areas which are plenty in number in the state. Because of lack of enough number of teachers in many schools the quality of education imparted is not up to mark.

Assam, demographically the biggest state in the Northeastern region has a large number of private unrecognised schools known as 'Venture Schools' and sizeable students pursue their elementary education in these schools. These schools have poor facilities and are generally ill equipped to impart education of satisfactory quality.

Teacher absenteeism and lack of accountability among the teachers are the two very crucial problems faced in elementary education sector of Assam. Lack of sufficient professionally trained teachers in the primary and upper primary schools of Assam is yet another problem that needs to be addressed to improve the education system. In remote areas of the state lack of place for teachers for stay is also a problem which hampers the proper functioning of the school in these areas.

One of the reasons for lack of trained teachers in the state is the shortage of intake capacity in the existing teachers' training institutions. These training institutions working in the state suffer from shortage of faculty and staff as well as infrastructure facilities and that is why their capacity to train more teachers is very limited.

The state has many big tea gardens and schools running in the tea garden areas lack basic facilities and have dearth of properly qualified and trained teachers. These schools are hardly visited by the inspecting staff and there is lack of proper monitoring of the activities of these schools.

Meghalaya, being a hill state, has unfriendly terrain and difficult weather conditions. The state mainly faces problem in the construction of the school buildings and the cost of construction in the state is very high. Prolonged monsoon further aggravates the problem and the time for completion of construction becomes longer. Provision of other facilities to be made available to the schools is also difficult and costly due to high cost of transport and bad weather conditions.

Basic facilities in the primary and upper primary schools of the state are generally lacking. Though the position of availability of buildings and classrooms in the schools is satisfactory but a large proportion of elementary schools do not have toilets, drinking water, boundary walls, barrier free access, playground and library, etc.

Training of the teachers, both pre-service as well as in-service, is an area of serious concern in the state. There is lack of properly qualified teachers and a considerable proportion of teachers is untrained. Barely 20 per cent teachers of the elementary schools fulfill the prescribed norms of qualification and training. A huge junk of the teachers need to be imparted training but the state do not have enough institutions for the said purpose.

Mizoram, though educationally quite advanced state has also several problems in the elementary education sector. It has been found that in this state there is hardly any coordination between the education department and other departments that are expected to be directly or indirectly involved in it. Convergence with other departments in the field of School Healthcare Scheme, water supply, electrification and sanitation is hardly found in Mizoram.

The classroom size of the primary and upper primary schools is a problem as most of the schools that are 20 years old or more have classrooms that cannot accommodate 40 or 35 children as is the RTE norm. However, so far since the enrollment is not very high in the classes the problem is not felt badly though in future it may create problem to accommodate more children.

A considerable proportion of teachers' positions are vacant in the primary and upper primary schools of the state which is adversely affecting the quality of education imparted in these schools. There is also the problem of uneven distribution of the teachers between rural and urban areas in the state. Due to shortage of teachers in rural areas the schools are unable to introduce Continuous and Comprehensive Evaluation (CCE) that is mandated under RTE in all the primary and upper primary schools.

Though teachers are properly qualified but the competence of many teachers is questionable. In view of the high standard of courses and the latest revised textbooks prescribed at the elementary level many teachers are found incapable of teaching the core subjects in a satisfactory manner. The institutions imparting in-service training of the teachers, for enhancing their competence and capability, are also not very strong in the state.

Nagaland has still quite a few single teacher primary schools and all these schools are government schools. It is, therefore, clear that there is shortage of teachers in the primary and upper primary schools in the state. In some schools the pupil teacher ratio is relatively quite high and it is especially true for the single teacher schools.

Availability of trained teachers is still a problem and a majority of the primary and upper primary school teachers are untrained. The problem of untrained teachers is a serious issue especially in the private unaided schools in the state as about 80 per cent teachers in these schools are untrained.

Sikkim, the smallest state, is the best performing state in the Northeastern region as far as the provision for elementary educational facilities are concerned. However, a typical problem faced in the state as described by the state officials is growing indiscipline among the students of primary and upper schools. Surprisingly it has been felt that it is because of the RTE Act that has a clause of providing fear free and trauma free education in elementary schools where students are free from any punishment and fine and moreover the students do not fear being detained in class up to the end of elementary education.

In the state there are hardly any facilities for the education of physically challenged children and ramps are available in less than 5 per cent primary schools of the state. The problem of availability of trained teachers is also found in Sikkim where more than 40 per cent teachers in the primary and upper primary schools are untrained and, therefore, the quality of elementary education imparted in Sikkim may also not be satisfactory.

Tripura faces the problem of lack of community involvement in the affairs of the schools and even adequate personnel are not available for the supervision and monitoring of the schools. The local bodies, whose role has been envisaged as very crucial under RTE Act, are hardly able to contribute in the development of education as they are over burdened with other works.

State does not have enough number of properly qualified persons to be appointed as teacher as per the norms prescribed by NCTE and therefore finding properly qualified teachers in Tripura is a big concern. This is especially true for the SC and ST category teachers whose posts are reserved.

Teacher training is a major problem in Tripura as the teachers training institutions are neither well equipped nor have sufficient staff to perform their functions properly. The four District Institutes of Education and Training (DIETs), the State Council of Educational Research and Training (SCERT) and the Institute of Advanced Study in Education (IASE) are all functioning with acute shortage of staff and infrastructure facilities. Huge proportion of teachers in the state is untrained and the possibility of training them also seems to be remote under the present conditions.

Future Challenges

The Northeastern region has its typical problems related to the access to elementary education. However, it is expected that all the eight Northeastern states will be implementing Right to Education (RTE) Act. The states may have to provide schools in all the habitations as per the state norm and may also have to provide all kinds of facilities in the primary and upper primary schools as per RTE norms. All states are supposed to implement all the clauses of RTE Act by 2013 and, therefore, the Northeastern states need to gear up to meet the provisions made under all these clauses in their primary and upper primary schools.

As discussed above many schools in the Northeastern region lack basic facilities and do not adhere to the RTE norms as prescribed in the Act. It may be noted that as per RTE norms each primary and upper primary school should have appropriate number of teachers depending upon the enrollment. Schools should also have all-weather building consisting of at least one classroom for every teacher and an office-cum-store-cum-head teacher's room, barrier free access, separate toilet for boys and girls, safe and adequate drinking water facility to all children, a kitchen where mid-day meal is cooked in the school, playground and boundary wall or fencing. Further, each school has to work for the minimum number of days in a year as per norms and for minimum number of working hours per week for the teacher. The schools should have teaching-learning equipment in each class as required and also should have library, play material, games and sports equipment. The data provided in this paper shows that in the Northeastern states there are many schools that do not have these facilities and infrastructure mentioned here. The need is to focus on these schools and make provision accordingly to ensure that these schools function properly and education of satisfactory quality is imparted in these schools.

The states of the Northeastern region lagging behind in provisions of elementary education are mainly Arunachal Pradesh and Assam which are the two biggest states in terms of geographical area. Especially in Arunachal Pradesh providing access of elementary education to all areas is a big challenge that the state need to face and resolve. These states need to take full advantage of the programme launched by the Central Government like Sarva Shiksha Abhiyan (SSA), mid-day meals (MDM) scheme, Mahila Samakhya (MS), Scheme for Providing Quality Education in Madarsas (SPQEM) and Scheme for Infrastructure Development in Minority Institutions (SIDMI). The last two schemes are quite relevant for Assam that has sizeable population of Muslims.

All the Northeastern states have the problem of lack of trained teachers in the primary and upper primary schools. Further, the provision for training of elementary teachers, both pre-service and in-service is also not adequate in these states. It is, therefore, required that the teachers training may be taken in a distance mode and specialised institutions from other regions may be contacted for providing support to undertake the training of elementary teachers in a big way. The services of the State Open Schools and the Open Universities may be accorded for this purpose.

References

Census of India. (2001) Series-1 India Provisional Population Totals, Paper 1 of 2001, Registrar General and Census Commissioner, India, New Delhi.

Census of India. (2011) 'Statewise: Population Census 2011 India Details and Analysis' retrieved from http://www.census2011.co.in/states.php.

Census of India. (2011) 'Literacy Rates in India 2011' retrieved from http://www.mapsof india.com/census2011/literacy-rate.html.

Government of India. (2005) 'Sarva Shiksha Abhiyan: Manual for Planning and Appraisal' MHRD Department of Elementary Education and Literacy, New Delhi.

Government of India. (2009) 'The Right of Children to Free and Compulsory Education Act, 2009' Ministry of Law and Justice (Legislative Department) New Delhi.

Government of India. (2011) 'Statistics of School Education 2009–1010' MHRD Bureau of Planning, Monitoring and Statistics, New Delhi.

National University of Educational Planning and Administration. (2012) 'Elementary Education in India: Progress towards UEE, Flash Statistics DISE 2010–11' NUEPA New Delhi.

National University of Educational Planning and Administration. (2012) 'Report of the Orientation Programme on Planning and Management of School Finances for North-Eastern States, 26 October – 01 November 2012' NUEPA New Delhi (unpublished).

Zaidi, S.M.I.A. (2005) 'Provision and Utilization of Elementary Educational Facilities in North East India' in *New Frontiers in Education*, Vol. XXXV, No. 3, July–September, 2005.

3

State of Universal Health Coverage in Northeast India

JAYANTA B. SARMA

Health systems consist of all the people and actions whose primary purpose is to improve health.[1] Promoting and protecting health is essential to human welfare and sustained economic and social development. This was recognised more than 30 years ago by the Alma-Ata Declaration signatories, who noted that Health for All would contribute both to a better quality of life and to global peace and security. Recognising this, in 2005, Member States of the World Health Organization (WHO) met to develop their health financing systems so that all people have access to services and do not suffer financial hardship paying for them.[2] This goal was defined as universal coverage, sometimes called universal health coverage, which must ensure that coverage is equitable and establish reliable means to monitor and evaluate progress.

However, the key question that arises here as to what restricts countries from moving closer to universal coverage? In fact, there are three fundamental and interrelated problems:

(1) availability of resources (in the poorest countries, few services are available to all)
(2) obligation to pay directly for services at the moment of need (include over-the-counter payments for medicines and fees for consultations and procedures)
(3) inefficient and inequitable use of resources (at a conservative estimate 20–40 per cent of health resources are being wasted), restrict countries from moving closer to universal coverage[3]

Therefore, countries must raise sufficient funds, reduce the reliance on direct payments by the patients to avail services when they need, and improve efficiency and equity.

In India, of all the limiting conditions cited above, obligation to pay directly for healthcare is the biggest handicap. According to WHO, India is one of the weakest countries in the world on overall health performances.[4]

Universal Health in India: Current State

Availability of Resources

Indian economy had high growth rates in recent years (9.4% in 2005–06 and 9.6% in 2006–07)[5] with a consistent 7.0 per cent growth rate even during the period of global economic slowdown. In contrast, the public spending on health was meagre 0.9 per cent of the Gross Domestic Product (GDP) in 2005, among the lowest in the world. In 2009, expenditure on public health increased to 1.4 per cent of GDP, which is still significantly lower than most developing countries.[6] For example, in 2009, Brazil and China spent 4.1 per cent and 2.3 per cent, respectively of its GDP on public health.[7] Notwithstanding, the Government of India (GOI) has made a commitment to increase public spending on health up to 2–3 per cent of the GDP by 2012.[8]

GOI allocation for Health in 2011–12	30,456 (INR in crores)
Allocations for National Rural Health Mission (NRHM) in 2011–12	18,172 (INR in crores)
Percentage (%) released funds in 2010–11	100 per cent

Free Services at the Point of Care

India boasts medical institutions in the private sector in the major cities that rival the best in the world.[9] However, private healthcare is one of the most commercialised in the world, where good care is overshadowed by frequently exploitative unregulated poor-quality (Patel et al., 2011a). Moreover, in the rest of country, that is, in the tier three cities and rural areas, availability of good quality healthcare remain limited. Health expenditure has become an important cause of household impoverishment as out-of-pocket expenditures on health in India are among the highest in the world. More than three-quarters of health spending is paid privately with about 39 million Indian people being pushed into the scourge of poverty every year (Kumar et al., 2011; Balarajan et al., 2011). Ironically, the healthcare needs of 47 per cent of rural India and 31 per cent of urban India are financed by loans and (or) sale of assets.[10]

Healthcare and Equity

'Economic transformation since early 1990s without corresponding positive change in social development with growing disparities across regions, castes, sex and other characteristics', this is how India's achievement has been described by the UNICEF.[11] Every second young child in India is malnourished, less than one-fourth of rural population uses toilets and only 4 out of 10 girls who enrol complete eight years of schooling.

In addition to this, the burden of infectious diseases (John et al., 2011) as well as that of chronic diseases (e.g. cardiovascular diseases, mental health disorders, diabetes, and cancer) and injuries is high in India. Coverage for chronic diseases are generally low, especially among the poor and rural population and much of the care for chronic diseases and injuries is provided in the private sector, which remain exorbitantly expensive (Patel et al., 2011b). Hence, imbalances in resource allocation, inadequate physical access to high-quality health services, scarce human resources and high out-of-pocket health expenditures are key challenges that India faces to achieve equity in healthcare and financially protecting the vulnerable (Balarajan et al., 2011).

Millennium Development Goals (MDG)[12] requires India reducing 'Under 5 Mortality' – U5MR (MDG–4) by two-thirds which is expected to decline to 70 per 1,000 live births in 2015 short of the target of 42 in the said year. The Infant Mortality Rate (IMR) has declined from 58 per 1,000 live births in 2005 to 47 in 2009, but still a long way to achieving target of 30 by 2015.[13] Key to significant progress in reducing U5MR and IMR rests with reducing neonatal deaths (infant deaths occurring within a year of birth) at a fast pace. From a Maternal Mortality Rate (MMR) of 437 per 1,00,000 live births in 1990–91, India is required to reduce MMR to 109 per 1,00,000 live births by 2015 (MDG–5). India is expected to fall short of the 2015 target by 26 points. Safe motherhood depends on the delivery by trained personnel, particularly through institutional facilities. HIV/AIDS, Malaria and other diseases (MDG–6), adult HIV prevalence has come down to 0.34 per cent in 2007 from 0.45 per cent in 2002 attributed to greater awareness and increasing condom use. Malaria diagnosis has declined from 1.74 per cent in 2005 to 1.52 per cent in 2009 with malaria prone states such as the Northeastern states recording fewer malaria deaths since 2006. Prevalence of Tuberculosis (TB) has steadily declined (India accounts for one-fifth of the global incidence) and treatment success rates have remained steady at 86–87 per cent. World Bank statistics show that in 2009, only 61 per cent of children (12–23 months) received full immunisation.[14]

Human Resource

Unarguably, the health sector in India suffers from a serious human resource deficit. Specialists are even harder to find; there was a 65 per cent shortfall in the required number of specialists at Community Health Centres in March 2010.[15] Moreover, the workforce is concentrated in urban areas. Medical education system has failed to keep pace with the demand in terms of quantity, quality (and required competencies) and appropriate proportion of the different categories of healthcare professional produced (Rao et al., 2011).

PANEL 1

State of Public Health[16]

1. Public health expenditure in India has declined from 1.3 per cent of GDP in 1990 to 0.9 per cent of GDP in 1999. The Union Budgetary allocation for health is 1.3 per cent while the State's budgetary allocation is 5.5 per cent. Union Government's contribution to public health expenditure is 15 per cent while States contribution stands at about 85 per cent.
2. Vertical Health and Family Welfare Programmes have limited synergy at operational levels.
3. Lack of community ownership of public health programmes impacts efficiency, accountability and effectiveness.
4. Lack of integration of sanitation, hygiene, nutrition and drinking water.
5. There are striking regional inequalities.
6. Population Stabilisation is still a challenge, especially in states with weak demographic indicators.
7. Curative services favour the rich: for every ₹ 1 spent on the poorest 20 per cent population, ₹ 3 is spent on the richest quintile.
8. Only 10 per cent Indians have some form of health insurance, mostly inadequate: hospitalised Indians spend on an average 58 per cent of their total annual expenditure.
    a. Over 40 per cent of hospitalised Indians borrow heavily or sell assets to cover expenses.
    b. Over 25 per cent of hospitalised Indians fall below poverty line because of hospital expenses.

National Rural Health Mission (2005–12)

The GOI's launch of the National Rural Health Mission (NRHM)[17] in 2005 is the largest public health programme in the world to address the issue of universal health in rural areas. The NRHM is to be transformed into the National Health Mission[18] extending coverage to urban areas. It is an umbrella programme subsuming many existing schemes, including the Reproductive and Child Health Project (RCH–II), National Disease Control Programme (NDCP), and Integrated Disease Surveillance Project (IDSP), which brought with it an influx of government funds. In 2011–12, NRHM constituted 61 per cent of total allocations for health, generally, 85 per cent of the funds come from the centre and the rest from the states. Allocation of funds is based on state Project Implementation Plans (PIP).[19]

The NRHM adopted several unique strategies, most notably, it is centrally financed but implemented in the districts, specifies explicit standards to be achieved and makes people's participation central to ensure accountability and transparency. It aims to strengthen the rural health infrastructure to the Indian Public Health Standards (IPHS) and integrates vertical health and family welfare programmes to provide an integrated healthcare, which remain free at the point of care. The health planning is decentralised involving Panchayati Raj Institutions (PRIs) to own, control and manage health services and ensure accountability and transparency by community ownership through the local Hospital Management Society *(Rogi Kalyan Samiti)*, which are key strategic planks. By mainstreaming doctors and practitioners who practice traditional Indian medicine, Ayurveda, Yoga, Unani, Siddha, and Homoeopathy (AYUSH), it seeks to alleviate the impact of scarce human resources in the healthcare in rural areas. Employment of female Accredited Social Health Activists (ASHA) in every village is one of its innovative ways to bring healthcare to the rural mass. It covers the entire country with special focus on 18 states including all the seven Northeastern states.

An external mid-term assessment in 2009 has suggested substantial achievements, at the same time urges that many major issues still need to be addressed (Bajpai et al., 2009).

PANEL 2

The Main Outcomes from the NHRM

- IMR reduced to 30/1,000 live births by 2012.
- Maternal Mortality reduced to 100/1,00,000 live births by 2012.
- TFR reduced to 2.1 by 2012.
- Malaria Mortality Reduction Rate – 50 per cent up to 2010, additional 10 per cent by 2012.
- Kala Azar Mortality Reduction Rate – 100 per cent by 2010 and sustaining elimination until 2012.
- Filaria/Microfilaria Reduction Rate – 70 per cent by 2010, 80 per cent by 2012 and elimination by 2015.
- Dengue Mortality Reduction Rate – 50 per cent by 2010 and sustaining at that level until 2012.
- Cataract operations-increasing to 46 lakhs until 2012.
- Leprosy Prevalence Rate – reduce from 1.8 per 10,000 in 2005 to less than 1 per 10,000 thereafter.
- Tuberculosis DOTS series – maintain 85 per cent cure rate through entire Mission Period and sustain planned case detection rate.

The Indian Public Health Standards (IPHS)

The IPHS are a set of uniform standards envisaged to improve the quality of healthcare delivery in the country.[20] The IPHS for Sub-centres, Primary Health Centres (PHCs), Community Health Centres (CHCs), Sub-District and District Hospitals were published in 2007 and used as the reference point for infrastructure planning and up-gradation. Last revised in 2012, these standards are flexible to suit the diverse needs of the states and regions. These IPHS guidelines are envisaged to act as the main driver for continuous improvement in quality and serve as the benchmark for assessing the functional status of health facilities.

Rogi Kalyan Samiti

Rogi Kalyan Samiti (RKS) is a registered society acting as a group of trustees to manage the affairs of the CHCs/hospitals. It consists of members from local Panchayati Raj Institutions (PRI), NGOs, local elected representatives and government officials, who are responsible for proper functioning and management of the CHCs/hospitals. The RKS is free to generate and use the funds as per its best judgment and is expected to play a crucial role in effort to upgrade the Community Health Institutions to IPHS.

Accredited Social Health Activist (ASHA)

One of the key components of the NRHM is to provide every village in the country with a trained female ASHA. Selected from the village itself, an ASHA is trained to work as an interface between the community and the public health system. Today, the ASHA programme has 8,50,000 activists across the country; they care for mothers, new-borns and children. Their services have shifted from promoting institutional delivery and immunisation to providing homebased care and counselling for pregnant women, new-borns and children. The other portfolio of ASHA services includes promotion of health products such as sanitary napkins and contraceptives not as commercial commodities but as behaviour change delivery vehicles.[21]

Rural Healthcare System in India

The healthcare infrastructure in rural India has been developed as a three-tier system (Figure 1) based on the following population norms:

PANEL 3

Population Norms

Centre	*Plain Area*	*Hilly/Tribal/Difficult Area*
Sub-Centre	5,000	3,000
Primary Health Centre	30,000	20,000
Community Health Centre	1,20,000	80,000

Figure 1

Three-Tier Rural Healthcare System in India

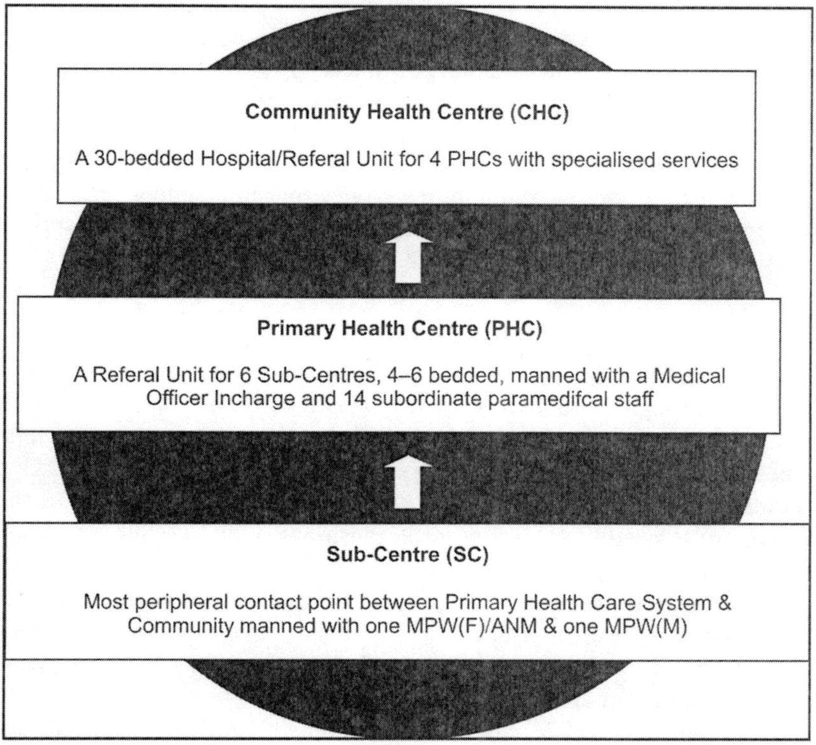

Source: Rural Health Care System in India, available at: http://www.gujhealth.gov.in/pdf/5_Ruralper cent20Healthcareper cent20Systemper cent20inper cent20India.pdf (accessed 25 October 2012).

Northeastern States: A Brief Demographic, Socio-Economic and Health Profile

Arunachal Pradesh (AP)

Arunachal Pradesh (land of the Dawn-Lit Mountains) with 83,743 sq km area has a long international border with Bhutan to the west (160 km), China to the north and Northeast (1,080 km) and Myanmar to the east (440 km). It stretches from snow-capped mountains in the north to the plains of the Brahmaputra valley in the south. Arunachal is the largest state in the region with respect to area.

The population of the state is 13,82,611 (79.2%, rural) according to 2011 Census and is scattered over 16 districts and 5,589 villages. The state has the lowest density of 17 persons per sq km. As against decadal growth rate of 17.64 per cent at the national level, the population of the state has grown by 25.92 per cent over the period 2001–2011. The sex-ratio of the state stands at 960 females to 1,000 males, which is higher than the national average of 914. Total female literacy is 66.95 per cent, while the crude birth, crude death and infant mortality rates are 20.5, 5.9 and 31 (national rates, being 22.1, 7.2 and 47), respectively (SRS, 2010).

There are 20 major tribes and a number of sub-tribes inhabiting the area. Most of these communities are ethnically similar, but their geographical isolation from each other has brought amongst them certain distinctive characteristics in language, dress and customs.

Assam

Assam, with an area of 78,438 sq km, is the land of hills and valleys, the land of the mighty river Brahmaputra. Except for a narrow corridor running through the foothills of the Himalayas that connects the state with West Bengal, the state along with other six Northeastern states are almost entirely isolated from India. In the east, the state is bordered by Arunachal Pradesh, while West Bengal, Meghalaya, Bangladesh are located in the west. To its north, lies Arunachal Pradesh and Bhutan while Nagaland, Manipur, Mizoram, Meghalaya, Tripura lies in the south. Assam's economy is based on agriculture and oil. It produces a significant amount of the total tea production of the world. It is also a home to more than half of India's petroleum. The humidity that is brought into Assam by the south-west monsoons, shower an average annual rainfall of 120 inches or more on the great Brahmaputra valley and the surrounding region. The monsoons are Assam's lifeblood; creating a bio-diversity that can compete with the equatorial rain forests, thereby painting the region with a thousand shades of green. There are many major tribes and a number of sub-tribes inhabiting the area.

According to 2011 Census, the population of the state is 3,11,69,272 (87.1%, rural) and is scattered over 27 districts and 26,395 villages. The state has the highest population density among Northeastern states, of 397 persons per sq km. As against decadal growth rate of 17.64 per cent at the national level, the population of the state has grown by 16.93 per cent over the period 2001–2011. The sex-ratio is 957 females to 1,000 males are higher than the national average of 914. Female literacy of the state rose to 73.18 per cent from 56.03 per cent in 2001. TFR is 2.5, rural 2.7 and urban 1.6 (SRS, 2010) against the crucial replacement level fertility of 2.1. Crude birth, crude death and infant mortality rates are 23.2, 8.2 and 58 (national rates, 22.1, 7.2 and 47), respectively (SRS, 2010). The average life expectancy for male is 58.6 years and for female, it is 59.3.

Manipur

Mizoram and Myanmar in the east, Assam in the West, Assam and Nagaland in the north and Mizoram and Myanmar in the south border Manipur. Manipur had been a union territory from 1956 and a full-fledged state from 21 January 1972. Handloom is the biggest industry in the state. Its area is 22,327 sq km and a population of 27,21,756 (73.4%, rural). There are nine districts and 2,588 villages. The state has population density of 122 per sq km. The decadal growth rate of the state is 18.65 per cent over the period 2001–2011 against the national rate of 17.64 per cent. The sex-ratio of Manipur is 934 females to 1,000 males. Female literacy of the state is 79.85 per cent. Crude birth, crude death and infant mortality rates are 14.9, 4.2 and 14 (national rates, 22.1, 7.2 and 47), respectively (SRS, 2010).

Meghalaya

Goalpara, Kamrup, Nagoan and Karbi Anglong districts of Assam, and on the east by the districts of Cachar and North Cachar hills, bound the state of Meghalaya on the north. In addition, on the south and west lies Bangladesh.

Meghalaya, 'the abode of clouds', was inaugurated as an autonomous state on 2 April 1970 and declared a full-fledged state on 21 January 1972. The total area of the state is 22,429 sq km, predominantly, inhabited by the Khasis, the Jaintias and the Garos. These tribal communities are the descendants of very ancient people having distinctive traits and ethnic origins. Meghalaya's capital, Shillong is situated at an altitude of 1,496 metres above sea level.

The population of Meghalaya is 29,64,007 (80.4%, rural) according to 2011 Census and is scattered over seven districts, 39 blocks and 6,839 villages. The state has the density of 132 persons per sq km. As against decadal growth rate of 17.64 per cent at the national level, the population of the state has grown by 27.82 per cent over the period 2001–2011. The sex-ratio of Meghalaya at 970 females to 1,000 males is higher than the national average. Female literacy of the state rose to 75.48 from 60.41 per cent in 2001. Crude birth, Crude death and infant mortality rates are 24.5, 7.9 and 55 (national rates, 22.1, 7.2 and 47), respectively (SRS, 2010).

Mizoram

The state is bordered by Myanmar in the east and south and by Bangladesh in the west. It occupies an area of great strategic importance in the region and bears an international boundary of 630 miles with Myanmar and Bangladesh. Mizoram has the most variegated hilly terrain: the hills are steep and are separated by rivers that flow to either the north or the south creating deep gorges between the hill ranges. The average height of the hills is about 900 metres. The highest peak in Mizoram is the Phawngpui (Blue Mountain) with a height of 2,210 metres.

Mizoram became the 23rd state of the union in February 1987. It was one of the districts of Assam until 1972 when it became a Union Territory. It is a state with one of the highest literacy rates in India.

The population of Mizoram is 10,91,014 (50.4%, rural) according to 2011 Census and is scattered over eight districts and 830 villages. The total area of the state is 21,081 sq km and has a density of 52 persons per sq km. As against the decadal growth rate of 17.64 per cent at the national level, the population of the state has grown by 22.78 per cent over the period 2001–2011. The sex-ratio of Mizoram at 971 females to 1,000 males is higher than the national average of 914. Female literacy of the state rose to 91.85 per cent from 86.13 per cent in 2001. Crude birth, crude death and infant mortality rates are 17.1, 4.5 and 37 (national rates, 22.1, 7.2 and 47), respectively (SRS, 2010).

Nagaland

Nagaland is a vibrant hill state bounded by Myanmar in the east; Assam in the west; Arunachal Pradesh and a part of Assam in the north and Manipur in the south. It offers rich incomparable traditional and cultural heritage. The population of Nagaland is entirely tribe, that is, there are many distinct tribes and a number of sub-tribes inhabiting the state. The distinctive character and identity of each tribe in terms of tradition, custom, language and dresses is clearly discernible to the visitors.

In January 1961, the GOI conferred the status of a state on Nagaland but the state of Nagaland was officially inaugurated on 1 December 1963.

The population of Nagaland is 19,80,602 (82.8%, rural) according to 2011 Census and is scattered over 11 districts and 1,428 villages. The total area of the state is 16,579 sq km and has the density of 119 persons per sq km. As against decadal growth rate of 17.64 per cent at the national level, the population of the state has contracted by –0.47 per cent over the period 2001–2011. The sex-ratio stands at 944 females to 1,000 males is higher than the national average. Female literacy rose to 80.11 per cent in 2011 from 61.92 per cent in 2001. Crude birth, crude death and infant mortality rates are 16.8, 3.6 and 23 (national rates, 22.1, 7.2 and 47), respectively (SRS, 2010).

Tripura

Tripura is bounded on the north, west, south and southeast by Bangladesh whereas in the east it has a common boundary with Assam and Mizoram. It was formally declared as union territory on 1 November 1957 and elevated to the status of a full-fledged state on 21 January 1972.

The population of Tripura is 36,71,032 (82.9, rural) according to 2011 Census and is scattered over four districts and 875 villages. The total area of the state is 10,486 sq km and has the density of 350 persons per sq km. As against decadal growth rate of 17.64 per cent at the national level, the population of the state has grown by 14.75 per cent over the period 2001–2011. The sex-ratio at 953 females to 1,000 males is higher than the national average of 914. Female literacy of the state rose to 87.75 per cent in 2011 from 65.41 per cent in 2001. Crude birth, crude death and infant mortality rates are 14.9, 5 and 27 (national rates, 22.1, 7.2 and 47), respectively (SRS, 2010).

The Healthcare Infrastructure in the Northeast

Sub-Centres

The Sub-Centre is the most peripheral and first contact point between the primary healthcare system and the community. Each Sub-Centre is manned by one Auxiliary Nurse Midwife (ANM) and one Male Health Worker MPW(M). In addition, one Lady Health Worker (LHV) is entrusted with the task of supervision of six Sub-Centres. The centres are assigned with tasks relating to bring about behavioural change and provide services in relation to maternal and child health, family welfare, nutrition, immunisation, diarrhoeal control and control of communicable diseases programmes. Each centre is provided with basic drugs for minor ailments needed for taking care of essential health needs of men, women and children. There are 1,48,124 Sub-Centres functioning as on March 2011 in the country as compared to 1,45,272 in 2007. Figure 2 demonstrates the number of Sub-Centres built in the states of Northeast India since 1981–85 till 2007–2012.

PANEL 4

Recommended Manpower at Sub-Centres (IPHS 2012)

Personnel	*Existing*	*Recommended*
Health Worker (Female)	1	1 or 2 (Optional)
Health Worker (Male)	1	1 or 0 (optional; may be replaced by female health worker)
Voluntary worker to keep the Sub-Centre clean and assisting ANM. She is paid by the ANM from her contingency fund @₹ 100 per month	1 (optional)	1 (optional)

Figure 2

Sub-Centres built in the Northeast since 1981–85

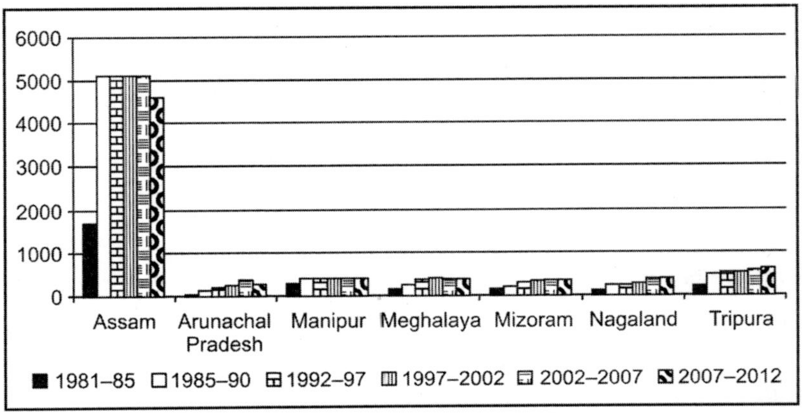

Note: Reduction in number of Sub-Centres is due to correction of actual status of functioning.

Primary Health Centres (PHCs)

PHC is the first contact point between village community and the Medical Officer. The PHCs were envisaged to provide an integrated curative and preventive healthcare to the rural population with emphasis on disease prevention and health promotion. The PHCs are established and maintained by the state governments under the Minimum Needs Programme (MNP)/Basic Minimum Services Programme (BMS). At present, a PHC is manned by a Medical Officer supported by 14 paramedical and other staff. It acts as a referral unit for six Sub-Centres. It has 4–6 beds for patients. The activities of PHC involve curative, preventive, primitive and family welfare services. There are 23,887 PHCs functioning as on March 2011 in the country as compared to 22,370 in 2007. Figure 3 illustrates the number of PHCs built in the state of Northeast India since 1981–85 until 2012.

PANEL 5

Recommended Manpower at PHCs (Indian Public Health Standards 2012)

Personnel	*Existing pattern*	*Recommended*
Medical Officer	1	2 (one may be from AYUSH and one other Medical Officer preferably a Lady Doctor)
Pharmacist	1	1
Nurse – Midwife (Staff Nurse)	1	3 (for 24 hour PHCs; 2 may be contractual)
Health Worker (Female)	1	1
Health Educator	1	1

Health Assistant (One male and One female)	2	2
Clerks	2	2
Laboratory Technician	1	1
Driver	1	Optional; vehicles may be out-sourced
Helpers	4	4

Figure 3

PHCs built in the Northeast since 1981–85

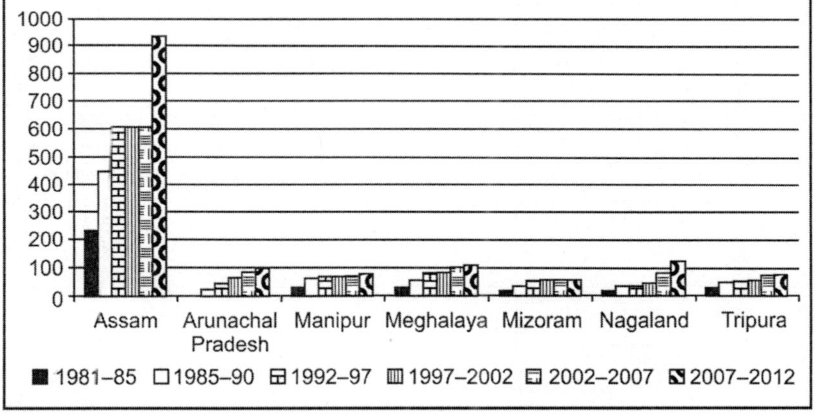

Community Health Centres (CHCs)

Figure 4 shows the number of CHCs built in the region since 1981–85, which are in operation. CHCs are being established and maintained by the state government under MNP/BMS programme. It is manned by four medical specialists, i.e. surgeon, physician, gynaecologist and paediatrician supported by 21 paramedical and other staff. It has 30 in-door beds with one operation theatre, X-ray room, labour room and laboratory facilities. It serves as a referral centre for four PHCs and provides facilities for obstetric care and specialist consultations. As on March 2011, there are 4,809 CHCs functioning in the country as compared to 4,045 in 2007.

Taken all the Primary Health Care Institutions together, Table 2 presents a snapshot of the average rural area and average radial distance covered by these institutions in the states of Northeast.

PANEL 6

Recommended Manpower at CHCs (Indian Public Health Standards 2012)

Personnel	*IPHS Norm*
Clinical Manpower	
General Surgeon	1
Physician	1

Obstetrician/Gynaecologist	1
Paediatrics	1
Anaesthetist	1, on contractual appointment or hiring of services from private sectors on case to case basis
Public Health Programme Manager	1, On contractual appointment
Eye Surgeon	1, for every 5 lakh population as per vision 2020 approved Plan of Action
Other specialists (if any)	
General duty officers (Medical Officer)	Recommended to undergo training in Sterilisation, IUD Insertions, Emergency contraception, RTI/STI, HIV/AIDS, New-born care, emergency obstetric care and any other relevant subjects.
Support Manpower Personnel	
Nursing Staff	7+2, 1 ANM and 1 Public Health Nurse for family welfare will be appointed under the ASHA scheme
Public Health Nurse	1
ANM	1
Staff Nurse	7
Nurse/Midwife	
Dresser	1
Pharmacist	1
Lab. Technician	1
Radiographer	1
Ophthalmic Assistant	1, Ophthalmic Assistant may be placed wherever it does not exist through redeployment or contract basis
Ward Boys/Nursing Orderly	2
Sweepers	3
Chowkidar	1 Flexibility may rest with the state for recruitment of personnel as per needs
OPD Attendant	1
Statistical Assistant/Data entry operator	1
OT Attendant	1
Registration Clerk	1

Table 1

Average Rural Area and Average Radial Distance Covered by Primary Healthcare Institutions

	Average Rural Area (sq km) covered by a			*Average Radial Distance (km) covered by a*		
	Sub Centre	*PHC*	*CHC*	*Sub Centre*	*PHC*	*CHC*
AP	NA	NA	NA	NA	NA	NA
Assam	16.83	82.60	717.37	2.31	5.13	15.11

Cont'd...

...Cont'd

Manipur	52.82	277.29	1,386.44	4.10	9.39	21.00
Meghalaya	54.81	203.66	765.49	4.18	8.05	15.61
Mizoram	55.39	359.55	2,277.12	4.20	10.70	26.92
Nagaland	41.49	130.41	782.46	3.63	6.44	15.78
Tripura	16.37	130.97	940.60	2.28	6.46	17.30
All India	21.05	130.54	648.43	2.59	6.44	14.36

Figure 4

CHCs built in the Northeast since 1981–85

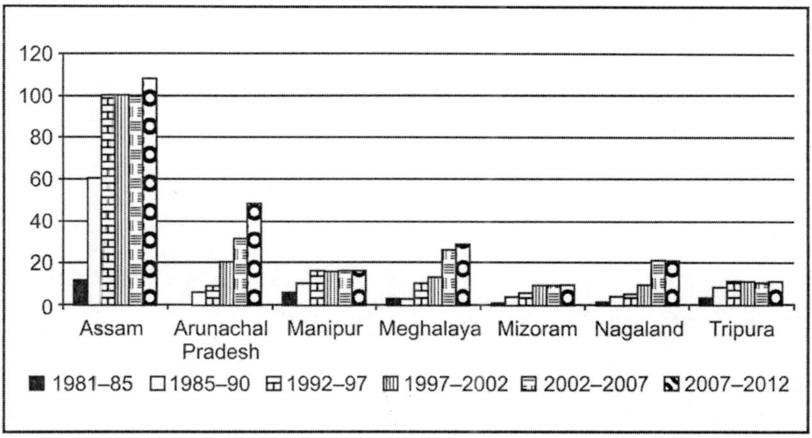

Shortfall in Health Infrastructure in the Northeast

With the launch of NHRM, all the Northeastern states have made considerable progress in terms of increasing the numbers of rural health infrastructure (please refer to Figure 2, Figure 3, Figure 4): gap between the required and in position Sub-Centres, PHCs and CHCs are reducing; in fact, there are surplus facilities in few states (Table 4). However, considerable progress needs to be made in terms of ANM staff quarters, water, electricity and motorable roads (please see, Table 5 and Table 6). The number of PHCs are functioning with labour room, operation theatre (Table 7); water, electricity, motorable roads, telephone and computers (Table 8); referral transport, RKS and as per IPHS (Table 9). However, still a long way to go but RKS are in place in nearly 100 per cent of the PHCs. The CHCs with four specialists, laboratory, labour room and operation theatre (Table 9), and with X-ray, doctor's quarters, transport, RKS and as per IPHS (Table 10) again RKS are in place in nearly 100 per cent of the CHCs but again there is a long way to go in terms of rest of the required facilities.

Table 2

Shortfall in Health Infrastructure as per 2011 Population (March 2011)

	Total Population in Rural Areas (Tribal Population)	*Sub Centres*			*PHCs*			*CHCs*		
		Required	*In Position*	*Shortfall*	*Required*	*In Position*	*Shortfall*	*Required*	*In Position*	*Shortfall*
AP	10,69,165 (7,44,996)	313	286	27	48	97	*	12	48	*
Assam	2,67,80,516 (36,38,841)	5,841	4,604	1,237	953	938	15	238	108	130
Manipur	18,99,624 (8,42,941)	492	420	72	77	80	*	19	16	3
Meghalaya	23,68,971 (21,37,702)	758	405	353	114	109	5	28	29	*
Mizoram	5,29,037 (5,09,316)	173	370	*	26	57	*	6	9	*
Nagaland	14,06,861 (13,18,698)	457	396	61	68	126	*	17	21	*
Tripura	27,10,051 (9,88,644)	673	632	41	106	79	27	26	11	15
India	83,30,87,662 (8,75,00,780)	1,78,267	1,48,124	35,762	29,213	23,887	7,048	7,294	4,809	2,766

Notes: The requirement is calculated using the prescribed norms based on provisional rural population from Census; 2011 and estimated rural tribal population in 2011 using per cent of tribal population out of rural population in 2001.

Table 3

Sub-Centres Functioning with ANM Quarters (March 2011)

	Sub-Centres Functioning	*Sub-Centres with ANM Quarter*		*Sub-Centres with ANM living in Sub Centre Quarter**	
		Number	*Per cent*	*Number*	*Per cent*
Arunachal Pradesh	286	114	39.9	114	100.0
Assam	4,604	2,542	55.2	507	19.9
Manipur	420	0	0.0	0	0.0
Meghalaya	405	401	99.0	171	42.6
Mizoram	370	350	94.6	350	100.0
Nagaland	396	68	17.2	66	97.1
Tripura	632	49	7.8	16	32.7
All India	1,48,124	81,422	55.0	49,470	60.8

Table 4

Sub-Centres Functioning with Water, Electricity and Motorable Roads (March 2011)

	Sub-Centres Functi-oning	*Without Regular Water Supply*		*Without Electric Supply*		*Without All-Weather Motorable Approach Road*	
		Number	*Per cent*	*Number*	*Per cent*	*Number*	*Per cent*
Arunachal Pradesh	286	12	4.2	63	22.0	95	33.2
Assam	4,604	439	9.5	3,111	67.6	689	15.0
Manipur	420	371	88.3	268	63.8	115	27.4
Meghalaya	405	294	72.6	265	65.4	73	18.0
Mizoram	370	296	80.0	0	0.0	69	18.6
Nagaland	396	210	53.0	195	49.2	132	33.3
Tripura	632	334	52.8	304	48.1	198	31.3
INDIA	1,48,124	36,663	24.8	36,250	24.5	10,217	6.9

Table 5

PHCs Functioning with Labour Room and Operation Theatre (March 2011)

	PHCs Functioning	*With Labour Room*		*With Operation Theatre*		*With at least 4 Beds*	
		Number	*per cent*	*Number*	*per cent*	*Number*	*per cent*
AP	97	67	69.1	11	11.3	59	60.8
Assam	938	686	73.1	33	3.5	511	54.5
Manipur	80	38	47.5	0	0.0	19	23.8
Meghalaya	109	109	100.0	0	0.0	109	100.0
Mizoram	57	57	100.0	57	100.0	57	100.0
Nagaland	126	88	69.8	39	31.0	123	97.6
Tripura	79	60	75.9	4	5.1	46	58.2
INDIA	23,780	15,629	65.7	9,131	38.4	14,830	62.4

Table 6

PHCs Functioning with Water, Electricity, Motorable Roads, Telephone and Computers

	PHCs Functioning	*Without Electric Supply*		*Without Regular Water Supply*		*Without All-Weather Motorable Approach Road*		*With Telephone*		*With Computer*	
		Number	*Per cent*	*Number*	*Per cent*	*Number*	*Per cent*	*Number*	*Per cent*	*Number*	*Per cent*
AP	97	31	32.0	29	29.9	11	11.3	13	13.4	0	0.0
Assam	938	83	8.8	392	41.8	29	3.1	447	47.7	562	59.9
Manipur	80	15	18.8	55	68.8	12	15.0	6	7.5	73	91.3
Meghalaya	109	4	3.7	13	11.9	59	54.1	18	16.5	85	78.0
Mizoram	57	0	0.0	57	100.0	57	100.0	57	100.0	45	78.9
Nagaland##	126	25	19.8	20	15.9	16	12.7	118	93.7	24	19.0
Tripura	79	5	6.3	12	15.2	50	63.3	29	36.7	57	72.2
INDIA	23,780	1,920	8.1	2,969	12.5	1,572	6.6	12,402	52.2	11,034	46.4

Table 7

PHCs Functioning with Referral Transport, RKS and as per IPHS

	PHCs Functioning	*Referral Transport*	*Registered RKS*	*PHCs Functioning as per IPHS*
AP	97	45	85	0
Assam	938	502	938	NA
Manipur	80	0	73	0
Meghalaya	109	55	109	3
Mizoram	57	57	55	0
Nagaland	126	33	126	21
Tripura	79	73	79	22
INDIA	23,780	9,657	18,702	3,594

Shortfall of Human Resources for Health

In terms of doctors posted at the PHCs, the shortfall is minimal and, interestingly, in Assam, Manipur and Tripura there remain an excess of doctors. The states have done well with the recruitment of ASHA (Table 12): ASHA in position[25] Selected Training up to Module 5 is complete for 100 per cent in all states. Except Assam, all states have completed two rounds of Module 6 and 7 training or are underway as of June 2012. The overall pattern of expenditure in Northeastern states reflects well-grounded programme, and Arunachal Pradesh, Assam, Mizoram, Nagaland and Sikkim have spent above ₹ 20,000 per ASHA over the period of 2005–12.[26] The two key challenges that states face today are in enabling ASHA to reach the most marginalised and to establish performance monitoring systems. Drug kits are distributed on annual basis, given to over 100 per cent of ASHA in 2011–12. Replenishment system from PHC on quarterly basis as per requirement is in place in Assam and Tripura.

In terms of specialist in the CHCs (Table 13), not surprisingly there is considerable shortfall but in Assam, this shortfall is in relation to obstetricians and gynaecologists, which is minimal and stands at 7 per cent (Table 14). However, there are surplus in cases of health worker (female)/ANM at Sub-Centre and PHCs (Table 15). Assam requires 1,322 (out of 1,657 required in the seven states) staff nurses (SN) at CHCs but data available on 30 June 2012 indicates nurses are yet to be recruited. Except for Mizoram (30/30), other states have shortfall in regards to staff nurses (Meghalaya 32/116; Nagaland 54/189).

Table 8

CHCs with 4 Specialists, Laboratory, Labour Room and Operation Theatre

	CHCs Functioning	*With all 4 Specialists*	*With computer/ Statistical Asst. for MIS/Accountant*	*With Functional Laboratory*	*With Functional OT*	*With Functional Labour Room*	*With Functioning Stabilisation Units for New Born*	*With New Born Care Corner*	*With at least 30 Beds*
AP	48	0	0	38	37	46	0	8	0
Assam	108	28	108	108	101	108	84	108	101
Manipur	16	0	16	14	7	16	NA	12	7
Meghalaya	29	0	29	29	6	29	3	12	29
Mizoram	9	0	9	9	9	9	2	9	9
Nagaland	21	0	10	21	21	21	0	21	21
Tripura	11	0	11	11	3	11	0	5	11
INDIA	4,809	641	4,158	4,545	4,190	4,557	938	2,884	3,354

Table 9

CHCs with X-Ray, Doctor's Quarters, Transport, RKS and as per IPHS

	CHCs Functioning	With Functional X-Ray	With Quarters for Specialist	With Specialist Living in Quarters	With Referral Transport	With Registered RKS	Functioning as per IPHS norms	Allopathic Drugs for Common Ailments	AYUSH Drugs for Common Ailments
AP	48	13	3	3	40	31	0	48	NA
Assam	108	60	NA	NA	108	108	NA	108	108
Manipur	16	12	16	0	16	16	0	16	16
Meghalaya	29	18	4	4	29	29	1	29	19
Mizoram	9	9	1	1	9	9	0	9	2
Nagaland	21	3	19	19	21	21	0	21	21
Tripura	11	8	3	0	11	11	1	11	11
All India	4,809	2,811	2,707	2,008	4,270	4,752	884	4,728	2,692

Table 10

ASHA In Position[27] Selected

	Proposed No. of ASHA	No. of ASHA Selected	Per cent of ASHA Selected
AP	3,862	3,757	97.28
Assam	29,693	29,172	98.4
Manipur	3,878	3,878	100.00
Meghalaya	6,258	6,258	100.00
Mizoram	987	987	100.00
Nagaland	1,700	1,700	100.00
Tripura	7,367	7,367	100.00

Table 11

Doctors at Primary Health Centres

		Required	Sanctioned	In Position	Vacant	Shortfall
Allopathic Doctors	Arunachal Pradesh	97	NA	92	NA	5
	Assam	938	NA	1,557	NA	*
	Manipur	80	240	192	48	*
	Meghalaya	109	127	104	23	5
	Mizoram	57	57	37	20	20
	Nagaland	126	NA	101	NA	25
	Tripura	79	NA	119	NA	*
	INDIA	23,887	30,051	26,329	7,246	2,866

Table 12

Specialists Community Health Centres

		Required	Sanctioned	In Position	Vacant	Shortfall
Surgeons	Arunachal Pradesh	48	NA	0	NA	48
	Assam	108	NA	42	NA	66
	Manipur	16	16	0	16	16
	Meghalaya	29	2	1	1	28
	Mizoram	9	NA	1	NA	8
	Nagaland	21	NA	12	NA	9
	Tripura	11	NA	0	NA	11
	INDIA	4,809	2,182	1,018	1220	3,052
Obstetricians and Gynaecologists	Arunachal Pradesh	48	NA	0	NA	48
	Assam	108	NA	101	NA	7
	Manipur	16	16	1	15	15
	Meghalaya	29	2	5	*	24
	Mizoram	9	NA	1	NA	8
	Nagaland	21	NA	11	NA	10
	Tripura	11	NA	0	NA	11
	INDIA	4,809	1,958	1,389	915	2,682

Cont'd...

...Cont'd

Physicians	Arunachal Pradesh	48	NA	0	NA	48
	Assam	108	NA	27	NA	81
	Manipur	16	16	1	15	15
	Meghalaya	29	2	2	0	27
	Mizoram	9	NA	0	NA	9
	Nagaland	21	NA	6	NA	15
	Tripura	11	NA	NA	NA	NA
	INDIA	4,809	1437	819	847	3,252
Paediatricians	Arunachal Pradesh	48	NA	1	NA	47
	Assam	108	NA	46	NA	62
	Manipur	16	16	2	14	14
	Meghalaya	29	2	1	1	28
	Mizoram	9	NA	0	NA	9
	Nagaland	21	NA	5	NA	16
	Tripura	11	NA	0	NA	11
	INDIA	4,809	1,731	1,041	849	3,029

NA: Not Available; * Surplus

Table 13

Health Worker (Female)/ANM at Sub-Centre and PHCs (as on March, 2011)

	Required[1]	*Sanctioned*	*In Position*	*Vacant*	*Shortfall*
Arunachal Pradesh	383	NA	395	NA	*
Assam	5,542	NA	8,723	NA	*
Manipur	500	984	661	323	*
Meghalaya	514	667	787	*	*
Mizoram	427	388	619	*	*
Nagaland	522	NA	907	NA	*
Tripura	711	NA	440	NA	271
INDIA[2]	1,72,011	1,77,103	2,07,868	8,835	6,555

[1] Requirement based on norm of one ANM per each existing Sub Centre and PHC; *: Surplus

Training Capacity

Table 14 and Table 15 show the number of Health and Family Welfare Training Centres and Multi-Purpose Worker (M) Training Centre and ratio of Healthcare Worker (F)/ANM schools to LHV/Health Assistant (F) training schools and average population covered as on March 2011. In Assam, an innovative idea was launched through introduction of Rural Health Practitioners with three year training for students completing higher secondary has facilitated improvement in the quality of health services in the rural areas.[28] The largest state, Assam, after the establishment of Assam Medical College, Dibrugarh (1947), Gauhati Medical College (1960) and Silchar Medical College (1968) prior to 1970 has failed to establish any new college, which severely constrained the number of doctors and specialists. To address this issue, Assam embarked on a rapid expansion programme with one new medical college functioning in Jorhat (2009) and three more are expected two start fully functioning: Barpeta in 2012, Tezpur in 2014 and Diphu in 2015.[29] Further, three more are planned to be established at Lakhimpur, Dhubri and Kokrajhar.[30] In addition, Assam has one Ayurvedic and three Homeopathy colleges. Tripura, Manipur and Meghalaya have one government medical college each[31] and Mizoram announced to set one up soon.[32]

Table 14

Health and Family Welfare Training Centres and MPW (M) Training Centre (March 2011)

	H&FW Training Centres	*MPW (M) Training Centre*
Arunachal Pradesh	0	0
Assam	1	0
Manipur	1	1
Meghalaya	1	0
Mizoram	0	1
Nagaland	0	0
Tripura	0	1
INDIA	49	49

Source: Training Division of Ministry of Health and Family Welfare, Govt. of India.

Table 15

Ratio of H.W. (F)/ANM Schools to LHV/Health Assistant (F) Training Schools and Average Population Covered as on March 2011

	No. of Training Schools		*Ratio of ANM per LHV School*	*Rural Population** – 2011 (lakhs) Covered by a*	
	ANM/HW (F)	*LHV/HA (F)*		*ANM School*	*LHV School*
Arunachal Pradesh	1	0	—	10.69	*
Assam	18	1	18	14.88	267.81
Manipur	3	1	3	6.33	19.00
Meghalaya	2	0	—	11.84	*
Mizoram	1	0	—	5.29	*
Nagaland	2	0	—	7.03	*
Tripura	2	1	2	13.55	27.10
INDIA	319	34	9	26.12	245.03

Source: Training Division of Ministry of Health and Family Welfare, Govt. of India.

Expenditure Performance

The state governments are able to use central funds to fill gaps identified by them in the infrastructure, human resources, equipment, and service outcome guarantees to ensure conformity with the IPHS. The NRHM also directly releases flexible funds to supplement the operations and maintenance budget. In 2005–06, only 73 per cent funds were spent which dropped to 55 per cent in 2007–08; 2008–09 saw a significant improvement when nearly 90 per cent funds were spent and no under spending, was reported in 2010–11. The funds are routed directly to RKS. Figure 5 shows the steadily increased spending capacity of all the seven states and Assam in particular considerably overspent making up for under spent amount in the previous years (Figure 6).

Figure 5

Amount of Expenditure by States under items Subsumed within NRHM (₹ in Crore)

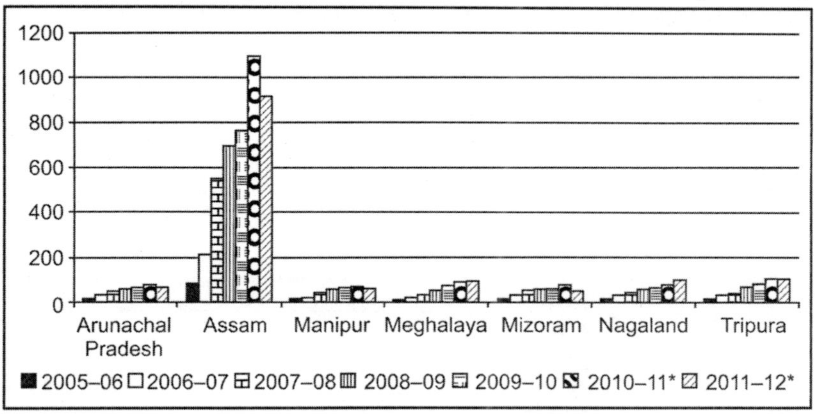

Figure 6

Unspent Amount Available with State out of Fund Released by GOI under items Subsumed within NRHM (₹ in Crore)

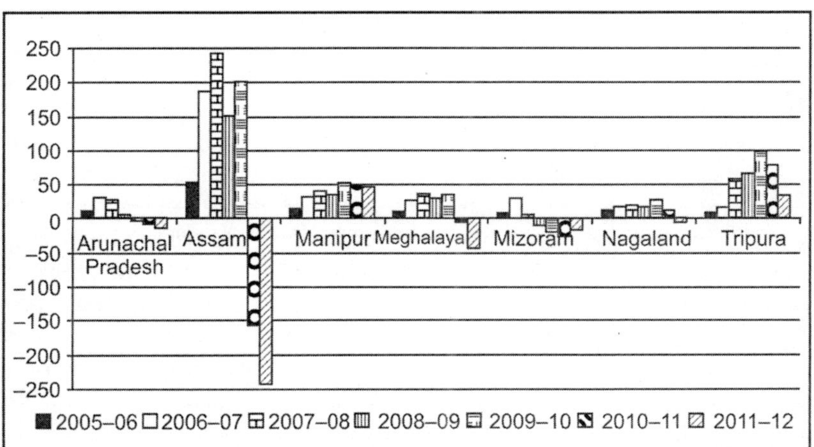

Janani Suraksha Yojana (JSY)

JSY is a conditional cash transfer scheme to encourage women to deliver in government health facilities or accredited private facilities by providing financial incentives.[33] Nationally, institutional delivery has increased since the launch of JSY from 57 per cent in 2006–07 to 79 per cent in 2010–11.[34] JSY has the largest number of beneficiaries for any such programme in the world, estimated to be 9.5 million women giving birth in 2010. Number of JSY beneficiaries in Assam has been increasing and doubled to over 4,00,000 in 2011–12 from under 2,00,000 in 2006–07 (Figure 7) with institutional delivery increasing by 212 per cent in 2011–12 (4,64,985) as compared to 2005–06 (1,49,003).

Figure 7

Number of Beneficiaries of JSY

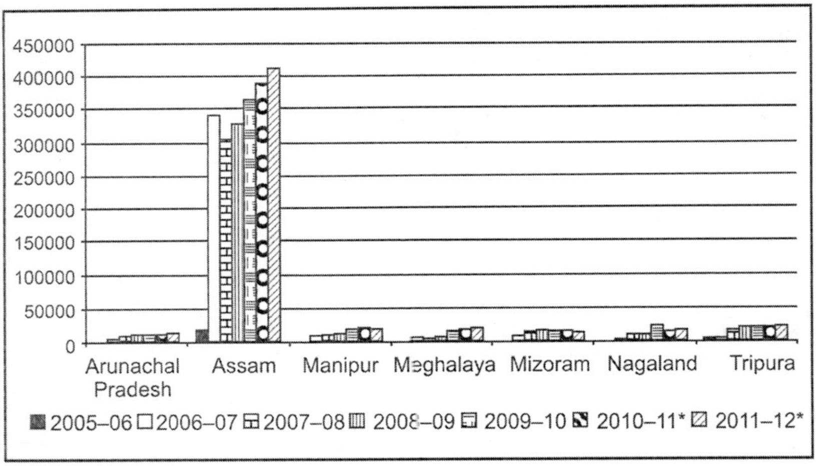

Burden of Cancer

This review revolves mainly around the NRHM, which is very much focused on pressing outcome measures such IMR and specific infectious diseases. However, among the chronic diseases, burden of cancer in the Northeast are among the highest in the country and warrants specific mention (Figure 8). A very high incidence of cancers of all types in general and tobacco and pesticide related cancers in particular has been reported in the region. There is extensive use of pesticides in tea gardens in the region, which can lead to widespread occupational and environmental exposures. The available data on tobacco usage and pesticide exposure alone is not sufficient to explain the high rate of incidence as

Figure 8

District-wise Distribution of the Average Annual Minimum Age Adjusted Incidence Rate (MAAR), Male[36]

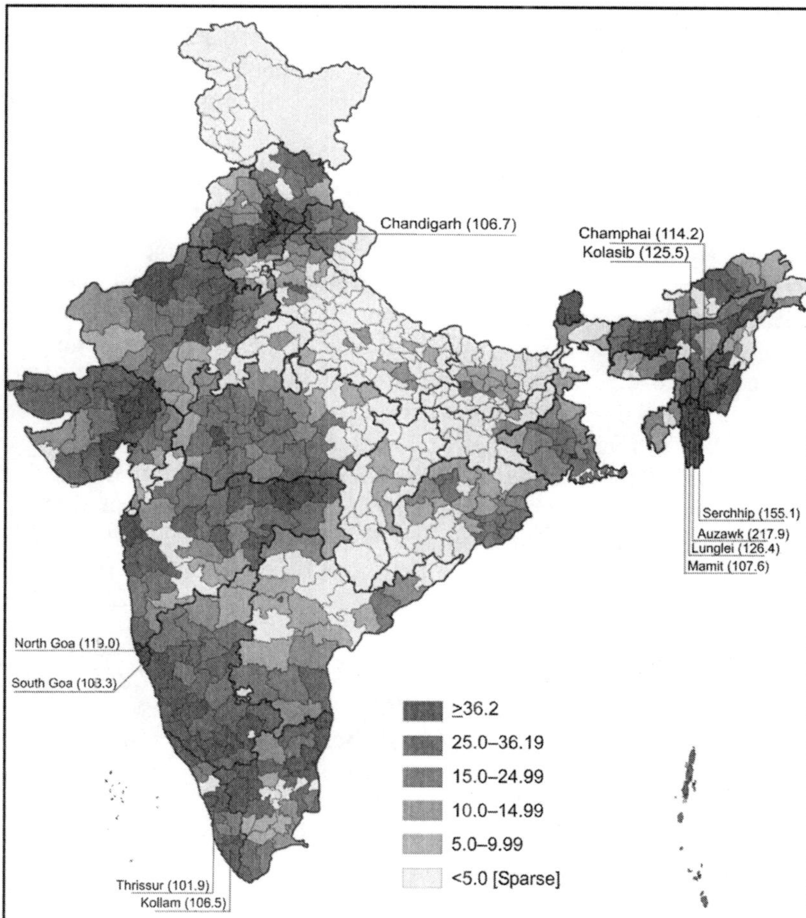

the region has different customs, food habits, lifestyle, diverse ethnic groups, and type and the pattern of tobacco use as compared to the rest of the country.[35] Assam has the highest number of patients with cancer of the oesophagus, pharynx (or throat), larynx and gallbladder in the country with betel nut and tobacco chewing being the major contributors. According to the data available from population-based cancer registries (2006–08) (Rahman, 2011), the Kamrup (metro) has the highest number of patients suffering from cancer of the oesophagus, pharynx and gall bladder, while Cachar tops the nationwide list for laryngeal cancer. In the case of male patients suffering from cancer of the oesophagus, Kamrup (metro) is second in the list in the country while Aizawl in Mizoram tops this list. Dibrugarh and Cachar are the third and fourth highest, respectively, in case of pharynx or throat cancer while Aizawl ranks second in the country. Kamrup (metro) was also found to have the highest cases of gall bladder cancer in the country.

Treatment Outside the Region

A large number of patients from Northeast travel to metropolis in search of advanced treatment. At a conservative estimate, 75,000 to 1,00,000 patients from Assam alone every year go to Chennai (and Vellore), a distance over 2,718 km from Guwahati, in search of better medical treatment.[37] There is a common perception rightly or wrongly that the good secondary and tertiary medical care is not available within the region.[38] According to a study conducted by Barman et al. (2012), approximately 26 per cent of the cancer patients preferred to go to big metropolis of India such as Delhi, Mumbai, and Chennai for advanced treatment after their diagnosis of the disease. The study found that the patients treated outside the state have better survival than that of patients treated locally. However, this is confounded by socio-economic status, because poor patients cannot afford treatment cost outside the home state.

Outcome Measures: Key Health Indices

Infant Mortality, U5MR, MMR and Immunisation Coverage

One of the key outcome measures of the NHRM is to reduce IMR to 30/1,000 live births by 2012. Latest figure available (Figure 9) indicates IMR for Assam stands at 55 (against the national rate of 43) in 2011. The IMR in Assam is steadily declining since 2006 from a base level considerably higher than the national. In other Northeastern states, IMR is considerably lower than the national rate and close to the target except for Meghalaya and Mizoram (Figure 10). The U5MR[39] for Assam was 83 (national 59) and Neo Natal Mortality is 33, same as the national rate (SRS, 2010).[40]

MMR for Assam was 390 against the national rate of 212 (2007–09). To tackle MMR, First Referral Units (FRUs) are being set up by upgrading the existing community health centres and sub-district hospitals for providing emergency obstetric care to pregnant women with complications as close to the community as possible. In June 2012, Assam has 60 FRUs (109 in total in Northeast), increasing from 46 in 2005.

Figure 9

Infant Mortality Rate (Time Series 2003–11)

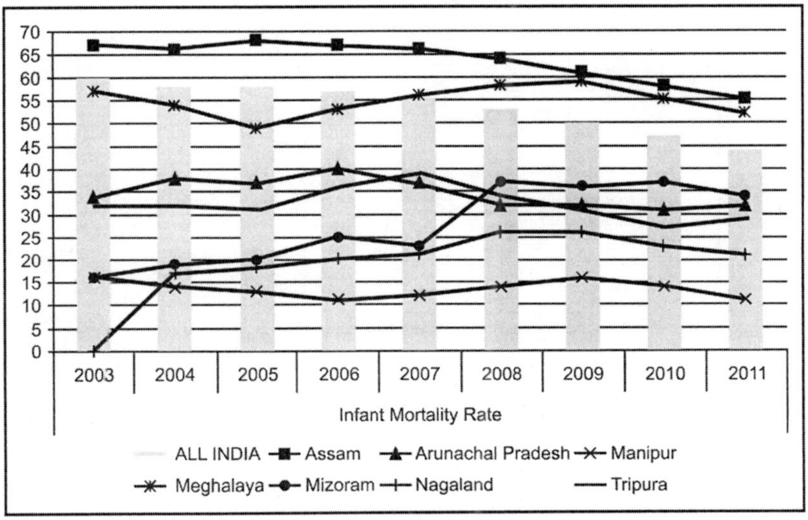

Figure 10

Infant Mortality Rates (Rural and Urban), 2010

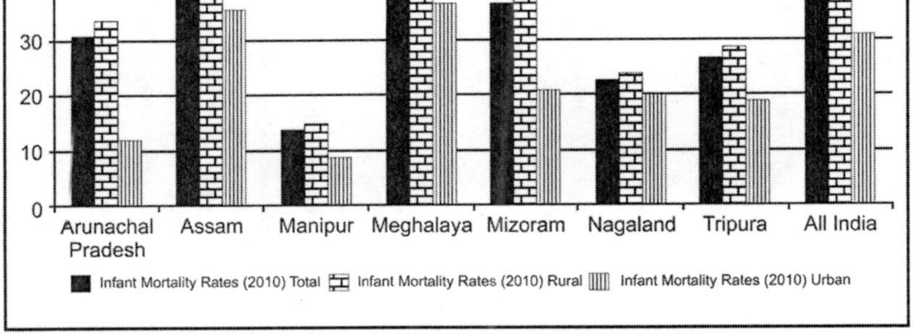

Source: SRS Bulletin December, 2011 Sample Registration System, Office of Registrar General, India.

NFHS-3 (2005–06) the immunisation coverage in the seven North-eastern states was poor ranging from 28 per cent to 50 per cent. Table 16

Table 16

Selected Key Indicators (Coverage Evaluation Survey 2009 – UNICEF)

	At least 1 ANC	*>3 ANC*	*Full ANC*[1]	*Institut-ional Delivery*	*Skilled Birth Atten-dance*[2]	*DPT3 Vaccine*	*Measles Vaccine*	*Full Immunis Ation*[3]	*DPT Booster Dose*[4]	*Vitamin A 1st Dose*	*Early Initiation of Breast Feeding (<1hr)*	*ORT or Increased Fluids for Diarrhoea*[5]	*Care Seeking for ARI in any Health Facility*[6]
AP	69.8	50.4	16.3	69.9	71.9	45.0	48.2	24.8	35.9	40.0	55.6	84.6	64.5
Assam	89.6	66.4	21.3	64.4	65.5	67.5	80.1	59.1	27.7	69.3	46.1	60.0	79.2
Manipur	93.7	85.0	28.4	80.0	82.7	62.7	60.3	51.9	39.9	47.9	75.1	82.9	77.8
Meghalaya	95.1	71.0	28.1	63.7	65.2	69.3	74.1	60.8	16.4	58.1	67.7	88.4	94.3
Mizoram	91.9	79.0	21.7	83.0	85.1	77.8	81.1	73.7	67.1	74.4	56.5	60.8	87.6
Nagaland	53.7	29.4	3.5	30.4	43.8	45.9	52.2	27.8	13.6	28.2	49.4	57.5	50.6
Tripura	90.9	83.1	21.5	82.6	83.1	70.6	68.8	66.0	50.7	68.0	7.1	76.4	95.5
INDIA	89.6	68.7	26.5	72.9	76.2	71.5	74.1	61.0	41.4	64.0	33.5	53.6	82.6

Note: Conducted during November 2009 to January 2010. All figures in per cent (available at http://www.unicef.org/india/health_6679.htm).

1. Women who received 3 ANC check-ups, one TT injection and consumed 100 + IFA tablets.
2. Delivery by Doctor, ANM/Nurse/LHV.
3. Children (12–23 months) receiving 1 dose BCG, 3 doses of DPT/OPV each and 1 measles vaccine.
4. Children aged 18–23 months who received DPT booster dose.
5. Among children <2 year of age who had diarrhoea in preceding 2 weeks.
6. Among children <2 year of age who had ARI in preceding 2 weeks.

summarises selected key reproductive and child health indicators including immunisation from more recent Coverage Evaluation Survey, 2009 conducted by the UNICEF.

Innovations

The NRHM encourages the states to appraise the need for innovation through decentralised planning.[41] It provides for funds for local innovative approaches that emerge as priorities during the bottom-up planning process. There is considerable emphasis by the states on meeting the RCH II overarching goal of reducing IMR, ensuring quality and service coverage for the un-served and underserved population.

PANEL 7

The innovations themes following the National Programme Implementation Plan of RCH II and the Implementation Framework of the NRHM

1. Safe Motherhood/Maternal Mortality Reduction
   a. Innovations to promote safe motherhood and institutional delivery
   b. Ambulance services and helplines for transport of obstetric emergencies
   c. Strengthening skills and capacity of providers
2. Immunisation and Infant and Young Child Feeding
3. Adolescent Reproductive and Sexual Health (ARSH)
4. Behaviour Change Communication (BCC)
5. Gender Mainstreaming
6. Service Delivery for RCH
   a. Mobile health units
   b. Social franchising networks
   c. Health financing
   d. Contracting out management of public health services
7. Programme Management
   a. Incentives to improve mobility, availability and attendance of staff
   b. Incentives to improve performance and range of services
   c. Alternatives to In service training for improved performance
   d. Community and panchayat involvement in planning, monitoring and management of health services and facilities
   e. Programme monitoring and management information systems
   f. Improving procurement and finance systems
8. School Health
9. Urban Health

Innovations by the Northeastern States

There are a number of innovations carried out by the Northeastern states. Following is a brief outline of selected initiatives, which provide a window to the unique nature of the problems faced by the respective states and the innovation piloted to overcome the constraint.

Management of PHCs by NGOs (Arunachal Pradesh): In a Public Private Partnership (PPP), management of 16 PHCs in 16 districts was handed over to NGOs. As per the Memorandum of Understanding (MoU) signed with the NGOs by the government, the NGOs provide manpower, equipment and administrative support and the range of outreach services. Sub-Centres under the respective PHCs are also managed by the NGOs who provide outreach services in the villages covered by the PHCs. The government provides 90 per cent of the funds with a 10 per cent contribution from the NGOs.

Chiranjeevi Yojana (Assam): This is a PPP initiative to increase access to emergency obstetric care and institutional delivery for the un-served population. The scheme contracts out services to the private doctors/hospitals, provides insurance coverage to all Below Poverty Line (BPL) pregnant women, neonates, and generates awareness about the scheme. Cash reimbursement provided for transport and for the patient's attendant wage loss.

Insecticide-treated Bed Nets for Pregnant Women (Assam): Insecticide-treated bed nets provided to all the pregnant women accessing institutions for delivery combined with the JSY incentive. This has been initiated in Sivasagar, Goalpara, Golaghat and Morigaon on pilot basis.

Emergency Management and Referral Institute (Assam): A toll-free number has been set up in Guwahati, which include emergency ambulance services in partnership with a non-profit organisation. The ambulances are placed strategically in the districts and functions 24/7 to cater to any kind of emergency with three teams: Information team (call taking, call processing and call dispatch), Response team (ambulance) and Care team (pre-hospital medical care). A state-wide toll-free emergency number connects informants to the Emergency Response Centre in Guwahati.

Mother and Child Health (MCH) Month (Assam): Specific months in a year are focussed (September and March) in all the districts for promoting awareness on child health and improving service delivery. During the MCH month, the emphasis is placed on the provision of the following services, which are provided at the Sub-Centres, *Anganwadi* centres, and out-patient departments of all health institutions: Vitamin A prophylaxis up to children of three years, de-worming of children between one to five years, treatment of anaemia in children between one to five years, treatment of ARI cases and cases of dehydration with ORS and zinc tablets.

ASHA Radio (Assam): Radio sets distributed to all the selected ASHA and radio programme for ASHA started from 8 October 2007 in All India Radio for two days in a week. Each programme is broadcast for half an hour all over the state weekly, produced in three languages and provides health education and information to the ASHA. Pre-paid postcards were distributed to the ASHA for giving feedback and according to the feedbacks, special topics are organised each week.

PPP with Private Hospitals/Tea Garden Hospitals (Assam): Partnership formed with private sector/trust hospitals/tea garden hospitals, refinery hospitals, army hospitals and other non-profit earning hospitals to deliver quality RCH services in urban and uncovered remote areas. The private hospitals will provide a range of services for promoting JSY, comprehensive Emergency Obstetric Care (EmOC), safe abortion facilities, new-born care services, sterilisation programmes and counselling on adolescent health. The hospitals rendering RCH services under PPP will be given an annual grant of ₹ 15 lakh each and will be supported in terms of honorarium for manpower, drugs, mobility support, JSY funds and social mobilisation and orientation. The state has established partnership with seven trust hospitals and 22 tea garden hospitals.

Mobile Boat Clinics in Riverine Areas (Assam): Launched phase-wise in five districts of Assam (Tinsukia, Dhemaji, Dibrugarh, Morigaon, Dhubri, Barpeta, Nalbari, Jorhat, Lakhimpur and Sonitpur). The boat clinic has provisions for providing routine primary healthcare services as well as emergency services. Health camps are held every month for providing antenatal care. During emergencies, that is, floods and other calamities, the boat clinic increases the frequency of visits.

Outsourcing of CHCs to NGOs (Assam): Management and operation of one CHC/block in four districts outsourced to private agencies, that is, charitable/army hospitals. That is, while the private partner will use the existing government infrastructure including the equipment, the state provides drugs and consumables to the partner and responsible for monitoring. In turn, the private agency/partner provides manpower and will be responsible for the service delivery in the CHCs.

Performance Incentives for Government Facilities to Improve Institutional Delivery (Assam): Performance-based incentives to hospitals for institutional delivery. Incentives will include normal and caesarean deliveries. The cash incentives will be paid to the institution, 50 per cent of the incentives will be deposited in the RKS, and the other 50 per cent will be paid to the team conducting the deliveries.

Cash Incentives for Staff in Difficult Areas (Assam): Difficult areas allowance paid to 40 specialists and 60 MOs posted in difficult areas. The doctor's salary will be at par with the Associate Professor of the medical colleges and Specialists with the Professor; ₹ 5,000 given to Specialist serving in rural area as allowance and difficult area allowance for all doctors serving in Karbi Anglong, NC Hills and five subdivisions.

Maternal and Perinatal Death Autopsy (Assam): This is an initiative to track maternal and perinatal death through verbal autopsies carried out by ASHA and ANM. All maternal deaths in a district/block reported directly to the DPM by the ANM, ASHA and the community within 24 hours of the death. This is followed by a detailed investigation of the case within 15 days of the occurrence of the death by an investigation team. A state-level assesses the quality of the maternal death investigation and provides feedback to the district on a quarterly basis.

Ensuring 100 per cent Birth Registration (Manipur): Incentives to Trained Birth Attendants (TBA) and others for ensuring 100 per cent birth registration.

Maternity Waiting Centres (Manipur): Pilot initiative for two NGO-managed maternity waiting centres each with a capacity for 20 beds. Each of these centres will include 14 ANM with two ANM on service 24/7. The centres are exclusively for women belonging to the poor families, who will be required to provide a nominal admittance and daily fees. Pregnant women will be shifted to the referral centres for delivery and in cases of emergencies.

Use of Satisfied Couples to Motivate Clients for Family Planning (Manipur): The scheme utilises the satisfied beneficiaries to generate demand.

Incentives to Sub-Centre Second ANM (Manipur): Performance-based incentives provided to additional ANM posted at Sub-Centres.

Incentives for Provision of Emergency Obstetric Care (Manipur): Performance-based incentives for MBBS doctors to train in comprehensive Emergency Obstetric Care (EmOC) and life-saving anaesthesia skills.

JSY Helpline (Mizoram): JSY helpline implemented by NGO.

Verbal Autopsy for New-born Deaths (Manipur): Verbal autopsy for deaths of new-borns.

Health Insurance for Poor (Mizoram): A family health insurance in partnership with a private insurance company and private sector hospitals. The state government/nodal agency will assist the insurance company in establishing the network of hospitals, finalising treatment protocols and costs and treatment authorisation and claims scrutiny. Private hospitals fulfilling the minimum criteria for standards will be empanelled. Pre-existing diseases will be covered and actual travel expenses as well as wage loss. The scheme will be subsidised for the BPL families.

Enabling Round-the-Clock Services for Institutional Delivery (Mizoram): Cash incentives for Medical Officers (MOs), staff nurses and Grade IV staff for conducting deliveries at night in primary health centres (PHCs).

PHC run Faith-Based Organisations (Mizoram): One PHC located in a very remote area in a district covering two Sub-Centres and six villages are managed by a church-based organisation. The State Health Society (SHS) provides the funds for the staff salaries, maintenance of the infrastructure, and all equipment to the Mission hospital. The Mission hospital is responsible for service delivery, recruitment of staff, managing the PHC in accordance with the norms provided by the SHS.

Incentives to Increase Mobility of Health Workers (Mizoram): Vehicle loan for health worker, health supervisor and community health worker.

Gender Budgeting (Nagaland): Gender budgeting integrating a gender perspective and ensuring that budgets respond to gender equality and requirements of women.

Communitarian Private Public Partnership for the Management of Health Centres (Nagaland): This is an on-going initiative in engaging community participation in management of health centre services from the Sub-Centre upwards to encourage ownership.

Cash Incentives for ANM (Nagaland): Incentive provided for ANM posted in Sub-Centres of remote districts.

Doli Initiative (Tripura): Referral transport in the form of a *doli* or palanquin for ensuring access to services for the people in the remote areas of the state, piloted in one district. The *doli* is used by the villagers/porters for transportation of sick mothers and children from the villages to the health facilities. The state expects to have 500 porter services in a year.

Mobile Helicopter Services (Tripura): Special services in 12 remote inaccessible areas through helicopter services.

Increasing Mobility to Enable the Monitoring of Sub-Centres (Tripura): A two-wheeler is provided to each CHC and all PHCs in a phased manner in Dhalai district for improving the supervision of the sub-centres. Visit report of the two-wheelers submitted to the district office and registers will be maintained for their movement.

Performance Incentives for Medical Officers in PHC, CHC and SDH (Tripura): Cash incentives paid to the MOs in PHCs and CHCs posted in the remote areas in all the four districts of the state. The bed occupancy rate of these facilities regularly monitored along with the performance of the staff chosen for the incentives.

Health Village Awards to Autonomous Development Councils (Tripura): In order to generate the interest of the community regarding the RCH programme, the Healthy Village award given to the top three general practitioners on Autonomous District Councils (ADCs) in the district every year, chosen by the District Selection Committee. The state provides a select list of indicators and the *Gram Pradhans* and health committees monitor the implementation of the various activities related to the indicators. The cash prizes for the top three villages are ₹ 3 lakh for the best village, ₹ 2 lakh for the second village and ₹ 1 lakh for the third best performing village, to be used for development activities in their respective areas.

Discussion

At the launch of the NHRM in April 2005, Prime Minister Singh admitted, 'What has been a fatal flaw in our approach is that we have gradually abandoned comprehensive health care and a public-health perspective for focused attention on selective diseases.'[42] He also said, 'We have grievously erred in the design of many of our health programmes. We have created a delivery model that fragments resources and dissipates energies. Most importantly we have paid inadequate attention to the public-health issues and the possibilities of social and preventive medicine.'[43] The NHRM is an attempt to remedy the situation with a clear policy direction and strategic objectives. There has been emphasis on developing adequate rural health infrastructure and meeting priority goals such as reducing IMR to meet the MDG obligation.

The findings suggest that there has been significant improvement in the rural health infrastructure since 2005 and fund utilisation capacity has increased significantly. In many respect, the Northeastern states fared better compared to the all India average. The NHRM has a strong and robust information capture and monitoring system via online Health Management Information System of all the programme components. The performance of Northeastern states in vital programme components such as number of districts which prepared annual district health action plan, beneficiaries of IUCD insertions and male and female sterilisations, antenatal care, delivery care, postnatal care, deliveries, children vaccinated, AYUSH components and number of Health *Melas* held, operational mobile medical unit and so on reveals variable performances but steady progress.[44] The gulf between the required and in position in terms of the physical infrastructure comprising Sub-Centres, PHC and CHS has reduced dramatically when compared to 2005. However, the main challenge is in meeting the human resources requirement, staffing being a serious concern particularly of specialist doctors and staff nurses at the CHC. However, Assam managed in recent time to fully meet the requirement of doctors and, in fact, has (with Manipur) surplus doctors in the PHC. Significant challenges remain in meeting the IPHS for the Sub-Centres, PHC and CHC in terms of staffing and amenities such as regular water and electricity, telephone, staff-quarter, all-weather motorable road, and, labour room and operating theatre, etc. However, states have done extremely well in forming registered RKS at PHC and CHC (100 per cent in Assam), together with clear explicit goal and roadmap, and performance continuously monitored, progress is likely to continue towards meeting

IPHS. Unlike in few other states,[45] there was no big fraud reported in Northeastern states so far, while this is no guarantee against the leakage of funds and misappropriation. The RKS and PRI hold the keys and could ensure much better utilisation of funds. The states have attained the target in appointing ASHA, all the preliminary training modules completed, and advanced training is underway in many states.

IMR is steadily declining from a very high base level compared to national rate; Assam still faces a significant challenge. The target of 30/1,000 live births by 2012 probably will not be met as IMR stands at 55 against the national rate of 43 in 2011. How sooner the significant progress was made in strengthening physical health infrastructure, full complementing ASHA, showing good performance in JYS and other components of reproductive and child health translate to achieve the IMR target is of great interest and has important implications. Similarly, MMR for Assam was 390 against the national rate of 212 (2007–09). In June 2012, Assam has 60 FRUs, an increase from 46 in 2005 to extend the reach of good obstetrics care. Whether MMR has reduced is yet to be reported. In Meghalaya and Mizoram, also, IMR remains a concern.

The innovations by the states provide a glimpse to the unique problems faced by the states, such as, remoteness and difficult access, lack of trained work force and government capacity to deliver services, overriding necessity to provide reproductive and child health services. The successful innovations need to be replicated and learning shared among all the stakeholders. ASHA radio is an interesting innovation; newer ICT technology should also provide great advantage to remotely deliver continuous professional learning and facilitate effective communication with the workforce. Similarly, incentive to MBBS doctors to upgrade skills, such as, in comprehensive emergency obstetric care to fill the specialist gap, is noteworthy. Continuous and relevant training is one of the most important activities of any service delivery enterprise. Access to such specialist training not only for doctors but also for other staff could be made easily deliverable by investing in simulation technology and creating interactive reusable digital learning material delivered in the form of webcast/podcast as internet penetration deepens. Boat clinic to make services available to remote, otherwise, inaccessible areas and during natural disasters is another noteworthy innovation. Partnership with private enterprise to deliver services is a standard policy but Northeastern states engaging in partnership with faith-based organisations and other not-for-profit organisations like military and tea garden hospitals are interesting experiment and worth closure look in terms of performance and outcome. In this regard, encouraging and empowering co-operative formed by patients to run services for its members could be quite effective. Introduction of competition with substantial cash reward to high performing institutions or units as in tried in some states is interesting. Innovations and replicating the successful ones are the way forward. Higher learning institutions such as universities need to be encouraged to do research on innovative practices, pilot ideas and generate otherwise much needed evidence to inform health policy formulation and future direction.

In the front of human resources, recruiting and training the healthcare professionals, from ASHA with basic curative and preventive competencies to doctors and nurses capable of specialist functions, curriculum update and meticulous work force planning to fill the gap for the next 25 years with expansion of training capacity are required. Assam has embarked on to establish a number of new medical colleges, which will fill the gap of doctors with first batch from the first new college qualifying in 2015. It is not sufficient to only produce doctors (and nurses and other health professionals) but with right mix of skills, competencies and attitude and in right proportion. In developed nations, the trend is for delegating more and more specialist tasks to trained nurses and non-doctor health professionals. In this context, the introduction of Rural Health Practitioners with three year training after 10+2 is a pioneering experiment in Assam. The current focus on infectious diseases, and reproductive and children health is understandable, but it soon has to be matched with equally urgent measures to combat the chronic disease epidemic, which equally affects the poor and rural population. A wide range of cost-effective primary and secondary prevention strategies are available for chronic diseases, which can be delivered by non-doctor healthcare professionals. As such, getting it right in terms of right mix of trained work force is a strategic priority for the Northeastern states lest it turns to be its Achilles' heel. The first and the only health university in the region established in Assam in 2009 could play an instrumental role in producing healthcare professionals in right numbers with right skills and competencies to serve the region.

The cancer care facilities in the region are comparatively poor relative to the burden of the disease. The states should pool their scarce resources and capability together, and create strategically located 'state-of-the-art' regional tertiary care centres instead of duplicating efforts and wasting resources. People travelling hundreds of kilometre from the region to metropolis in search of medical care must stop, not only from the equity point of view but also from economic point of view. It is an economic imperative for the region as a whole to prevent drainage of money from the region.

Overall, with much strengthened physical infrastructure in place in most states and progress towards IPHS, what is waiting to emerge is a strong professional leadership and replicable ground breaking innovations enabling the Northeastern states to make a leap towards universal health coverage in this strategic corner of the country.

Notes

1. World Health Organization (WHO). The World Health Report (2000). Health Systems: Improving Performance. Geneva: WHO, retrieved from http://www.who.int/whr/2000/en/whr00_en.pdf (accessed 10 December 2012).
2. Resolution WHA58.33 (16–25 May 2005). Sustainable Health Financing, Universal Coverage and Social Health Insurance. In *Fifty-eighth World Health Assembly,* Geneva: WHO, retrieved from http://apps.who.int/gb/ebwha/pdf_files/WHA58/WHA58_33-en.pdf (accessed 23 June 2010).
3. World Health Organization (WHO). The World Health Report (2010). Health Systems Financing: the Path to Universal Coverage. Geneva: WHO, retrieved from http://www.who.int/whr/2010/whr10_en.pdf (accessed 1 December 2010).
4. World Health Organization (WHO). World Health Statistics (2008). Geneva: WHO, retrieved from http://www.who.int/whosis/whostat/EN_WHS08_Full.pdf (accessed 05 January 2013).
5. World Bank (WB). GDP Growth (annual %). Washington DC: WB, retrieved from http://data.worldbank.org/indicator/NY.GDP.MKTP.KD.ZG (accessed 12 January 2013).
6. World Bank (WB). Health expenditure, public (% of GDP). Washington DC: WB, retrieved from http://data.worldbank.org/indicator/SH.XPD.PUBL. ZS (accessed 12 January 2013).
7. National Rural Health Mission, Government of India (NRHM, GOI, 2012–13). Accountability Initiative Report, retrieved from http://Econ Papers.repec.org/RePEc:ess:wpaper:id:4867 (accessed 30 December 2012).
8. National Rural Health Mission, Government of India (NRHM, GOI, 2012–13). Accountability Initiative Report, retrieved from http://Econ Papers. repec.org/RePEc:ess:wpaper:id:4867 (accessed 30 December 2012).
9. PWC. Addressing the unfinished agenda Universal healthcare. http://www.pwc.in/assets/pdfs/healthcare/background-paper.pdf
10. Indians' medicine bills concern WHO. http://articles.timesofindia.indiatimes.com/2011-11-02/india/30349668_1_drug-procurement-therapeutics-committee-medicines
11. Millennium Development Goals (MDGs), India, retrieved from http://www.unicef.org/india/overview_3696.htm (accessed 02 January 2013).

12. United Nations Development Programme (UNDP), About India. Retrieved from http://www.in.undp.org/content/india/en/home/countryinfo/(accessed 01 January 2013).
13. Millennium Development Goals Indicators-The Official United nations Site for the MDG Indicators, Infant Mortality rate (0–1) per 1,000 live births. Retrieved from http://unstats.un.org/unsd/mdg/SeriesDetail.aspx?srid=562 (accessed 01 January 2013).
14. National Rural Health Mission, Government of India (NRHM, GOI, 2012–13). Accountability Initiative Report, retrieved from http://EconPapers.repec.org/RePEc:ess:wpaper:id:4867 (accessed 30 December 2012).
15. National Rural Health Mission, Government of India (NRHM, GOI, 2012–13). Accountability Initiative Report, retrieved from http://EconPapers. repec.org/RePEc:ess:wpaper:id:4867 (accessed 30 December 2012).
16. National Rural Health Mission (NRHM). Mission Document (2005–2012). Retrieved from http://www.mohfw.nic.in/NRHM/Documents/Mission_Document.pdf (accessed 01 January 2013).
17. National Rural Health Mission (NRHM). Mission Document (2005–2012). Retrieved from http://www.mohfw.nic.in/NRHM/Documents/Mission_Document.pdf (accessed 01 January 2013).
18. National Rural Health Mission: Framework for Implementation (2010). MHFW, Government of India. Retrieved from http://mohfw.nic.in/NRHM/Documents/Urban_Health/UH_Framework_Final.pdf (accessed 02 January 2013).
19. NRHM Implementation Plans, 2012–13. Retrieved from http://pipnrhm-mohfw.nic.in/PIP2012-13_files/State_PIP.htm (accessed 24 December 2012).
20. Indian Public Health Standard (IPHS). National Rural Health Mission. Retrieved from http://mohfw.nic.in/NRHM/iphs.htm (accessed 01 January 2013).
21. Update on the ASHA Programme (July 2012). National Rural Health Mission. Retrieved from http://nhsrcindia.org/pdf_files/resources_thematic/Community_Participation/NHSRC_Contribution/Asha_Update_July_2012.pdf (accessed 09 December 2012).
22. Sample Registration System (SRS) Bulletin (December 2011). Office of Registrar General, India.
23. District Level Household and Facility Survey (DLHS). Retrieved from http://www.rchiips.org (accessed 10 January 2013).
24. National Family Health Survey (NFHS), India. Retrieved from http://www.rchiips.org/NFHS/index.shtml (accessed 10 January 2013).

25. Update on the ASHA Programme (July 2012). National Rural Health Mission. Retrieved from http://nhsrcindia.org/pdf_files/resources_thematic/Community_Participation/NHSRC_Contri-ution/Asha_Update_July_2012. pdf (accessed 09 December 2012).
26. Update on the ASHA Programme (July 2012). National Rural Health Mission. Retrieved from http://nhsrcindia.org/pdf_files/resources_thematic/Community_Participation/NHSRC_Contri-ution/Asha_Update_July_2012.pdf (accessed 09 December 2012).
27. Update on the ASHA Programme (July 2012). National Rural Health Mission. Retrieved from http://nhsrcindia.org/pdf_files/resources_thematic/Community_Participation/NHSRC_Contriution/Asha_Update_July_2012.pdf (accessed 09 December 2012).
28. Evaluation Study of National Rural Health Mission (NRHM) in 7 States (2011). Programme Evaluation Organisation Planning Commission, Government of India. Retrieved from http://planningcommission.nic.in/reports/peoreport/peoevalu/peo_2807.pdf (accessed 12 December 2012).
29. Medical Education in Assam. Retrieved from http://www.jmch.org.in/showsubpage.asp?subid=54&id=120 (accessed 06 January 2013).
30. Kokrajhar Medical College foundation laid (12 February 2011), *Assam Tribune*. Retrieved from http://www.assamtribune.com/scripts/details new.asp?id=feb1211/state05 (accessed 06 January 2013); Dhubri to get medical college (28 January 2011) *The Telegraph,* Calcutta India. Retrieved from http://www.telegraphindia.com/1110128/jsp/north east/story_13500498.jsp (accessed 06 January 2013); Foundation of Lakhimpur Medical College laid (21 February 2011). *The Assam Tribune*. Retrieved from. http://www.assamtribune.com/scripts/detailsnew.asp?id=feb2111/at09 (accessed 06 January 2013).
31. List of Colleges Teaching MBBS. *Medical Council of India*. Retrieved from http://www.mciindia.org/InformationDesk/MedicalCollegeHospitals/ListofCollegesTeachingMBBS.aspx (accessed 06 January 2013).
32. Mizoram to get medical college. *The Hindu - Businessline.* Retrieved from http://www.thehindubusinessline.com/industry-and-economy/econmy/article1523380.ece (accessed 06 January 2013).
33. Janani Suraksha Yojana, Guidelines for Implementation (2005). MHFW. Government of India. Retrieved from http://www.ilo.org/dyn/travail/docs/683/Janani%20Suraksha%20Yojana%20%20Guidelines%20for%20implementation%20-%20Ministry%20of%20Health%20and%20Family%20Welfare.pdf (accessed 11 January 2013).
34. National Rural Health Mission, Government of India (NRHM, GOI, 2012–13). Accountability Initiative Report, retrieved from http://Econ

Papers.repec.org/RePEc:ess:wpaper:id:4867 (accessed 30 December 2012).

35. Cancer in North-East Regions of India. Retrieved from http://icmr.nic.in/annual/2004-05/icpo/cancer_neregion.pdf (accessed 10 January 2013).
36. First All India Report 2001–2002: Atlas of cancer in India. Retrieved from www.ncrpindia.org/Cancer_Atlas_India/map.aspx (accessed 10 January 2013).
37. Chennai Assam Bhawan likely to be a reality (07 February 2008). *The Assam Tribune*. Retrieved from http://www.assamtribune.com/scripts/details.asp?id=feb0708/State9 (accessed 10 January 2013).
38. Healthcare improves but people still eye big cities (26 April 2012). *The Times of India*. Retrieved from http://articles.timesofindia.indiatimes.com/2012-04-26/guwahati/31409490_1_cleft-surgeries-patients (accessed 12 January 2013).
39. U5MR and MMR figures for smaller States are not available.
40. State-Wise Progress as on 30.06.2012, National Rural Health Mission (NRHM). Retrieved from http://www.mohfw.nic.in/NRHM/Documents/MIS/Statewise%20Progress%20under%20NRHM_Status%20as%20on%2030.06.2012.pdf (accessed 02 January 2013).
41. Directory of Innovations: Implemented in the Health Sector (December, 2008), Supported by Department for International Development. Retrieved from http://planningcommission.nic.in/reports/genrep/health/Directory_ of_innovations_march.pdf (accessed 31 December 2012).
42. India's Medical Emergency (01 May 2008). *Time*. Retrieved from http://www.time.com/time/magazine/article/0,9171,1736516-1,00.html (accessed 09 January 2013).
43. Directory of Innovations: Implemented in the Health Sector (December, 2008), Supported by Department for International Development. Retrieved from http://planningcommission.nic.in/reports/genrep/health/Directory_ of_innovations_march.pdf (accessed 31 December 2012).
44. State-Wise Progress as on 30.06.2012, National Rural Health Mission (NRHM). Retrieved from http://www.mohfw.nic.in/NRHM/Documents/MIS/Statewise%20Progress%20under%20NRHM_Status%20as%20on%2030.06.2012.pdf (accessed 02 January 2013).
45. NRHM scam: CBI files Chargesheet against ex-UP Babu, others (03 April 2012). *The Times of India*. Retrieved from http://articles.timesofindia.indiatimes.com/2012-04-03/india/31280630_1_cbi-files-chargesheet-charge-sheet-nrhm (accessed 10 January 2013).

References

Bajpai, N., J.D. Sach and R.H. Dholakia. (2009) 'Improving Access, Service Delivery and Efficiency of the Public Health System in Rural India – Mid-Term Evaluation of the National Rural Health Mission', *Working Papers Series*, Center on Globalization and Sustainable Development, New York: Columbia University.

Balarajan, Y., S. Selvaraj and S.V. Subramanian. (2011) 'Health Care and Equity in India'. *The Lancet*. 377 (9764). pp. 505–511.

Barman, M.P., J. Hazarika and K. Dutta. (2012) 'Survival Status of Oesophageal Cancer Patients in Assam, India: A Bio-Statistical Analysis'. *International Journal of Statistika and Mathematika*. 3(2). pp. 42–49.

John T.J., L. Dandona, V.P. Sharma and M. Kakkar. (2011) 'Continuing Challenge of Infectious Diseases in India'. *The Lancet*. 377(9761). pp. 252–69.

Patel, V., A.K. Shiva Kumar, V.K. Paul, K.D. Rao and K.S. Reddy. (2011a) 'Universal Health Care in India: The Time is Right'. *The Lancet*. 377(9764). pp. 448–449.

Patel, V., S. Chatterji, D. Chisholm, S. Ebrahim, G. Gopalakrishna, C. Mathers, V. Mohan, D. Prabhakaran, R.D. Ravindran and K.S. Reddy. (2011b) 'Chronic Diseases and Injuries in India'. *The Lancet*. 377(9763). pp. 413–28.

Rahman, D. (13 April 2011) 'Cancer Rages in Assam – Betel nut, Tobacco Culprits'. *The Telegraph*, Calcutta, India. Retrieved from http://www.telegraphindia. com/1110413/jsp/northeast/story_13845916.jsp (accessed 10 January 2013)

Rao, M., K.D. Rao, A.K. Shiva Kumar and, T. Sundararaman Chatterjee. (2011) 'Human Resources for Health in India'. *The Lancet*. 377 (9765). pp. 587–598.

Shiva Kumar, A.K., L.C. Chen, M. Choudhury, S. Ganju,V. Mahajan, A. Sinha and A Sen. (2011) 'Financing Health Care for All: Challenges and Opportunities. *The Lancet*. 377 (9766). pp. 668–679.

4

Internal Displacement in the Northeast

WALTER FERNANDES

Studies indicate that India has deprived an estimated 60 million people of their sustenance 1947–2000 in the name of national development. Some of them have been physically relocated and are known as displaced persons (DP). Others are deprived of their sustenance without physical relocation and are called project affected persons (PAP). The tribes that are a little over 8 per cent of the population account for around 40 per cent of the DP-PAPs. Many consider tribal deprivation necessary because their regions are resource-rich and those riches should be used for the whole country. But they ignore the impoverishment and marginalisation that it causes and the legal status of their land that allows the State to displace them without rehabilitation or compensation and with no possibility of beginning life anew. Tribal proportion is higher in the Northeast. Also conflicts and disasters displace people. This paper will study the impact and possible solutions to the impoverishment of the DP-PAPs especially tribal.

Disaster and Conflict IDPs

Internally displaced persons (IDPs) are caused by development projects, conflicts and disasters. This section concentrates on disaster and conflict IDPs with focus on the Northeast. In the late 1990s, UN agencies put the number of conflict and disaster IDPs in the world at 20–25 million (Sheikh, 2005: 63).

Conflict IDPs

If the DPs remain in their country they are called IDPs. Those who cross international borders and go to another country become refugees. This difference is conditioned also by the size of the country. For example, persons who fled from Sri Lanka to India 100 kilometres away or the Rohingiyas who crossed over from Myanmar to Bangladesh (Abrar, 2000: 45–47) or the estimated 40,000 Myanmar refugees in Mizoram or the 1,30,000 Bhutanese residents who escaped to Nepal less than 200 km away (Acharya, 2004) and the 1,20,000 families whom 'settlers' forced out of the Chittagong Hill Tracts of Bangladesh and took refuge in Northeast India in the 1980s (Guhathakurtha and Begum, 2005: 186–187) are called refugees. But those who travelled 1,200 kilometres to Uttar Pradesh from Gujarat during the 2002 anti-Muslim pogrom are considered IDPs.

The number of conflict IDPs has grown in the world during the last decade. For example because of the intervention of foreign troops to control the minerals worth USD five trillion in Afghanistan and petroleum in Iraq and southern Sudan, 15 per cent of the population of Iraq, 28 per cent of Afghanistan and 47 per cent of South Sudan had become IDPs by 2007. Many more had fled the country (Ferris, Mooney and Stark, 2011: 25–26). The exact number of conflict IDPs is difficult to know since many of them take refuge in their relatives' houses. The UN figure of 5,07,000 IDPs in India in 1999 (Majumdar, 2002: 102) is an underestimate. Studies point to more than 30,00,000 conflict IDPs in India during the last three decades. They include 3,50,000 Kashmiri Pandits, 50,000 IDPs of the 1985 caste riots and 1,00,000 of the 2002 anti-Muslim pogrom in Gujarat, 5,00,000 of the border villages of Kashmir and over 2,00,000 of the anti-Muslim riots in 1989 and the 1892 after Babri Masjid demolition (Das, 2005: 122–134). Communal tension is considered their major cause but in reality there are many conflicts around shortages and could be for political power and are not necessarily religious.

Disaster IDPs

Studies rarely mention the desertification displaced as disaster IDPs because they are often invisible and its impact is not felt in one event like an earthquake but it is lasting (Dasgupta, 2007: 30–33). Till recently studies put the number of disaster DPs at 5,00,000 per year except in years of extraordinary events like the 2001 Gujarat earthquake and the 2004 Kashmir earthquake, each of which seems to have killed 20,000–30,000 persons and caused 2,00,000 IDPs and the tsunami that killed 3,00,000 and displaced 5,00,000 (Das, 2005: 112–113). The number of disaster IDPs is growing mainly because of human intervention in the environment and because the level of rivers has risen as a result of siltation caused by deforestation in their catchment area (Gadgil and Guha, 1995: 35–36). Floods displace a few million persons temporarily every year. The extent and intensity of floods, droughts and landslides has increased because of desertification and environmental degradation. Moreover, today many

IDPs of floods are unable to begin life anew when they return home because they lose most of their belongings including the year's crops (Bandyopadhyay, 2007: 5).

Because of environmental degradation through human interventions in the name of development the situation of disasters deteriorating further and the number of disaster IDPs is growing (Dekens, 2007: 7). For example even the official figure of flood-related deaths that is an underestimate shows that in India, as a whole, they caused 524 deaths in 1953 on 24.28 million hectares affected. The number went beyond 1,000 in the mid-1960s but the big rise is from the 1980s with 40,593 deaths in 1985 from 59.59 million hectares, 37,023 in 1995 from 35.93 million hectares and 58,459 from 68.72 million hectares in 1998. The number declined in the drought year of 2002 and is rising again (Prasad, 2005). A component of recent floods and other disasters is permanent loss of the natural resources whose impact the poor feel more than the rich do because with the decline in their resource base, the traditional coping mechanisms and techniques that were linked to a different environment have become outdated and non-viable. So the victims are unable to adapt them to the changed situation. But very few new coping mechanisms have been developed (Dekens, 2007: 10–11). Disasters have both human and economic costs. They destroy the infrastructure built over years and force families and the State to divert development funds for relief. The World Bank (2003) puts the loss incurred by disasters in India 1965–2000 at $35 billion (₹ 3,57,000 crores at January 2013 rate).

Whatever their type and impact, the situation of the IDPs remains serious. By and large, disaster IDPs are well looked after because many agencies have developed skills for their long-term rehabilitation though there are cases of neglect, for example of Muslims and Dalits after the Gujarat earthquake and of Dalits after the tsunami in Tamil Nadu. Women and children receive inadequate attention (Banerjee, 2005: 270–272). Moreover, because of the emotional outburst after a disaster financial aid flows somewhat fast. Conflict IDPs get some attention in the camps but tend to be forgotten later. Development IDPs are all but ignored.

Disaster IDPs in the Northeast

The negative impacts are clearly visible in the Northeast in the form of loss of the natural resources and subsequent disasters. Forests have been lost to industry and forestland to development projects. Also some natural heritage has been lost, for example, about 35 per cent of the Majuli Island in Assam, the world's biggest river island, lost to erosion (Goswami, 2003: 9). Another negative impact is loss of resilience in natural resource management and of agricultural operations adapted to the ecosystem. For example, in Assam, which depends mostly on the south-west monsoons, annual floods were a part of life. Most regions depending on these monsoons celebrate the harvest festival in August–September but Bhogali Bihu, the harvest festival of Assam is in January, the month in which regions depending on the Northeastern monsoons celebrate it. It is because in the past, farmers began cultivation before the first floods in July, reaped what remained of it and transplanted again using the silt from the floods as soil nutrient. As a result, the main harvest was in December (Bhattacharyya, 2003: 2–3) and Bihu symbolises it.

Such resilience was possible because floods were an annual event coming in one phase. Today too they are annual but are more intense and widespread than in the past and come in many phases. For example, the 2004 floods considered the worst in Assam in 50 years, came in three phases and destroyed crops worth ₹ 990 crores (Patowary, 2004). Flash floods in Goalpara district came on 4 October which is two weeks before the end of the weeding season. Today, the last phase is usually in September when traditionally the farmer completed transplantation. Siltation does not always allow a second crop after the floods since the silt is mostly sand and not fertile as it was in the past. As a result people's resilience has declined. They have become more vulnerable to the negative impact than in the past since they lack support to rebuild their lives.

Conflict IDPs in the Northeast

Also the number of conflict IDPs is growing in the region because of many ethnic conflicts for two decades, most of them due to shortage of resources caused by environmental degradation and encroachment of land by the immigrants. The Anti-Foreigner Movement in Assam, 1979–85 displaced 1,37,000 persons. Western Assam experienced conflicts after the 1993 accord on a Bodo Autonomous Council. Since the Assam Government refused to include over 1,000 villages in it, since they did not have a Bodo majority, efforts to 'create a majority' resulted in attacks on Bengali Muslims in 1993, Bengali Hindus in 1995 and Santhals in 1996. They caused 3,50,000 IDPs. The tribal-Bengali conflict in Shillong in Meghalaya in the 1980s caused 25,000–35,000 IDPs. Some 1,400 Bengalis and 280 tribals were killed and 1,90,000 persons were displaced in the same decade in Tripura. The Kuki-Paitei and Naga-Kuki conflicts in Manipur in the 1990s resulted in the burning of 10,000 houses, death of 2,000 and displacement of more than 50,000. In Mizoram, over 30,000 Reang (Bru) tribals have been displaced by attacks on them (Bhaumik, 2005: 150–165). In Assam, conflicts in North Cachar Hills in 2007 displaced 1,00,000 persons and in Karbi Anglong district they displaced 50,000 in 2005 (Mangattuthazhe, 2008: 60–61).

The Northeast confirms that the distinction between refugees and IDPs is tenuous. Some refugees give rise to internal conflicts. For example, because of Bangladeshi Hindu immigration, the tribal proportion in Tripura has declined from 58.1 per cent in 1951 to 31.1 per cent in 2001. The tribes had lost 20 to 40 per cent of their land to the immigrants by 1970 when the State announced the Dumbur dam that submerged 32,000 acres more of their land. This combination resulted in the tribal uprising that was called terrorist (Bhaumik, 2003: 84–85). The presence in Arunachal of 60,000 Chakma and Hajong tribals displaced by the Kaptai dam in the erstwhile East Pakistan has led to ethnic tension in the State (Chakraborty, 2002: 162–164). Assam experiences tensions around Bihari and Bangladesh immigrants.

Development-Induced Displacement

Unlike disasters and conflicts, development projects are planned. So it should be possible for the project authorities to plan land takeover in such a way that people's lives are not disrupted and to rehabilitate their DP-PAPs. In practice it does not happen. This section will study its causes and the process leading to it.

The Extent of Displacement in India

The number of development DP-PAPs is enormous but no official database exists on them. However, fairly reliable studies that have been done till now in 13 of India's 28 states give a total 20.41 million DP-PAPs (Table 1). Studies have not been done in the high displacement states of Madhya Pradesh, Maharashtra and Chhattisgarh. In Orissa, Andhra Pradesh, Assam, West Bengal and Tripura only around 80 per cent of the data could be accessed and in Mizoram, Jharkhand, Kerala, Meghalaya and Sikkim it was 60 per cent. Secondly, many studies are for 1951–95 and are being updated to 1947–2010. Extrapolation based on them and on case studies brings one to 60 million DP-PAPs in the period 1947–2000. Tribal proportion among the DP-PAPs is much than in the state population (Table 1, last column). The caste-tribe of around 15 per cent of the DP-PAPs is not known. There are indications that most of them are tribal but they are marked as NA since one is not absolutely certain about it.

The tribal proportion is more than a third of the DP-PAPs whose caste-tribe is known. Once the tribal DP-PAPs in the NA category are added to them, they would not be less than 40 per cent. Dalits are probably around 20 per cent. Till the 1980s, the Backwards were included in the general category. Data available from studies indicate that the poorest among them like the quarry and fish workers are around 20 per cent of the DP-PAPs but one does not assert it because even today many states include them in the general category. Based on the studies one can surmise that the voiceless tribal-dalit-BC combine is as high as 80 per cent of the total. But the official sources that depend on the eminent domain based colonial

Table 1

Caste-Tribe of DP-PAPs from Some States with Tribal Percentage in 2001

State	*Tribal*	*%*	*Dalits*	*%*	*Others*	*%*	*NA*	*%*	*Total*	*Tribal %*
Andhra	9,70,654	30.19	6,28,824	19.56	14,67,286	45.63	1,48,856	04.63	32,15,620	6.6
Assam	4,24,253	22.14	NA	NA	6,09,509	31.81	8,82,323	46.05	19,16,085	12.4
Goa	NA	NA	NA	NA	NA	NA	66,820	100	66,820	0
Gujarat	18,21,283	44.43	4,62,626	11.29	17,91,142	43.70	23,818	0.58	40,98,869	14.8
Jharkhand	6,20,372	40.08	2,12,892	13.75	6,76,575	43.71	38,178	02.47	15,48,017	26.3
Kerala	NA	NA	NA	NA	NA	NA	5,52,233	100	5,52,233	1.1
Meghalaya	1,10,258	100	0	0	0	0	0	0	1,10,258	85.9
Mizoram	2,00,139	100	0	0	0	0	0	0	2,00,139	94.5
Nagaland	62,675	100	0	0	0	0	0	0	62,675	89.1
Orissa	6,16,116	40.38	1,78,442	11.64	6,71,351	48.01	0	0	14,65,909	22.1
Sikkim	20,178	36.14	1,190	2.13	25,720	40.79	8,747	15.66	55,835	22.0
Tripura	1,00,195	56.66	20,518	11.60	NA	NA	56,082	31.72	1,76,795	31.1
W. Bengal	13,30,663	19.16	16,89,607	24.33	25,66,223	36.95	13,57,999	19.55	69,44,492	5.5
Total	62,76,786	30.75	31,94,099	15.65	78,07,806	38.25	31,35,056	15.36	2,04,13,747	8.2

Source: AP, Fernandes et al., 2001: 88; Assam, Fernandes and Bharali 2011: 220; Goa, Fernandes and Naik 2001: 57; Gujarat, Lobo and Kumar 2009: 109; Jharkhand, Ekka and Asif 2000: 87; Kerala, Muricken et al., 2003: 203; Orissa, Fernandes and Asif 1997: 94; West Bengal, Fernandes et al., 2012: 237; Meghalaya, Mizoram and Tripura, Fernandes and Bharali 2010: 90; Govt of India 2007: 87–88. Nagaland and Sikkim: Fernandes et al., 2011: 85 and 100.

land laws, that recognise individual ownership alone, exclude from the list of DP-PAPs the common property resource (CPR) dependants and other landless groups like those sustaining themselves by rendering services to the village as a community (Ramanathan, 2008: 28–29). The official lists do not treat them as DPs, do not compensate or rehabilitate them. Its consequence is impoverishment and marginalisation.

The second facet of the process is weak resettlement and rehabilitation. One needs to distinguish between resettlement and rehabilitation. Resettlement is people's relocation by the project with or without other support. Rehabilitation is rebuilding the economic resources, cultural systems, social structures and community support mechanisms that they lose at their dispossession. One speaks of rebuilding, not replacing them because the cultural, social and other intangibles that have sustained their societies for centuries cannot be reproduced in their pristine form. They have to be rebuilt in a new way to suit the changing conditions to enable them to begin life anew. Only the DPs need resettlement but also the PAPs require rehabilitation. Steps for it have to begin long before loss of sustenance and have to continue long after it (Fernandes and Bharali, 2011: 10). Most policies ignore this distinction and deal only with resettlement though are called R&R (Resettlement and Rehabilitation).

Table 2

Number of DPs and Resettled

State	*DPs*	*Resettled*	*%*
Andhra	15,26,813	4,40,090	28.82
Assam	3,07,024	11,000	03.59
Goa	15,950	5,375	33.63
Gujarat	6,90,322	1,64,498	23.82
Kerala	2,19,633	30,036	13.68
Meghalaya	26,973	00	00
Mizoram	1,80,474	2,833	1.57
Orissa	5,48,794	1,92,840	35.27
Tripura	1,14,085	14,911	13.07
W. Bengal	36,34,271	4,00,000	11.18
Total	72,64,339	12,61,583	17.37

Source: as in Table 1

A reason why resettlement very rarely leads to rehabilitation is that even the projects that have a rehabilitation component do not go beyond physical relocation to provide facilities required to rebuild even the economy of the DP-PAPs and all but ignore the social, cultural and psychological components. For example, Mayurakshi in West Bengal, Ukai in

Gujarat, Nagarjunasagar in Andhra and some other dams with an irrigation component and a rehabilitation package built colonies and gave some land to the DPs but did not provide them irrigation facilities. Secondly, resettlement is based on the eminent domain principle of individual ownership and excludes the CPR dependants, service providers and others who do not have a legal title to the land acquired under the present law. That forces the subalterns into a new society and economy with no economic, social, cultural and psychological preparation for it and impoverished most of them. Even individual landowners cannot cope with the change if they are only paid compensation. The quantum of compensation is based on the 'market price' interpreted as the average registered for 3 years (Ramanathan, 2008: 29). It is a public secret that what is registered is not more than 40 per cent of the amount paid for it. CPRs, most of them in the tribal areas, are not compensated. The 'market price' of the little private land they own in the 'backward' area is low. So most tribal DP-PAPs and a very big number of others get inadequate compensation.

The rehabilitation status of 10 states is given in Table 2. The remaining three states resettled none. Thus the actual number resettled is lower than the 17.37 per cent given in Table 2. A majority of the rest are of the tribal-Dalit-BC group and they have to fend for themselves. Impoverishment is its consequence though some PAPs from the better off sections, living in 'advanced' districts, improve their lifestyle if they get a fairly high price for their not so fertile land. Most Dalit and tribal DP-PAPs are impoverished because of the loss of their sustenance. Michael Cernea (2000) has given the main impoverishment risks so they need not be repeated here. One can only add that the status of those who were poor before their alienation deteriorates further.

The next step is marginalisation. It goes beyond economic deprivation to the weakening of their social, cultural and psychological base and reduces the DP-PAPs to fatalism and helplessness. They accept their state as their fate and lose all hope of improvement. One of its signs is loss of the sustainable resource management culture. In the absence of other income, many tribal and other rural communities that had developed a sustainable management system begin to treat the resources as commodities or as sources of present income. They overexploit them by cutting trees for sale as firewood or for timber as workers under contractors, or by overfishing or shortening the *jhum* cycle from around 18 to 6 or even 3 years. Many extend the culture of treating the resource as a commodity also to the human body. Many adults whom land loss deprives of work treat their children not as assets for the future but as sources of present income. For example, 49 per cent of the displaced families in West Bengal and 56 per cent in Assam kept their children out of school or withdrew them from it to turn them into child labourers. In the absence of other income many women use their bodies as sources of income through prostitution. Even among the subalterns women pay the highest price and are further marginalised (Fernandes et al., 2012: 23–27).

Marginalisation cannot be remedied by economic incentives alone because displacement and deprivation take the DP-PAPs beyond economic loss to deterioration of their social, cultural and psychological status. By alienating the resources that are the centre of their economy, culture and identity, the project dispossesses the powerless communities of their cultural heritage, spiritual beliefs, history, legends and myths and disrupts their traditional lifestyle, social networks and cultural practices and provides no alternatives (Pamei, 2001). With their loss their dependants lose the social, cultural and psychological support that the CPRs provided them and are pushed into the powerful formal economy and society. From it follows the cultural, psychological and social change of accepting impoverishment as their fate. They begin to view themselves not as people with a right to a life with dignity but as communities incapable of developing themselves (Good, 1996). The culture of treating the natural resources, children and women's bodies as sources of present income symbolises their marginalisation.

Displacement in the Northeast

The extent of displacement in the Northeast is not fully known. The total in five of the seven states studied comes to 22,46,952 DP-PAPs (Table 1). Studies are yet to be completed in Arunachal Pradesh and Manipur. The population of the five states studied was around 34 millions in 2011 so their DP-PAPs are 6.5 per cent against around 5 per cent in much of India. Moreover, in Assam, Meghalaya, Mizoram and Tripura, the study stopped at 2000 and much displacement has taken place in the last decade. In much of India, water resources displace the biggest number followed by industries and mines. In the Northeast a disproportionately big number belongs to transport and communications and defence and security. Only Nagaland has a big number of dam affected persons because the Doyang dam was completed in the last decade. Meghalaya has a big number of them because of one dam built by Assam in the 1960s to provide power to the rest of the state. The remaining States have very few water resource DP-PAPs.

However, 48 hydro-power dams are being planned for the present decade and 120 more later but the industrial base is weak. It would mean that most dams are meant to supply power to the remaining states of India. On 12 March 2002, speaking in the Rajya Sabha the then Minister for Power put the hydro-electrical potential of the region at 58,000 MW that is 38 per cent of the country's total and added that the 13 major dams being planned were the first of the 48 in a decade. There is another list of 156 possible dams. On 24 May 2003, the then Prime Minister Atal Bihari Vajpayee, launched the Northeast Initiative of 50,000 MW meant to turn the region into a powerhouse of India and of South-East Asia (*The Telegraph* 25 May 2003). That turns major dams into a crucial issue in the region.

That the dams are not meant for industries in the region is seen also from the small number of DP-PAPs of industries against the big number of IDPs of defence and security and refugee rehabilitation. Thus, the region seems to be treated primarily as borderlands that need to be protected and not developed with productive jobs. Many projects are meant to secure the territory and to supply raw materials of tea and petroleum and now to be a 'powerhouse' for the rest of India. Many of the 166 industries that existed in 1996 have been declared sick (Fernandes and Bharali, 2011: 81–82).

High Tribal Proportion, Poor Rehabilitation

The tribal proportion among the DP-PAPs is higher in the region than in the rest of India (Table 1). Against 40 per cent tribals among the 60 million DP-PAPs in India as a whole they are 8,97,520 out of 24,65,952 (36.4%) in the five states where studies have been done. They are 1,00,195 out of 1,76,828 DP-PAPs (56.73%) in Tripura, 4,25,253 of 19,16,085 (22.21%) in Assam, 100 per cent in Meghalaya, Mizoram and Nagaland. The caste-tribe of 8,82,323 DP-PAPs (45.98%) in Assam and 56,082 (31.72%) in Tripura is not known. Among those whose caste-tribe is known, tribals are 40.93 per cent in Assam and 82.98 per cent in Tripura. There are indications that most DP-PAPs in the NA category are tribal. Thus, more than 50 per cent of the DP-PAPs in Assam and 90 per cent in Tripura are tribal (Fernandes and Bharali, 2010: 69). Preliminary data from Manipur point to a tribal majority among them and 100 per cent of the DP-PAPs in Arunachal where they are 64 per cent of the population.

Equally important is poor rehabilitation. As Table 2 shows, only Assam in the region had some weak rehabilitation components. Among the more than 3,000 files studied, one found cases of partial rehabilitation in nine projects that gave a job or a colony. Neither leads to rehabilitation. In Mizoram official sources claim to have rehabilitated the more than 1,00,000 persons displaced for defence projects. In reality 1,68,853 persons from 516 of its 764 villages were displaced and put behind barbed wires in 110 villages in reorganisation as a counter-insurgency strategy (Nunthara, 1989: 48). That is not rehabilitation.

Land Laws and Displacement

The officials claim that the abundance of resources in the tribal areas should result in displacement supported by the second draft of the national rehabilitation policy which states that after the New Economic Policy of 1991, i.e. liberalisation, 'It is expected that there will be large scale investments, both on account of internal generation of capital and increased inflow of foreign investments, thereby creating an enhanced demand for land to be provided within a shorter time-span in an increasingly competitive market ruled economic structure. Majority of our mineral resources ... are located in the remote and backward areas mostly inhabited by tribals' (MRD, 1994: 1.1–2).

Apart from the abundance of resource also the legal status of their land is basic to their impoverishment. Much of tribal sustenance is CPRs. But the colonial land laws that continue to be in force today recognise only individual ownership. That explains why most official figures are underestimates. For example, by official count the Hirakud dam in Orissa displaced 1,10,000 persons (Government of Orissa, 1968) but researchers put their number at 1,80,000 (Pattanaik, Das and Mishra, 1987). By official count Assam used 3,90,302 acres of land for development projects and displaced 3,43,262 persons 1947–2000. In reality the State had 19 lakh DP-PAP from 14.1 lakh acres but it counted only private land acquired through Gazette notifications (Fernandes and Bharali, 2011: 216).

Most of those who are not counted are tribal and other dependants of CPRs like tribal or fish and quarry workers. The law turned their habitat of centuries into state property and made them encroachers on it (Ramanathan, 2008: 29–30). They are 'evicted', not displaced from it under this law and the state does not even count them among the DP-PAPs. In Assam too most of what was excluded was CPRs but is marked as NA because of some ambiguity around it. Not surprisingly, tribals who are 12.4 per cent of the population are a majority of the DP-PAPs. The same holds good for the remaining states of the region.

A deliberate effort too is made to alienate tribal land by changing the laws. For example, the Tripura Land Revenue and Land Reforms Act 1960 was enacted in order to facilitate tribal land acquisition to rehabilitate the more than 8,00,000 East Pakistani refugees and immigrants who had entered Tripura during the preceding decade (Shimray, 2006: 14). It recognised only individual land registered with the state. Most tribes being illiterate and not familiar with the formal law did not register even the private land they owned. Their CPRs became state property (Deb Barma, 2009: 120–121). Around 80,000 acres of their land were used for refugee rehabilitation and more was alienated to moneylenders (Fernandes and Bharali, 2010: 77). As much as 32,000 acres were acquired for the Dumbur dam in the early 1970s but the project authorities counted only 2,558 *patta* owning families out of 8,000 to 9,000 displaced families (Bhaumik, 2003: 84). Today, they form 31.1 per cent of the population but 83 per cent of the 1,20,717 DP-PAPs whose caste-tribe is known.

In Mizoram and Meghalaya, CPR proportion is low due to poor record keeping and because their land classification is different from that of the formal law. So it is difficult to record it in the language of the formal law (Nongkynrih, 2009: 34–35) so much of the land lost is not counted. Tribal land loss is much higher after liberalisation. The statement of the Government of India that there would be more land takeover than in the past and that much of it would be tribal has turned out to be true. Much of the land acquired during the last decade or planned to be acquired in the present one is tribal CPRs. Most land that the private sector is eyeing as mining land in Jharkhand, Orissa and Chhattisgarh and for mega-dams in the Northeast is tribal (IWGIA, 2004: 314).

Change of Lifestyle

A result of loss of sustenance is change of lifestyle. The DP-PAPs are pushed from a CPR-based informal society to an individual-based formal system without preparation for the new society, economy and culture in which land is only a commodity valued at the market price. They lose all rights over their forests and other CPRs since the law recognises only individual ownership. By thus treating them as encroachers, the law denies them their rights under Article 21 of the Constitution. It is right to life that the Supreme Court has interpreted as every citizen's right to a life with dignity (Vaswani, 1992: 158). This attack continues at every step leading to their deprivation and even rehabilitation. For example, according to official documents the proposed Lower Subansiri dam in Arunachal will submerge two villages and displace 38 families. It does not count 12 more villages. The state insists that the 38 families will be rehabilitated on a land for land basis according to its rehabilitation policy of one hectare per family (*The Assam Tribune,* 17 August 2008) and ignores the fact that they are *jhum* cultivators. These 38 families cultivate 986 hectares of CPRs. By resettling them on one hectare each, the project pushes them into settled agriculture with no preparation for it (Menon, 2009: 133–136). Studies show that such measures impoverish and marginalise them. Also most other projects impoverish their DP-PAPs by not preparing them for the change and not replacing the assets that are the basis of their economy, culture, social systems and identity. Even when a project has an R&R package, very few of its staff members give importance to it because their career and promotion depend on the efficiency with which they implement the project, not on the extent and quality of rehabilitation (Singh, 2006).

Impoverishment to Marginalisation

One does not have to go into all the steps of impoverishment and marginalisation. Suffice its to state that landlessness is its first step. For example, before the project the 594 families studied in Meghalaya, Mizoram and Tripura owned a total of 2,655.89 acres of *patta* land and

460.94 acres of commons. Each family cultivated an average of 5.25 acres. After the project, *patta* land came down to 1,659.54 acres and commons to 162.44 acres or a total of 1,821.98 at an average of 3.07 acres. Private land declined by 37.52 per cent and commons by 64.76 per cent because most projects use a high proportion of the commons. Eighty of the 594 families became landless, seven became tenants and the rest own less land than what they did in the past. In Meghalaya, private land declined from 1,092.34 to 757.34 acres (30.67%), the commons from 358.34 to 236.84 acres (33.91%) and the average cultivated area from 8.2 to 5.62 acres. In Mizoram, private land declined by 47.44 per cent, CPRs by 63.27 per cent and the cultivated area from 6.07 to 2.95 acres. In Tripura, private land declined by 36.05 per cent, the commons by 63.08 per cent and the average cultivated area from 5 to 2.68 acres (Fernandes and Bharali, 2010: 103–104). In Assam, landlessness grew from 15.56 to 24.38 per cent and the average area declined from 3.04 to 1.45 acres per family (Fernandes and Bharali, 2011: 244–245).

Joblessness is the next step because the resources alienated by the project had provided them work and security. They lose both but the project resettles very few DPs and gives fewer jobs. In Assam, three projects gave some jobs and five resettled the DPs. Some jobs were given by the World Bank funded highway project in Mizoram and the Agartala Railway in Tripura. One is not aware of any other project giving jobs. Moreover, tribals get fewer jobs than the other castes do. Most DP-PAPs, particularly tribal, also experienced downward occupational mobility. In Assam, access to work declined from 77.27 to 56.41 per cent and 50 per cent of the cultivators became landless agricultural labourers or daily wage earners (Fernandes and Bharali, 2011: 288–289). A reason for low employment generation is mechanisation that deprives the DP-PAPs of jobs. Most skilled jobs go to outsiders since very few land losers have the skills they require. For example, in the 1960s, only 27 per cent of the industrial employees in Assam were locals and very few of them held skilled and semi-skilled jobs. Resentment against it was expressed during the Assam Movement (Chattopadhyay, 1990: 101). Tribal proportion was much lower among the 27 per cent employed but that was not highlighted during the Movement. Even today because of mechanisation of projects like Gas Cracker, each job will cost around ₹ 20 lakh.

The next step is marginalisation which begins with a low self-image. Every step of land acquisition contributes to it. That is also internalisation of the dominant value system by the subalterns is the next step because no unequal society can survive without the subalterns internalising the dominant ideology (Gaventa, 1980: 27–30). The process of land alienation confirms the tribes of Assam and Tripura who already had a low self-image. In Meghalaya the project created this image in them

(Fernandes and Bharali, 2010: 112–113). The denial of compensation confirms them further in their low self-image. In the eminent domain based legal system the market price rules supreme. The *patta* land losers are paid a meagre compensation in the 'backward' areas. The project tends to treat even rehabilitation as welfare, not as a right. Despite Article 21, the steps leading to land acquisition reduce the independent workers to the status of cheap labour. The remaining inputs devalue their culture and social life, treat them as people without rights and their sustenance as commodity. That gives them the message that they and their sustenance are dispensable commodities. These components confirm them in their low self-image (Heredero, 1989: 33–34).

The whole family suffers the impact of impoverishment and marginalisation but women and children feel it more than men do. Many men take to alcohol as coping mechanisms to deal with the trauma of forced displacement. Domestic violence and drinking did exist in the past but drunkenness as a coping mechanism and the rise in domestic violence is different from the past. A majority of women in Assam and Orissa mentioned more drinking and violence than in the past (Fernandes and Bharali, 2011: 312–313). Tribal men accept dominant values when they come face to face with the formal society. Tribal women accept them by beginning to believe that they are incapable of being active economic agents. Tribal children are forced to accept them by becoming child labourers who are deprived of a future. They come to believe that they are made only for a life of labour. The whole community internalises the ideology of the natural resources being only a commodity. Women are the worst victims of the cultural changes that are based on an economic model that treats them as commodities.

Conclusion

This bird's eye view of IDPs especially tribal in the Northeast shows that tribal proportion among the DP-PAPs is much higher than their share in the population because they live in resource rich regions and the State monopolises their sustenance. These resources are the centre of their culture and identity and they are deprived of them with no transition to a new society. They are forced into the new society with no preparation and without alternatives to the material assets lost to the project. That begins the process of their impoverishment and marginalisation. All the DP-PAPs feel its negative impact but because of their distance from the formal society and dependence on the commons, tribals feel it more than the others do. Even among them women and children are the worst affected. When their economic and social status deteriorates, they find coping mechanisms in alcohol and crime and in internalising the dominant ideology of their community or women being inferior. Thus, most studies show that the tribes in general and women and children among them in particular pay the price of the development of another class. That is bound to lead to many conflicts and more repression. A solution to it requires a new look at the development paradigm that takes their impoverishment for granted.

References

Acharya, Jagat Mani. (2004) *Bhutanese Refugees in Nepal: A Source Book.* Kolkata: Calcutta Research Group.

Banerjee, Paula. (2005) 'Resisting Erasure: Women IDPs in South Asia,' in Paula Banerjee, Sabyasachi Basu Ray Chaudhury and Samir Das (eds) *Internal Displacement in South Asia.* New Delhi: Sage Publications. pp. 280–315.

Bhaumik, Subir. (2003) 'Tripura's Gumti Dam Must Go'. *The Ecologist Asia,* 11 (n. 1, January–March). pp. 84–89.

Chakraborty, Sanat. (2002) 'Chakma and Hajong Refugees of Arunachal Pradesh: Still a 'No Where People'' in C. Joshua Thomas (ed.) *Dimensions of Displaced People in Northeast India.* New Delhi: Regency Publications. pp. 159–178.

Chattopadhyay, Dilip Kumar. (1990) *History of the Assamese Movement Since 1947.* Calcutta: Minerva.

Das, Samir. (2005) 'India: Homelessness at Home,' in Paula Banerjee, Sabyasachi Basu Ray Chaudhury and Samir Das (eds) *Internal Displacement in South Asia*, pp. 113–143.

Dasgupta, Rajdeep. (2007) *Disaster Management and Rehabilitation.* New Delhi: Mittal Publications.

Deb Barma, Sukhendu. (2009) 'Refugee Rehabilitation and Land Alienation in Tripura,' in Walter Fernandes and Sanjay Barbora (ed.). *Land, People and Politics Contest over Tribal Land in Northeast India.* Guwahati: North Eastern Social Research Centre and IWGIA. pp. 88–112.

Dekens, Julie. (2007) *Local Knowledge for Disaster Preparedness: A Literature Review.* Kathmandu: International Centre for Integrated Mountain Development.

Ekka, Alexius and Mohammed Asif. (2000) *Development-Induced Displacement and Rehabilitation in Jharkhand: A Database on its Extent and Nature.* New Delhi: Indian Social Institute (mimeo).

Fernandes, Walter and Mohammed Asif. (1997) *Development-Induced Displacement and Rehabilitation in Orissa 1951–1995: A Database on its Extent and Nature.* New Delhi: Indian Social Institute. (mimeo).

Fernandes, Walter, Nafisa Goga D'Souza, Arundhuti Roy Choudhury and Mohammed Asif. (2001) *Development-Induced Displacement In Andhra Pradesh 1951–1995: A Quantitative Study of Its Extent and Nature*. New Delhi and Guwahati: Indian Social Institute and North Eastern Social Research Centre (mimeo).

Fernandes, Walter and Niraj Naik. (2001) *Development-Induced Displacement in Goa 1965–1995: A Database on Its Extent and Nature.* Guwahati: North Eastern Social Research Centre and Panjim: INSAF (mimeo).

Fernandes, Walter and Gita Bharali. (2010) *Development-Induced Displacement 1947–2000 in Meghalaya, Mizoram and Tripura: A Quantitative and Qualitative Database on Its Extent and Impact.* Guwahati: North Eastern Social Research Centre (mimeo).

Fernandes, Walter and Gita Bharali. (2011) *Uprooted for Whose Benefit? Development-Induced Displacement in Assam 1947–2000.* Guwahati: North Eastern Social Research Centre.

Fernandes, Walter, Shanti Chhetri, Sherry Joseph and Satyen Lama. (2012) *Progress: At Whose Cost? Development-Induced Displacement and Deprivation in West Bengal 1947–2000: A Study of its Extent and Impact.* Guwahati: North Eastern Social Research Centre.

Fernandes, Walter, Thejanuo Fidelia Sekhose, Medonuo Pienyu, Alibo Achumi, Sungtemmenla Aier, Mhonthung Yanthan and V. Sherpa. (2011) Development-Induced Displacement and Deprivation in Nagaland 1947–2008 and in Sikkim 1975–2008: A Quantitative and Qualitative Database on Its Extent and Impact. Guwahati: North Eastern Social Research Centre (mimeo).

Ferris, Elizabeth, Erin Mooney and Chareen Stark. (2011) *From Responsibility to Response: Assessing National approaches to Internal Displacement.* London: The Brookings Institution, London School of Economics.

Gadgil, Madhav and Ramachandra Guha. (1995) *Ecology and Equity: The Use and Abuse of Nature in Contemporary India.* Penguin Books.

Gaventa, John. (1980) *Power and Powerlessness: Quiescence and Rebellion in an Appalachian Valley.* Oxford: Clarendon.

Good, Byron J. (1996) 'Mental Health Consequences of Displacement and Resettlement,' *Economic and Political Weekly,* 31 (n. 24, June 15). pp. 1504–1508.

Goswami, D.C. (2003) 'Flood Problem of Assam: Causes and Remedies,' in Prabhat Chandra Sabhapandit (ed.) *Flood Problem of Assam: Cause and Remedies.* New Delhi: Omsons Publications. pp. 8–14.

Government of Orissa. (1968) *Report on the Benefits of Hirakud Irrigation: A Socio-Economic Study.* Cuttack: Bureau of Statistics and Economics.

Guhathakurta, Meghna and Suraiya Begum. (2005) 'Bangladesh: Displaced and Dispossessed' in Paula Banerjee, Sabyasachi Basu Ray Chaudhury and Samir Kumar Das (ed.) *Internal Displacement in South Asia*, pp. 175–212.

Heredero, J.M. (1989) *Education for Development: Social Awareness, Organisation and Technological Innovation.* New Delhi: Manohar.

IWGIA. (2004) *The Indigenous World 2004.* Copenhagen: International Work Group for Indigenous Affairs.

Lobo, Lancy and Shashikant Kumar. (2009) *Development-Induced Displacement in Gujarat 1947–2004.* Vadodara: Centre for Culture and Development.

Mangattuthazhe, Tom. (2008) *Violence and Search for Peace in Karbi Anglong, Assam.* Guwahati: North Eastern Social Research Centre.

Menon, Manju. (2009) 'Land Alienation due to Large Hydro-Power Projects in Arunachal Pradesh,' in Walter Fernandes and Sanjay Barbora (ed.) *Land, People and Politics Contest over Tribal Land in Northeast India.* Guwahati: North Eastern Social Research Centre and IWGIA. pp. 128–141.

MRD. (1994) *The Draft National Policy for Rehabilitation of Persons Displaced as a Consequence of Acquisition of Land.* New Delhi: Ministry of Rural Development, Government of India (Second Draft).

Murickan, Jose et al. (2003) *Development Induced Displacement: The Case of Kerala.* Jaipur: Rawat Publications.

Nongkynrih, A.K. (2009) 'Privatisation of Communal Land of the Tribes of North East India: A Sociological Viewpoint,' in Walter Fernandes and Sanjay Barbora (ed.) *Land, People and Politics Contest over Tribal Land in Northeast India.* Guwahati: North Eastern Social Research Centre and IWGIA. pp. 16–36.

Pamei, Aram. (2001) 'Havoc of Tipaimukh High Dam Project,' *Economic and Political Weekly,* 36 (No. 13, pp. 1045 and 1148).

Patowary, Ajit. (2004) 'Floods Inflict 990 crore Loss on Farm Sector,' *The Assam Tribune,* 27 September.

Pattanaik, S.K., B. Das and A.B. Mishra. (1987) 'Hirakud Dam: Expectations and Realities,' in PRIA (ed.). *People and Dams.* New Delhi: Society for Participatory Research in Asia. pp. 47–59.

Prasad, K. (2005) *Manual on Community Approach to Flood Management in India.* New Delhi: Institute for Resource Management and Economic Development.

Ramanathan, Usha. (2008) "The Land Acquisition Act 1894: Displacement and State Power,' in Hari Mohan Mathur (ed.) *India: Social Development Report 2008: Development and Displacement.* Council for Social Development and Oxford University Press. pp. 27–38.

Sheikh, Attaur-Rehman. (2005) 'Pakistan: Development and Disaster,' in Paula Banerjee, Sabyasachi Basu Ray Chaudhury and Samir Das (eds) *Internal Displacement in South Asia*, pp. 62–112.

Singh, Shekar. (2006) 'Displacement and Rehabilitation: A Comparison of Two Policy Drafts,' *Economic and Political Weekly* 41 (n. 52, 30 December). pp. 5307–5308.

Vaswani, Kalpana. (1992) 'Rehabilitation laws and Policies: A Critical Look,' in Enakshi Ganguly Thukral (ed.) *Big Dams, Displaced People: Rivers of Sorrow, Rivers of Change.* New Delhi: Sage Publication. pp 155–169.

World Bank. (2003) *Financing Rapid Onset Natural Disaster Losses in India: A Risk Management Approach.* Washington D.C.: The World Bank.

5

Gender Inequality in Northeast India

BIDISHA MAHANTA AND PURUSOTTAM NAYAK

The past few decades have witnessed a steadily increasing awareness of the need to empower women and achieve gender equality through measures to increase social, economic and political equity, and broader access to fundamental human rights, improvements in nutrition, basic health and education. The concept of gender equality has been gaining importance as the subordinate status of women in relation to men has been seen in almost every facets of life. Gender equality is understood as that stage of human development at which the rights, responsibilities and opportunities of individuals are not to be determined by the fact of being born as male or female. It is a stage when both men and women realise their full potential and become partners in every sphere of their lives. Realising the extent of gender inequality throughout the world, the United Nations Development Fund for Women (UNIFEM) was established as a separate fund within the United Nations Development Programme (UNDP) in 1984. The General Assembly at that time instructed to ensure women's involvement with mainstream activities. The Platform of Action resulting from the 1995 Beijing World Conference on Women expanded the concept and called it as 'gender mainstreaming', i.e. the application of gender perspectives to all legal and social norms and standards, to all policy development, research, planning, advocacy, development, implementation and monitoring – as a mandate for all member states. The gender factor was no longer to be only a supplement to development but central to the practice of development. As a result of the Beijing Conference and many years of work leading up to it, more than 100 countries announced new initiatives to improve the status of women. In

2000, the follow-up Beijing+5 Conference further strengthened the application of the mainstreaming concept and used it to highlight the need for more progress in reaching equality worldwide.

Similarly, on human development front, it was gradually realised that if the women who constituted almost half of the population remained as passive, human development in its real sense could not be possible. Therefore, in 1995 main emphasis on gender equality was given in the Human Development Report (UNDP, 1995). At the global level for the first time just before the Fourth World Conference on Women held in Beijing two important gender indices were constructed by UNDP (1995): the Gender-related Development Index (GDI) and the Gender Empowerment Measure (GEM). The GDI considered inequalities by gender in the Human Development Index (HDI) dimensions. It measured the inequalities confronted by women in achievement of those which were very essential for overall development of human being. The GEM focused on political participation (measured by women's shares of parliamentary seats), economic participation (shares of high level and professional positions) and power over economic resources (income gaps).

The disadvantages facing women and girls are a major source of inequality. Very often, women and girls are discriminated against health, education and in labour markets - with negative repercussions for their freedoms. In 2010 report, UNDP further introduced a third measure of inequality known as Gender Inequality Index (GII) built on the same framework as the HDI and the Inequality adjusted Human Development Index (IHDI) in order to better expose differences in the distribution of achievements between women and men. The GII is unique in including educational attainment, economic and political participation and female-specific health issues and in accounting for overlapping inequalities at the national level. Thus it became an important advancement on existing global measures of gender equity.

According to the latest human development report (UNDP, 2011: 139):

- Gender inequality measured for 187 countries varied tremendously across countries – the losses in achievement due to gender inequality (not directly comparable to total inequality losses because different variables were used) ranged from 4.9 per cent to 76.9 per cent. Sweden topped the list of the most gender-equal countries, followed by Netherlands, Denmark and Switzerland.
- Countries with unequal distribution of human development also experienced high inequality between women and men, and countries with high gender inequality also experienced unequal distribution of human development. Among the countries doing very badly on both fronts were Central African Republic, Haiti and Mozambique.

The GII which was estimated for 138 countries in 2010 report also revealed gender disparities in reproductive health, empowerment and labour market participation. The losses in those achievements due to gender inequality, as expressed by the GII, ranged from 17 per cent to 85 per cent, with larger losses concentrated in the Arab States and South Asia (UNDP, 2010).

Along with those measures of gender inequality another measure to capture the magnitude and scope of gender-based inequalities is known as Global Gender Gap Index (GGGI). This was introduced by the World Economic Forum (WEF) in 2006. The Index benchmarks gender gaps on economic, political, education and health-based criteria, and provide country rankings that allow for effective comparisons across regions and income groups, and over time. The GGGI examines the gap between men and women in four fundamental categories: *economic participation and opportunity, educational attainment, health and survival* and *political empowerment.*

Gender Gap at Global Level

According to the reports of World Economic Forum, WEF (2005–2011), the large populous nations such as India, Pakistan, Turkey and Egypt held some of the lowest ranks in respect of gender gap. The study put Sweden, Norway, Denmark and Iceland on the top of the list. These countries were characterised by strong liberal society, with an impressive record of openness and transparency in government and comprehensive safety net which provided security to vulnerable group of the population. As a result, women of those parts of the world enjoyed greater access to education, work opportunity and a higher standard of living. Although no country yet succeeded in eliminating the gap, it was narrowed in case of Nordic countries. In 2009, 25 countries fully closed the gap on educational attainment as compared to 24 countries in 2008 and 15 countries in 2007. On the health and survival sub index, 39 countries fully closed the gap, compared to 36 in 2008 and 32 in 2007. However no countries in the world have been able to eliminate gender inequality. The 2010 report threw a valuable snapshot of the performance of 134 countries. On an average, over 96 per cent of the gap on health outcomes, 93 per cent on educational attainment, 60 per cent on economic participation and 17 per cent on political empowerment had been closed. The three highest ranking countries – Iceland, Finland and Norway – had been able to close their gender gaps significantly (over 80%), while the lowest ranking country, Yemen, had closed only around 46 per cent of its gender gap. India's position was 112 among 134 countries.

The 2011 report aggregated last six years of data and provided a snapshot of the situation as well as the changes over time, revealing a positive trend as the majority of countries continued to make progress on closing the gender gap. It also provided unique information on the policy frameworks that supported women's economic participation. It showed that the 135 countries covered in the report, representing over 90 per cent of the world's population, had closed almost 96 per cent of the gap in health outcomes between women and men and almost 93 per cent of the gap in educational attainment. However, the gap between women and men on economic participation and political empowerment remained wide: only 59 per cent of the economic outcomes gap and only 19 per cent of the political outcomes gap had been closed. The four Nordic countries that had consistently held the highest positions in the previous reports of the GGGI continued to hold those privileged positions, with Iceland still holding the top spot, closely followed by Norway, Finland and Sweden. Although no country had yet achieved gender equality, all of the Nordic countries, with the exception of Denmark, had closed over 80 per cent of the gender gap and thus served as models and useful benchmarks for international comparisons. While many developed economies had succeeded in closing the gender gap in education, few had succeeded in maximising the returns from the investment. India with 113th position, the Islamic Republic of Iran with 125th, Nepal with 126th and Pakistan with 133rd position occupied the last places in the regional rankings. India and Pakistan performed above the average on the political empowerment of women, particularly India, but they lagged behind in the other three categories. In particular, the persistent health, education and economic participation gaps remained as detrimental to India's growth. India was the lowest ranked among the BRIC economies.

Area of Study

The Northeast India comprises eight states namely Arunachal Pradesh, Assam, Manipur, Meghalaya, Mizoram, Nagaland, Sikkim and Tripura. The region is multiethnic with heterogeneous cultural background and is different from mainstream homogeneous culture. Due to the prevalence of tribal and indigenous culture it is generally perceived that women of the region are relatively much liberal than rest of the country. The general presumption is that women of the region are equal partners with their male counterparts in different spheres of lives. This belief is rooted because unlike northern, southern, western and eastern part of India, the entire Northeastern region is almost free from social evils like dowry, *sati pratha*, female foeticide, and female infanticide. However, various gender studies reveal a totally different picture. The gender attainment study by Shiv Kumar (1996) revealed that Assam, one of the largest Northeastern states, ranked 10th among 16 major states of India. According to the National Human Development Report, the GEI at the national level was

0.620 in the 1980s which improved marginally to 0.676 in the early 1990s (Government of India, 2002). The study showed that Northeastern states like Manipur, Meghalaya, Arunachal Pradesh, Mizoram, and Nagaland ranked above the national average in terms of GEI in 1990s. However, the states like Assam, Sikkim and Tripura remained far below the national average in the same study. Moreover, in the last few decades, insurgency has been the part and parcel of the life of the people of the region. Various ethnic strife, rebel, militancy have been affecting the normal lives of the people and women are the worst victims of it. The region has been witnessing the violation of human rights. Due to armed conflict and militant activities women in the region has been more vulnerable. Keeping all these points in mind an attempt has been made in the present paper to analyse the issues of gender gap in the region.

Review of Literature

Wallace and March (1991) in their work explained the effects of global issues on the lives of women and explored the conceptual basis of gender awareness planning and implementation of development project. Moser (1993) focused on the inter-relationship between gender and development, formulation of gender policy and implementation of gender planning and practices. Anand and Sen (1995) tried to develop a measure of gender inequality. They focused on the use of gender-equity-sensitive indicators and the formulation and utilisation of measures of gender equality and inequality. Nussbaum (2001) held the view that international political and economic thought must be sensitive to gender difference as a problem of justice, and feminist thought must begin to focus on the problems of women in the Third World. Hicks (2002) critically examined Sen's view on gender inequality and capability approach and its applicability in religious ethics. The edited volume of Mahanta (2002) sought to explain the question of women's access to or deprivation of basic human rights as the right to health, education and work, legal rights, rights of working women besides issues like domestic violence, all the while keeping the peculiar socio-cultural situation of the Northeast in mind. Sullivan (2004), in her article, examined the changing gender relations between heterosexual couples in the domestic spheres. While doing so, she presented evidences for change of gender relation at home. She also discussed the changes in attitude to gender equality, images of masculinity and intimacy in personal relationship. She presented cross national quantitative evidence based on time-use diaries suggesting long term changes in gender practices around the domestic division of labour. Gender gap reports of World Economic Forum assessed the status accorded to women in a broad range of countries. The first report on global gender gap published in 2005 attempted to measure gender inequality among 58 countries. India secured 53rd position among those 58 countries. Seven reports have been published so far and the coverage of countries has increased to 187. Global Monitoring Report reviewed the evidence on the relationship between gender equality, poverty reduction and growth (IBRD, 2007). There was also compelling evidence that gender equality and women's empowerment were channels to attain universal primary education, lower under-five mortality rate, improve maternal health and lower likelihood of contracting HIV/AIDS. Rout and Panda (2008) opined that ensuring gender parity have become a great challenge for the modern world. Gender equality formed part of development strategy in many countries of the world including India. When both men and women had equal access to services and resources, enjoyed equal rights, and got equal opportunities to develop skills and capabilities then the country would be fast and balanced. Gaye, et al. (2010) reviewed ways to measure and monitor gender inequality. They provided a critique to the existing measures, including the first global gender indices that were launched in the 1995 Human Development Report, i.e. the Gender-related Development Index and the Gender Empowerment Measure. Further they also introduced a new index that was presented in the 2010 Human Development Report.

The sixth human development report put special emphasis on women empowerment (UNDP, 1995). It mainly concerned formulation and utilisation of measure of gender inequality and the identification of efforts and contribution made by women that went unrecognised in standard national income and employment statistics. The concepts of GDI and GEM evolved out in that report. Assam Human Development Report threw light on inequality in the achievement between men and women of Assam in different spheres of life (Government of Assam, 2003). The report viewed that poverty, violence and lack of political participation were the main issues of concern for South-Asian Women, and Assam was no exception. Human development reports of the Northeastern states also showed that women of the region were at disadvantageous position relative to men. However, the status of women in the region in areas like education, employment, health, etc. were far better than that of the nation as a whole.

Bardhan and Klasen (1999) criticised GEM as an inadequate index of measuring women empowerment at aggregate level. While supporting the need to develop indicators that reliably track women's empowerment as well as the impact of gender inequality on overall human development, they argued that the particular ways in which these indices are constructed and the assumptions are made to overcome data gaps severely limit their usefulness and result in very misleading international comparisons. A paper prepared for the World Bank by Malhotra, Schuler and Boender (2002) highlighted the methodological aspects of measurement and analysis on women empowerment. Institute of Social Sciences and South Asia Partnership, Canada, organised a workshop in 2003 which dealt with women's empowerment through political participation wherein presentations were made on various theoretical works and case studies. The workshop addressed issues like 'proxy women' which was the shorthand term used by some who perceived that women elected to Panchayat bodies were merely 'proxies' or puppets in the hands of their husbands, relatives and other male panchayat members. Underscoring how deconstructing the idea of proxy women was, the workshop emphasised on training programme for elected women for their capacity building. In the keynote address, Mathew (2003) viewed that the equity and empowerment approaches merged together to form the 'gender and development concept'. Findings of Kishor and Gupta (2004) revealed that average women in India were disempowered absolutely and there have been little change in their empowerment over time. The authors viewed that there were several cogent and pressing reasons for evaluating, promoting and monitoring the level of women's empowerment in India, not the least of which was that household health and nutrition were generally in the hands of women and their empowerment was necessary to ensure not just their own welfare but the well-being of households. They also asserted that empowerment was critical for the very development of India, as it enhanced the quality and quantity of human resources available for development. Blumberg (2005) viewed that economic empowerment of women was the key to achieve gender equality as well as wealth and well-being of a nation. The author opined that financial autonomy would enhance women's capacity of decision making in various arenas of life. Moreover, it would lead to less corruption, less armed conflict and less violence against female in the long run. Kabeer (2005) discussed the third Millennium Development Goal (MDG) on gender equality and women's empowerment. It explored the concept of women empowerment and highlighted ways in which the indicators associated with this Goal. January 2008 issue of a journal on rural development focused mainly on women's empowerment and opined that although women were the active agents for sustainable development, and their empowerment was very important for the process of development, they had not actively participated in their own emancipation mainly due to low economic independence (Government of India, 2008). The above review of literature reveals that a number of studies have been undertaken on the issue of gender inequality at the national and global level but no such serious attempt has been made in case of Northeast India. The present paper in this regard is a humble attempt to bridge the research gap.

Data and Methodology

The present paper is solely based on secondary sources of data. The extent of gender gap in Northeastern region has been examined in four fundamental areas like economic participation and opportunity, education, health and political participation using the indicators like work participation rate (WPR), literacy rate, enrollment ratio, sex-ratio, infant mortality rate (IMR), life expectancy at birth and political participation.

Gender Issues in Northeast India

To examine the status of women in Northeast India let us first have a look at the GDI values of all the individual states of the region as well as India (Table 1). The figures reveal that all the states have satisfactory GDI values. Mizoram has the highest GDI value and is placed in the first rank among the Northeastern states as against Arunachal Pradesh which is placed in the last rank. Assam, Nagaland, Arunachal Pradesh and Meghalaya are placed below the national average in terms of GDI ranking while the other four states have GDI values far above the national average indicating that women of the region enjoy greater autonomy and less disparity in the attainment of various indicators of lives.

Let us now examine the status of gender gap in Northeast India using indicators like literacy rate, enrollment ratio, WPR, sex-ratio, IMR, life expectancy and women's political participation.

Gender Differential in Educational Attainment

Education is one of the important factors which determines the status of women. Taking into account the literacy rate and enrollment rate at various levels of education, one can find out if there exists any discrimination and the extent of discrimination which prevails in a society at a given period of time. The gender gap in education in Northeast India has been analysed using these indicators in the following paragraphs:

Literacy Gap

Literacy is the first step to formal education. It is seen that for all the Northeastern states the gender gap in literacy rate exists and males were observed to be more literate than that of the females (Table 1). However, the gender gap in literacy rate was lower in the region than that of the national literacy rates of 21.6 per cent and 16.68 per cent in 2001 and 2011, respectively. It was significantly lower for Mizoram, Meghalaya and Nagaland. Arunachal Pradesh had the highest gender gap in literacy rate. However, in the last decade, there has been significant improvement in literacy rate. Besides, the gender gap in literacy has been narrowed down for all the states in the region excepting Assam. Surprisingly, the gap has been widened in case of Assam. Huge influx of Bangladeshi population might be one of the reasons for widening gender gap in literacy rate.

Table 1

GDI and Male-Female Literacy Gap in Northeast States

State/Country	*GDI in 2001**	*Literacy Gap in 2001***	*Literacy Gap in 2011***
Ar. Pradesh	0.48	20.33	14.12
Assam	0.49	8.64	11.54
Manipur	0.58	18.17	13.32
Meghalaya	0.51	5.73	3.39
Mizoram	0.67	4.56	4.32
Nagaland	0.42	9.19	6.60
Sikkim	0.59	15.60	10.86
Tripura	0.56	16.10	9.03
India	0.54	21.60	16.68

Sources: * National Human Development Report 2001; ** www.indiastat.com.

Enrollment Gap

Enrollment ratio at different levels of education is another dimension in which gender gap is witnessed. When we compare the enrollment ratio of classes I to V and VI-VII over the period from 1999–2001 to 2009–10, a noticeable change was observed over a period of 10 years (Table 2). In 1999–2001 the gender gap in enrollment ratio existed in all the states for the class I-V. The gap was highest for Assam (18.89%) and lowest for Sikkim (0.84%). However it was still above the national average. In 2009–10, the gender gap was narrowed down. Except Assam and Meghalaya, all other states of the region had gender gap more than the national average. However, the states like Assam and Meghalaya performed well and gender gap became negative implying the fact that enrollment ratio for girls exceeded that of boys. But in classes VI-VII, the enrollment rate for girls in some states exceeded that of the boys. For instance in Meghalaya, Nagaland and Sikkim the enrollment rates of girls at high school were more than that of boys and the gender gap were narrowed for other Northeastern states excepting Assam as compared to the national average in 1999–2001. However, in 2009–10, the gender gap was narrowed down. Tripura and Assam were able to reduce the gender gap to a significant level. In states like Meghalaya, Nagaland, Sikkim and Assam the gender gap in enrollment ratio in classes VI-VII were negative. Contrary to this, in Arunachal Pradesh, the gender gap was increased. In Arunachal Pradesh and Manipur gender gap was less than that of the national average.

When we analysed the gender gap in enrollment in high school and higher education, we found that all the Northeastern states had lesser gender gap in enrollment at IX-X level as compared to all India average

Table 2

Gross Enrollment Ratio in Primary and Secondary Education in NE States

State/Country	Classes I-V (6–10 Years)						Classes VI-VIII (11–13 Years)					
	1999–2001			2009–10			1999–2001			2009–10		
	Boys	Girls	Gap	Boys	Girls	Gap	Boys	Girls	Gap	Boys	Girls	Gap
Ar. Pradesh	126.14	108.55	17.59	169.99	163.42	6.57	72.42	66.68	5.74	106.14	96.21	9.93
Assam	124.25	105.36	18.89	91.67	94.15	–2.48	81.02	64.63	16.39	67.32	70.32	–3.00
Manipur	101.87	87.41	14.46	189.66	182.26	7.40	79.62	71.34	8.28	107.21	99.19	8.02
Meghalaya	119.46	111.64	7.82	169.95	174.09	–4.14	57.42	62.28	–4.86	80.45	91.44	–10.99
Mizoram	121.84	107.52	14.32	173.95	162.2	11.75	78.77	76.17	2.60	100.83	94.98	5.85
Nagaland	92.21	87.78	4.43	99.63	98.89	0.74	58.67	61.14	–2.47	59.13	60.70	–1.57
Sikkim	139.32	138.48	0.84	157.91	152.75	5.16	70.96	76.59	–5.63	70.89	86.59	–15.70
Tripura	118.28	100.86	17.42	146.81	143.72	3.09	69.96	60.26	9.70	93.33	93.14	0.19
India	104.08	85.18	18.90	115.55	115.39	0.16	67.15	49.66	17.49	84.53	78.30	6.23

Source: www.indiastat.com.

(Table 3). Even for most of the states it was negative, implying that the enrollment of girls was more than that of boys. However, in classes XI-XII, Manipur and Tripura had more gender gap as compared to national average. In case of higher education, i.e. above class XII, the enrollment rate of boys and girls were significantly lower as compared to classes IX-X and XI-XII. But gender gap in enrollment at higher education was higher for all the Northeastern states compared to all India average (3.2%) except in Meghalaya, Mizoram and Nagaland. Sikkim (5.7%) had highest gender gap in higher education followed by Assam (5.0%). However, in Meghalaya with prevalence of matriarchal society, gender gap was observed to be negative.

Table 3

Gross Enrollment Ratio in High School and Higher Education in Northeast States

State/Country	*Classes IX–X (14–15 Years) Year 2010–11*			*Classes XI–XII (16–17 Years) Year 2010–11*			*Above Class XII (18–23 Years) Year 2008–09*		
	Boys	*Girls*	*Gap*	*Boys*	*Girls*	*Gap*	*Boys*	*Girls*	*Gap*
Ar. Pradesh	73.3	67.9	5.4	49.1	45.7	3.4	15.5	11.4	4.1
Assam	52.0	46.9	5.1	18.2	14.6	3.6	10.7	5.7	5.0
Manipur	83.5	80.1	3.4	39.0	32.1	6.9	14.5	11.1	3.4
Meghalaya	49.0	49.9	–0.9	13.7	17.3	–3.6	15.4	17.0	–1.6
Mizoram	75.4	78.3	–2.9	41.2	40.2	1.0	25.0	22.4	2.6
Nagaland	27.4	29.5	–2.1	18.3	16.7	1.6	13.4	11.6	1.8
Sikkim	44.9	50.3	–5.4	27.6	29.5	–1.9	25.2	19.5	5.7
Tripura	73.0	73.3	–0.3	31.9	25.0	6.9	19.4	15.8	3.6
India	69.0	60.8	8.2	42.2	36.1	6.1	12.3	9.1	3.2

Source: www.indiastat.com.

Gender Differentials in Employment

Female work participation rate is one of the indicators of employment status of women. The gender differential in employment is presented in Table 4 and analysed taking the difference in male and female work participation rates of rural and urban areas of various states. It is found that for all the Northeastern states, except Manipur, the difference was positive implying existence of gender gap in the region. But the gender gap in work participation rate was relatively more in urban areas than that of rural areas. Work participation rate of rural women was relatively more than urban women. Except for Sikkim, Tripura and Assam, all other Northeastern states were having the gender gap in rural areas less than that of the national average. In case of urban area, the situation was adverse for Assam and Tripura where gender gap was above the national average.

Table 4

Work Participation Rate in Northeast States 2004–05

State/Country	*Rural*			*Urban*		
	Male	*Female*	*Gap*	*Male*	*Female*	*Gap*
Ar. Pradesh	50.0	41.0	9.0	46.1	14.8	31.3
Assam	55.1	20.9	34.2	55.1	10.9	44.2
Manipur	52.4	35.1	17.3	45.6	55.1	–9.5
Meghalaya	57.2	47.8	9.4	45.4	30.3	15.1
Mizoram	59.4	44.1	15.3	48.4	28.1	20.3
Nagaland	54.9	50.4	4.5	45.7	25.7	20.0
Sikkim	55.4	31.8	23.6	54.5	16.8	37.7
Tripura	54.9	8.5	46.4	50.4	10.0	40.4
India	54.6	32.7	21.9	54.6	16.6	38.0

Source: www.indiastat.com.

Gender Differentials in Health and Wellbeing

Health is one of the broad indicators in which gender disparity is seen all over the world. An improved sex ratio always indicates a better status of women in the society. As far as Northeastern states are concerned we examined it using the indicators like sex ratio, infant mortality rate, and life expectancy at birth.

Table 5

Sex Ratio and Infant Mortality Rates in Northeast States

State/Country	*Sex Ratio in*		*Infant Mortality Rate in 2009*								
			Total			*Rural*			*Urban*		
	2001	*2011*	*M*	*F*	*Gap*	*M*	*F*	*Gap*	*M*	*F*	*Gap*
Ar. Pradesh	893	919	31	34	–3	na	na	na	na	na	na
Assam	935	953	58	64	–6	61	67	–6	35	38	–3
Manipur	978	987	14	18	–4	na	na	na	na	na	na
Meghalaya	972	985	59	59	0	na	na	na	na	na	na
Mizoram	938	975	33	38	–5	na	na	na	na	na	na
Nagaland	909	931	23	28	–5	na	na	na	na	na	na
Sikkim	875	889	35	33	2	na	na	na	na	na	na
Tripura	948	961	33	30	2	na	na	na	na	na	na
India	933	940	49	52	–3	54	56	–2	32	35	–3

Source: www.indiastat.com.

Note: na stands for not available.

Sex-Ratio

The sex-ratio for all the Northeastern states was higher than the national average except for Arunachal Pradesh, Nagaland and Sikkim both in 2001 and 2011 (Table 5). However, in 2011, all the states of the region experienced a better sex-ratio as compared to 2001. Sex-ratio for Manipur (987), Meghalaya (985) and Mizoram (975) were significantly higher than that of the national average (940). Yet sex-ratio was not favourable to women in all the states of the region.

Infant Mortality Rate

The influence of tradition and its valuing of the girl child has been a positive influence on health and nutritional status of girl children. The impact is seen from the favourable figures on female infant mortality rates that Northeastern states cherished (Table 5). When disaggregated by gender, we found that the gap between boys and girls was narrow and the mortality profiles of female infants were lower in most of the states of the region in comparison to the national figure. Gender gap was highest in Assam as compared to other Northeast states and nation as a whole. However, the male and female infant mortality rates were equal in case of Meghalaya implying no gender gap in the state. As regards to the data on rural-urban segregation it was available only for the state of Assam. Gap was observed to be more in rural Assam as compared to urban Assam.

Life Expectancy at Birth

Life expectancy at birth is another indicator which shows the longevity of life of a person. It is one of the indicators of human development index too. In the absence of life expectancy tables for different states in the region we had to be dependent on various sources to present a sketchy idea about the region. The life expectancy at birth was higher for women than that of men both at the national level and in different states in the region. However, the states like Arunachal Pradesh (54.51 years) (Govt. of Arunachal Pradesh, 2005: 93) and Manipur (61.5 years) (Government of Manipur, 2011) and Assam (58.1 yrs) (SRS based Abridged Life Table, 1998–2002) had lower life expectancy at birth for women than that of the national figure (63.3 years) (SRS based Abridged Life Table, 1998–2002). Tripura (74 years) had longer life expectancy at birth for women than men (Government of Tripura, 2007: 17). But female life expectancy was always higher than that of male life expectancy for all the states of the region.

Gender Differentials in Political Participation

Women's political participation is another input to their empowerment. It is one of the important factors that contribute to their well-being. Empowered women have political freedom which in turn translates into their decision-making capacity at the community, state and national level. Women's representation in political field even in its most modest form of local government has the ability to transform and reinterpret the practice of politics (Mathew, 2003). It helps to create better village communities based on harmony and cooperation achieved through gender balance and justice. However, in case of India and even in the North-East, the strong family based structure of Indian politics makes it difficult for women to assert independent political choices, as distinct from the male headed families. Therefore, judging women's political agency on the basis of their representation in political bodies is hazardous; women standing proxy for men are quite common in India (Government of Assam, 2003).

When we analysed the gender differentials in women's political participation in Northeastern states, we found that elected women members in Legislative Assembly of the states were negligible. For instance in Assam, in 1972, there was not even a single woman MLA. However, the number and percentage had increased over time. In 2006, about 10 per cent of MLAs were women. Similarly, in Arunachal Pradesh, percentage of women MLA never exceeded 5 per cent. In the last 25 years, there had been only one woman MP from the state. However, at the local level, women's representation was almost one-third. Participation of women at village, intermediate and district panchayat level of Arunachal Pradesh was 39.6 per cent, 34.99 per cent and 33.82 per cent, respectively (Government of Arunachal Pradesh, 2005). Mizoram also tells the same story. In the past only once a single woman was elected as a Member (Lalthansangi, 2005). In Manipur at the local level the participation of women was about one third of the total. However, in hilly districts of Manipur, women were not allowed to have any representation in any political institution (Government of Manipur, 2011). In Tripura no woman had been elected as MP till date. However only one woman was elected to the State Legislative Assembly, but representation in local bodies had been good and about one third of the total members (Government of Tripura, 2007). In Nagaland also no woman had been elected till date. But representation in local bodies had been relatively good (Government of Nagaland, 2004). Till date Meghalaya had represented one woman in the Parliament. Although representation in local bodies did not always indicate empowerment of women as in most cases they acted as proxies to their male counterparts yet it is desirable from the point of view of progress in the long run. It is believed that elected women in the long run no longer remain as proxies rather they become politically active and empowered. Overall information revealed that there had been a huge gender gap in political participation at higher bodies in Northeastern states but grounding was being prepared for future as revealed from their participation at local bodies.

Findings and Conclusion

In the analysis, an endeavour has been made to study the extent of gender inequality in Northeastern states of India in four different areas, viz., education, employment, health and political participation. The gender related development indices of the eight states were compared with the corresponding national figure. It was found that four states had GDI above national level and the remaining four states had GDI values marginally below than that of India implying that women of the region enjoyed less disparity in terms of longevity, educational attainment and thus control over resources. The gender gap was estimated in the areas like literacy rate, enrollment rate, work participation rate, sex ratio, infant mortality rate, life expectancy at birth and women's political participation, etc. We found that the gap was narrow for the states like Meghalaya, Mizoram and Nagaland in respect of literacy rate. The gender gap in literacy was the largest for Arunachal Pradesh among Northeastern states. However it was always better than national figure. Similarly Meghalaya, Nagaland and Sikkim had done well in case of enrollment rate. Even in high school level the enrollment rate of girls was more than that of boys in those states. But in Arunachal Pradesh and Assam, the gender gap was wide in enrollment rate at different levels of education. Gender gap in work participation rate was less in Manipur, Nagaland and Mizoram. The prevalence of women market in Manipur might be the cause of the low gender gap in the state. However, the situation was worse in Tripura, Assam and Sikkim where tribal population were relatively lower in comparison to other Northeastern states. As regards sex-ratio, we found that Meghalaya, Manipur, Mizoram, Tripura and Assam had better sex ratio and states like Sikkim, Arunachal Pradesh and Nagaland had sex ratio much lower than that of national average. Infant mortality rate was lower for Northeastern states. Female infant mortality rate was higher than male infant mortality rate in the region except in the states of Sikkim and Tripura. Similarly, life expectancy at birth was more for women than for men in the Northeast and India. So it seems that the women of the region enjoyed better health status as compared to national level. Political participation of women at state and national level was lower for those states except Assam. However, the participation at local level was almost one-third for all the states of the region. But this might not indicate that women of the region were politically empowered or aware. There might be influence of male members of the family on the women as a result of which they acted as proxies of their male counterparts in the political domain. Although the status of women was relatively better in Northeastern states, viz., Mizoram, Nagaland, Manipur and Meghalaya as compared to national level yet there were gaps in educational attainment, access to employment, health, political participation, etc. Giving property right, access to employment and educational opportunity to women thus might not change the picture. A revolutionary change in the social and cultural values and behavioural pattern is necessary to foster the process of achieving gender equality. As soon as women feel that they have the capability to operate the society at the same term as men then achieving gender equality would not remain as a distant dream.

References

Anand, S. and A. Sen. (1995) 'Gender Inequality in Human Development: Theories and Measurement' in Fukuda Parr and A.K. Shiv Kumar (eds.) *Readings in Human Development*. New Delhi: OUP.

Bardhan, K. and S. Klasen. (1999) 'UNDP's Gender related Indices: A Critical Review', *World Development*, 27(6). pp. 985–1010.

Blumberg, R.L. (2005) 'Women's Economic Empowerment as the Magic Potion of Development? Paper presented at the 100th Annual Meeting of the American Sociological Association, Philadelphia.

Gaye Amie, J. Klugman, M. Kovacevic, S. Twigg, and E. Zambrano. (2010) 'Measuring Key Disparities in Human Development: The Gender Inequality Index', Paper provided by Human Development Report Office (HDRO), United Nations Development Programme in its series Human Development Research Papers (2009 to present) with number HDRP-2010–46.

Government of Arunachal Pradesh. (2005) *Arunachal Pradesh Human Development Report*, Itanagar.

Government of Assam. (2003) *Assam Human Development Report*, Planning and Development Department, Dispur, Assam.

Government of Manipur. (2011) *State Human Development Report* (Draft Report). Retrieved from <http://manipur.nic.in/planning/DraftMSDR/Draft_SDR_ pdf/Chapter%2015_Health.pdf>, Visited on 12 September 2010 at 9.30 a.m.

Government of Meghalaya. (2008) *Meghalaya Human Development Report*.

Government of Nagaland. (2004) *Nagaland State Human Development Report*.

Government of Sikkim. (2001). *Sikkim Human Development Report*.

Government of Tripura. (2007) *Tripura Human Development Report*.

Government of India. (2008) *Kurukshetra: A Journal on Rural Development*, 56(3), January, Ministry of Rural Development.

Government of India. (2002) *National Human Development Report, 2001*, Planning Commission, New Delhi.

Hicks, D.A. (2002) 'Gender Discrimination and Capability: Insights from Amartya Sen', *The Journal of Religious Ethics*, 30(1). pp. 137–154.

I.B.R.D. (2007) *Global Monitoring Report.* Millennium Development Goals: Confronting the Challenges of Gender Equality and Fragile States. Retrieved from <http://siteresources.worldbank.org/INTGLOMONREP 2007/Resources/3413191-1176390231604/1264-FINAL-LO-RES.pdf>. Visited on 7 February 2011 at 11.37 a.m.

Kabeer, N. (2005) 'Gender Equality and Women's Empowerment: A Critical Analysis of the Third Millennium Development Goal', *Gender and Development,* 13(1). pp. 13–24.

Kishor, S. and K. Gupta. (2004) 'Women's Empowerment in India and its States: Evidence from the NFHS', *Economic and Political Weekly,* 39(7). pp. 694–712.

Lalthansangi. (2005) 'A Situational Analysis of Women and Girls in Mizoram', National Commission for Women.

Mahanta, A. (ed.) (2002) *Human Rights and Women of North East India.* Dibrugarh: Centre for Women's Studies, Dibrugarh University..

Malhotra, A., S.R. Schuler and C. Boender. (2002) 'Measuring Women's Empowerment as a Variable in International Development', World Bank. Retrieved from <www.unicef.org/pubsgen/humanrights-children/ index.html>. Visited on 11 January 2011 at 5 p.m.

Mathew, G. (2003) Keynote address in the workshop on 'A Decade of Women's Empowerment through Local Governance' organized jointly by Institute of Social Sciences and South Asia Partnership, Canada sponsored by International Development Research Centre.

Moser Caroline O. (1993) *Gender Planning and Development: Theory Practice and Training,* Place?: Women, Ink.

Nussbaum, M.C. (2001) *Women and Human Development: The Capability Approach.* Cambridge: Cambridge University Press.

Rout, H.S. and P.K. Panda. (eds) (2008) *'Gender and Development in India: Dimension and Strategies',* Retrieved from <http://www.pnayak.webs. com>. Visited on 16 September 2010 at 9.30 p.m.

Shiv Kumar, A.K. (1996): 'Gender Related Development Index: A Comparison for Indian States', *Economic and Political Weekly,* April 16.

Sullivan, Oriel. (2004) 'Changing Gender Practices within the Household: A Theoretical Perspective'. Retrieved from <http://www.pnayak.webs. com>. Visited on 13 September 2010 at 9.30 p.m.

UNDP (1990–2010) *Human Development Report.* Oxford: Oxford University Press.

Wallace, T. and C. March. (eds) (1991) *Changing Perception: Writing on Gender and Development,* Oxfam Press, Oxford.

World Economic Forum (2005–2010) *Global Gender Gap Report.*

www.indiastat.com Visited on 14 November 2012 at 9.30 p.m.

6

Countering Regionalism in Northeast India

A Study of Development Initiatives

HARENDRA SINHA

Regionalism is related with region. In the geographical sense, it means any more or less familiar part of earth's surface. In Indian context, regionalism generally refers to assertion of distinct ethnic, linguistic or economic interest by various groups within the nation. Since regional consciousness is based on linguistic, economic, ethnic and cultural identities of the people living in a specific geographical area, the political scientists have chosen to treat economic regionalism, linguistic regionalism, political regionalism and even sub-regional movements in general frame of regionalism (Sikri, 1994: 236). It has its wider and narrower connotations. In the former sense, regionalism means the love for one's area of living or a particular region to which one belongs. It is something natural and presence of such regionalism in a federal polity in particular, is natural. Here one can also include all demands and movements directed against excessive centralism and in favour of decentralisation and financial autonomy. In the latter sense, it means love for one's own region over and above the country as a whole. When the people of region make regional and parochial demands on the political system, which are opposed to the interests of other regions or the country as a whole it tantamount to regionalism in its worst form which is a big strain upon nationalism and the nation as a whole. The demand for secession, separate statehood, full statehood, autonomy and regional autonomy within a state, inter-state disputes, sons of the soil policy, militant regionalism and linguistic regionalism are the main forms of regionalism that plague Indian political system (Ghai, 2008: 436). The

Northeast India has also been afflicted with regionalism in the form of demand for secession in Mizoram[1], Nagaland, Manipur and demand for regional autonomy within a state like Bodoland and son of the soil principle as a manifestation of regionalism. In all the Northeastern states, there is a strong resentment over the presence of persons who have migrated from Bangladesh in particular on their soils and the passions generated by such a demand do not spare the fellow Indians belonging to different states of the Indian Union, and a demand is made that they should also quit these states. The whole of Northeast continues to be affected by inter-communal clashes (Nagas and Kukis) and the like, as well as by sub-nationalism. (ibid., 440–43).

The growing intensity of terrorism and militancy as means of pursuing narrowly conceived regional goals is indeed alarming and its immediate and effective handling is needed. At the same time, identification of the causes of regionalism and its solution is also requires. Out of the various causes of regionalism in India, like large diversity, linguistic attachment, appeasement policy, socio-cultural differences, administrative decentralisation, ethnicity, geography, etc. the uneven economic development of the country and consequent backwardness of certain regions is the main factor that gives rise to regionalism. This is true to a great extent in case of Northeast India. Backward economy is one of the main reasons behind the regionalism in Northeast region. The backwardness is unequivocally manifested in every sector of the economy. Since Independence, the policy initiatives followed by the Central Government for the Northeast have, by and large, failed to satisfy the needs and aspirations of the people. The present paper attempts to examine the development initiatives undertaken by the Government of India for growth and thereby help in countering regionalism in the Northeast and suggests some fresh initiatives for further development of the region. This paper is organised from published and unpublished works, findings of some scholars and fieldwork findings of the authors which is required for this paper.

All the aspects relating to regionalism and development initiatives undertaken by the Central Government for Northeast are not covered in this paper but efforts have been made to cover up some of the major initiatives undertaken and the need for fresh initiatives, which may serve as highlights for further research and some feedbacks for administrators and policy makers.

Regionalism and the Present Economic Scenario of the Northeast

The continuous problem of regionalism in the Northeast is due to the interaction of diverse psychological, historical, social, political and economic factors. The deep sense of perpetual grudge in the minds of the people, antagonism and mistrust among various sections of the society, lack of sense of belongingness and the continuing communication gap aggravate the situation. Indian leadership, barring Mahatma Gandhi, is charged with having agreed to the Cripps Mission proposal of grouping Assam with East Pakistan. It is often alleged that Nehru abandoned the people of Assam in the face of the Chinese aggression. The vested interest groups try to perpetuate the memory of these happenings in the minds of the people suffering from a bottle-neck psychology. The psychology of blaming the Centre for most of the present day ills and the growing sense of alienation in post-Independence India has its roots in the perpetuation of colonial theories (Kumar, 1995: 17–18). Factionalism is inextricably tied up with ethnic politics, giving it a centrifugal continuity (Chaube, 1999: 256). All the groups of people who demanded secession withdrawal from India had specific grievances and were confronting crisis – political, economic, social, structural or related to identity (Nag, 1994: 315).

Table 1

Economic Indicators of Northeast India

	Unit	*NER**	*All India*
1. Credit Deposit	%	16.8–38.3	56.7
2. Per Capita Power Consumption	KWH	97	355
3. Industrial production	% of GDP	2.16	27
4. Unemployment	%	12	7.7
5. Rail length	Km	2,578 (4%)	63,140
6. Road length	Lakh km	1.74 (7%)	25

* Northeastern Region

Source: Annual Report 2006–07, Ministry of Development of NER.

The Northeast India comprises eight small states (Arunachal Pradesh, Assam, Manipur, Meghalaya, Mizoram, Nagaland, Tripura and Sikkim) comprising the total area of the region of 2,55, 036 km of which 70 per cent is hilly terrain and deep valley It represents about 7.5 per cent of India's landmass and 3.5 per cent of India's population (2001). Its population density of 143 per sq km is much lower than the all India figure of 313. Significantly, it accounts for 26 per cent of the national forest cover. About 90 per cent of the regions boundaries form India's international border with Bangladesh, Bhutan, China and Myanmar. The region is extremely rich in terms of mineral and natural resources, yet suffers with low economic indicators. The document prepared by the national Institute of Public Finance and Policy for Northeast Council says the per capita gross state domestic product (GSDP) of Northeast India is 31 per cent less than the national average. In 2004–05, the entire region's GSDP, a measure of the standard of living for people, was ₹ 18,027 against the national average of ₹ 25,968. Even within the region, there are vast differences in the plains and hills. To reach all-India level of per capita income in 2020, the Northeast Vision 2020 Document Paper says that the GSDP of the Northeast region will have to grow at 11.8 per cent annually on an average (GOI, 2007). Table 1 shows that credit deposit, power consumption, industrial production is less than national average and also the rail and road length. The percentage of unemployment is much higher than the all India average.

About 84.49 per cent of the people live in rural areas compared to around 72.21 per cent for all India. The topographical isolation, bad communication network, limited cultivable land and going down of agricultural workers due to increasing population and consequent rise of rural work force, poor irrigation facilities, recurrence of flood, poor infrastructure, low level of resource utilisation, poor institutional financing are some of the major causes of economic backwardness of the region. The continued underdeveloped position even after six decades of Independence of the Northeast region has induced many political outfits to clamour for rights of self-determination and even sovereignty (Borkakoti, 2002: 118). The level of resource utilisation in the region is very low. Even in case of land-use it is found that thousands of hectares of land remains unused throughout the year. The total number of educated job-seekers stands more than 2 million now. Lack of employment in the secondary and tertiary sectors and increasing pressure of population are the main reasons for unemployment in the region (Taher, 2007: 277). Such a crisis situation has driven the youths to the wall. And since a hungry man is like an angry man, the Northeast youths now see things in anger. However, anger always burns the angry man himself the most. So the Northeasterners have suffered themselves in and due to innumerable agitations and struggles more than half a century of independent era. The rest of the country never bothered about the political upheavals in this region as long as the flow of raw materials from here remains undisturbed (Borkakoti, 2002: 120). The situation can be redeemed only if the causes of economic backwardness are carefully analysed and removed as quickly as possible through development initiatives. Let us examine some of the policy measures initiated by the Central Government for the development of the region since Independence.

Development Initiatives

With abundant natural resources, oil, natural gas, coal deposits, limestone reserves, clay, granite deposit, huge hydroelectric power potential and over 60 per cent of total geographical area under forest cover, the region has immense potential for development. The Central Government has taken a number of initiatives in terms of overall development of the region.

The Northeast Council

The Northeast Council (NEC) was constituted by an Act of Parliament in December 1971 followed by the Presidential assent on 1 August 1972 which was inaugurated at Shillong on 7 November 1972. It came into being along with the reorganisation of the Northeastern areas. The Northeastern Areas Reorganisation Act of 1971 and the Northeastern Council Act of 1971 are the twin products of the initiative of the Government. It is the nodal agency for the economic and social development of the Northeastern region which consists of the eight states of Arunachal Pradesh, Assam, Manipur, Meghalaya, Mizoram, Nagaland, Sikkim and Tripura. Nagaland, which had some reservations, finally joined the Council in 1976 and Sikkim became a member on 23 December 2002 following an amendment to the NEC Act (GOI, 1971). The constitution of the Council has marked the beginning of a new chapter of concerted and planned endeavour for the rapid development of the region. The primary purpose of NEC is the development of the region for better human welfare. It is not a super government. Nor does it curtail the power of the states, an advisory and not supervisory body. The NEC was described as an index of the Central Government's concern for the development of a neglected region. The Central Government will naturally be in touch with the problems of economic planning and security of the region (Chaube, 1999: 232). The functions of the Council as mentioned in the Act centre around the necessity of a fast and balanced socio-economic development of the entire region, through a regional planning with a set of priorities suited to the felt needs. There are differences in the states with regard to resource endowments, levels of industrialisation and infrastructure facilities. The region has to be treated as one unit, for the purpose of social and economic planning, strengthening inter-regional and intra-regional economic relations.[2] The NEC is focusing on various inter-state projects and the major areas taken up include agricultural and allied activities, horticulture, animal husbandry, industries and mineral, sericulture, flood control, forest wealth, bio-gas, solar energy, manpower and entrepreneurship development. Over a period of time, it has established an identity as a mechanism to promote regional economic development (Bandyopadhyay, 2005: 96–99). The NEC is a new experiment in inter-state and centre state relations.

Ministry of Development of the Northeast

The Ministry of Development of Northeastern Region (DoNER) is a Government of India ministry, established in September 2001, which functions as the nodal department of the Central Government to deal with matters related to the socio-economic development of the eight states of

Northeast India. It acts as a facilitator between the Central Ministries/Departments and the State Governments of the Northeastern region, including the economic development, removal of infrastructural bottlenecks, provision of basic minimum services, creating an environment for private investment and to remove impediments to lasting peace and security in the Northeastern region. The DoNER accorded the status of a full fledged ministry on May 2004. The ministry is mainly concerned with the creation of infrastructure for economic development of Northeastern region. The Northeastern Council (NEC), Northeastern Development Finance Institution (NEDFI), Northeastern Regional Agricultural Marketing Corporation Limited (NERAMAC), Sikkim Mining Corporation Limited. (SMC), Northeastern Handlooms and Handicrafts Development Corporation (NEHHDC) are functioning under it. The main activities and functions of the DoNER are Non-Lapsable Central Pool of Resources (NLCPR), Northeastern Council (NEC), coordination with the Central Ministries and the state governments of the Northeastern states, capacity building, advocacy and publicity, international cooperation and enterprises of the department. Many infrastructure related projects are being undertaken with the funds released from the Non-Lapsable Central Pool of Resources (NLCPR) to the Northeastern states.

The Brahmaputra Board

The Brahmaputra Board was set up by the Government of India under an Act of Parliament, i.e. The Brahmaputra Board Act, 1980 (46 of 1980) under the Ministry of Irrigation (now renamed as Ministry of Water Resources) for the planning and integrated implementation of measures for the control of floods and bank erosion in the Brahmaputra Valley and for matters connected therewith (GOI, 1980). The Board office started functioning with its headquarters at Guwahati with effect from 11 January 1982. The jurisdiction of the Board includes both the Brahmaputra and Barak Valleys and covers all the states of the Northeastern region either in full or in part. The main functions of the Board are to carry out surveys and investigations in the Brahmaputra Valley and prepare a Master Plan for the control of floods and bank erosion and improvement of drainage in the Brahmaputra Valley, to prepare detailed reports and estimates in respect of the dams and other projects proposed in the Master Plan as approved by the Central Government and indicate in each case the cost attributable to different purposes or uses and maintain and operate such dams and works. However, the Board is virtually a non-functioning body which does little work by itself barring of carrying out some investigations, surveys, etc. as most of the specialised items of work are done by expert agencies as and when needed (NECCC[I], 1995: 105).

Power Generation through NEEPCO

The region has 30 per cent of nation's estimated total hydel potential, the largest being in Arunachal Pradesh. It is now producing a bare 3 per cent of that (ibid.). The North-Eastern Electric Power Corporation Limited (NEEPCO) is assuring the region a bright future towards a power surplus region. The NEEPCO, a Schedule 'A' Government of India Enterprise under the Ministry of Power was set up on the 2 April 1976 to plan, investigate, design, construct, generate, operate and maintain power stations in the Northeastern region of the country. NEEPCO has an installed capacity of 1,130 MW which is 49 per cent of the total installed capacity of the Northeast region. NEEPCO's authorised share capital is ₹ 5,000 crore at present and its net worth as on 31 March 2009 is ₹ 4,182.31 crore. With its headquarters at Shillong, the capital of Meghalaya, NEEPCO is a power sector enterprise with projects located in various states of the Northeast. Its mission is to harness the vast hydro and thermal power potential, to produce pollution free and inexhaustible power through planned development of power generation projects and to play a significant role in the integration and development of hydroelectric and thermal power in the Central Sector covering all aspects such as investigation, planning, designs, construction, operation and maintenance of hydroelectric and thermal projects which in turn would effectively promote the development of the nation as a whole. The NEEPCO is to responsibly exploit the vast hydro and thermal power potential for sustainable development of Northeast region, to undertake execution of new hydro/thermal schemes and undertake timely renovation and modernisation of existing old hydro and thermal plants, to execute on-going hydro/thermal projects as per targets set, so as to achieve commissioning of such projects as per schedule or ahead of schedule, to ensure optimum utilisation of installed capacity so as to achieve maximum generation and optimum machine availability, to improve the Quality Management System, NEEPCO is already registered as an ISO: 9001–2008 Company, NEEPCO has also been accredited with OHSAS 18001 for occupational health and safety risk management system and ISO 14001 for environmental management system, to complete DPR of new schemes for hydro/thermal projects as per schedule or ahead of schedule as and when estimated by Central Electricity Authority (CEA), to promote industrial growth and prosperity of the Northeastern region by fulfilling the need of supply of electricity thereby improving the quality of life of the region and to improve the socio-economic condition of the neighbourhood by providing infrastructure, medical schooling and the creation of productive environment opportunities.

The Look East Policy

The Look East Policy (LEP), which was initiated in 1991, marked a strategic shift in India's perspective of the world. It was developed and enacted during the government of Prime Minister P.V. Narasimha Rao and rigorously pursued by the successive governments of Atal Bihari Vajpayee and Manmohan Singh. The essential philosophy of the LEP is that India must find its destiny by linking itself more and more with its Asian partners and the rest of the world and that India's future and economic interest are best served by greater integration with East and South-East Asia. An agreement for co-operation in this field was signed by India and Myanmar in 1994. The immediate outcome of pursuing the LEP by India was to counter-act Chinese monopoly over Burmese resources and to effectively block the Chinese plan of extracting natural resources and gas in Arakan (Doungel, 2010: 8). The LEP is expected to usher in a new era of development for the Northeast through network of pipelines, road, rail and air connectivity, communication and trade. However, several hurdles need to be overcome of which the region is embroiled for the past several decades before any meaningful activity can take place. Starting from various forms of insurgent activities to the problem of illegal migration and drug trafficking, which are all transnational in character, the Government of India need to forge cooperation from the neighbouring countries? Such cooperation with the neighbouring countries should not antagonise the people of this region. The trans border communities can be restored through border trade and inter-country trade which the border region should not act merely as a transit corridor but as a source of local manufacture and enhancing people-to-people contact. The emphasis should be on industrialisation and growth. The Indian Government and the Northeastern states must adopt proactive role and provide not only infrastructures but also political stability and good governance (Haokip, 2011).

Border Area Development Programme

Border Area Development Programme (BADP), a 100 per cent central assistance programme, was started with the objective of balanced development through the provision of infrastructure facilities to promote a sense of security among the local populations of international border and sensitive areas. This programme was started in the year 1986–87 for balanced development of border areas of states bordering Pakistan, namely Jammu and Kashmir, Punjab, Gujarat and Rajasthan. During the Eighth Plan, the programme was revamped and its coverage was extended to the states on the eastern border with Bangladesh. In the Ninth Plan period, the programme has been extended to all the land borders in response to the demands of the state governments and the Ministry of Home Affairs. Thus, in 1997–98, BADP was extended to states bordering Myanmar. In 1998–99, the states bordering China were included under the programme and from 1999–2000, the Programme was further extended to include the states bordering Nepal and Bhutan also. The main objective of

BADP is to meet the special needs of the people living in remote and inaccessible areas situated near the border. Successful implementation of BADP in the remote areas by creating sustainable income generation is very essential by giving highest priority to all weather road connectivity. Spending huge amount of money on construction of market sheets under BADP, for example, will be of no use without marketing links and communication (Sinha, 2006: 230). However, BADP implementation is infected with high level of corruption. In state like Mizoram, for example, its implementation had little impact on the life of the people. The CAG report has revealed that in Mizoram, the Rural Development Department drew an amount of ₹ 46.76 crore during 2005–10 presenting false bills to the government treasury before actual commencement of approved works (http://www.marinews.com/mizoram).

Control of Jhum Cultivation

Jhum[3] cultivation has been widely practiced in the hill areas of the region leading to soil erosion, damages soil fertility, creates environmental problem, denudation of forest cover, etc. Table 2 shows that jhuming continues unabated throughout the Northeast and the strategies of the government for providing alternatives to jhum is yet to be entrenched to the jhumia families.

Table 2

Shifting Cultivation in the Northeast Region

State	*Annual Area under Shifting Cultivation (sq kms)*	*Fallow Period (in years)*	*Minimum Area under Shifting Cultivation one time or Other (sq kms)*	*No. of Families Practicing Shifting Cultivation*
Arunachal Pradesh	700	3–10	2,100	54,000
Assam	696	2–10	1,392	58,000
Manipur	900	4–7	3,600	70,000
Meghalaya	530	5–7	2,650	52,290
Mizoram	630	3–4	1,890	50,000
Nagaland	190	5–8	1,913	1,16,046
Tripura	223	5–9	1,115	43,000
Total	3,869 (1.5%)	—	14,660 (5.7%)	4,43,336

Source: Basic Statistics of NER, 2002, Government of India, NEC, Shillong.

The National Forest Policy, 1952 which laid stress on weaning people away from shifting cultivation by persuasion, was unable to achieve any notable success. Efforts to regulate, control and contain shifting cultivation have been made in several states from time to time with varying results. The North-Eastern Council took up programmes in the North-eastern states for control of shifting cultivation. These were mainly aimed at soil and water conservation by building terraces for development of agriculture and the production of horticultural crops including tree crops. The most recent scheme initiated by the Government of India as strategy for the control of jhum is Watershed Development Project in Shifting Cultivation Areas (WDPSCA). The Planning Commission approved WDPSCA scheme in seven states of Northeastern region, namely Arunachal Pradesh, Assam, Manipur, Meghalaya, Mizoram, Nagaland and Tripura with 100 per cent special Central assistance to the states as per directions of National Development Council (NDC) in 1994–95. The main objectives of the programme are to: (a) protect hill slopes of jhum areas through soil and water conservation measures on watershed basis and to reduce further land degradation (b) encourage and assist jhumia families to develop jhum land for productive uses with improved cultivation and suitable package of practices leading to settled cultivation. (c) improve socio-economic status of jhumia families through household/land based activities (d) mitigate ill effects of shifting cultivation by introducing appropriate land use as per land capability and improved technologies with the adoption of watershed approach for treatment of degraded jhum areas as cluster and contiguous manner, integration of sectoral measures for comprehensive watershed development and to mitigate ill effects of shifting cultivation by introducing appropriate land use as per land capability and adoption of improved technologies, etc.

The WDPSCA scheme succeeded to a limited extent to decrease in shifting cultivation area and in overall increase in income of the jhumia families. Families practicing jhum in the Northeastern states is still very high and jhum cultivation continues to be a major method of farming despite the efforts to encourage farmers to move away from this traditional practice.

Moreover, the Government of India has taken a number of new initiatives in terms of special package for the region. These initiatives cover areas like identifying gaps in infrastructure and basic minimum services and initiating measures to remove them, generation of employment, earmarking of 10 per cent of each Central Ministry's budget for specific programme in the region, separate industrial policy, separate export promotion policy for the region, improved credit flow, improvement and expansion of the railway services, water management and flood control measures, border trade and deployment of export trade routes, massive investment in telecommunication, electronics and tourism. (Bandyopadhyay, 2005: 99–101).

The analysis of some of the policies and initiatives presented in this paper is laudable and it seems that every effort is being made by the Union

Government to develop the Northeastern region covering all sectors of development. The region is also rich in natural resources and does not lack hard working, skilled and un-skilled manpower. In spite of all these factors, the region remains under-developed. The achievements on various development programmes in the region are mainly enclose on the aggregate physical and financial targets which does not include any record of the impact of the programmes on general economic condition of the people. Therefore, revamping the programmes initiated and searching fresh initiatives for the development of the region is indispensable.

Suggestions

Designing and implementing people-centric schemes by harnessing the natural resources of the Northeastern region through participatory development strategy and grassroots planning is desirable. In Northeast India, the majority of the people live in its villages and so planning strategy should aim at developing rural areas. Development of agriculture by controlling the rage of floods and by providing scientific technology for jhum cultivation and its alternatives is essential. Building up of infrastructure by giving top priority to roads, railways, power and inland waterways is important. Planning strategy for the Northeast should aim at the establishment of growth foci and through linking the different villages, service centres and growth centres in an integrated manner (Bhattacharya, 2002: 115).

Lack of good communication facility is the major problem faced by the rural population of the region. Due to remoteness and scattered nature of the villages and lack of road transport facilities, the farmers of the remote villages cannot market their products even to the block headquarters. Regulated markets and cold storage facilities in the region are inadequate. Although the agro climatic condition of the region is conducive, dairy, poultry, fishery, etc. has not been developed as a means of livelihood. Veterinary services in the rural areas are inadequate. The efforts of the government in developing small-scale industries are not quite satisfactory and also this sector has a direct link with road transport, power, and water resources. Middleman's share has been one of the main reasons behind increasing food prices at the retail level. How to eliminate the middleman and thus cut costs and to reach the actual profit to the rural development beneficiaries are not taken into consideration while implementing rural development schemes (Sinha, 2006: 256).

Effective implementation of development initiatives is vital. More infrastructure development ensuring better link roads, market connectivity, cold storage facilities, irrigation are required. Initiatives for more farmers' cooperative societies should be encouraged, which will help in eliminating the middleman. Understanding of the technical factors involved while implementing development programmes, timely supply of appropriate inputs, flow of assistance, marketing of outputs, strict and continuous monitoring are essential.

While not ignoring the political and cultural roots of the violence in the Northeast, certainly the extent of this violence among our young people has to be attributed, to a great extent, to their frustration due to lack of opportunities for gainful and dignified employment (Minamparampil, 2007: 72). Providing gainful and productive employment opportunities is essential for which capacity building, focusing on development of skills and training, is extremely important. Local means and production suited to the genius of the people needs to be identified and explored. Industrial development programmes announced by the government from time to time lack efficiency in management and there is lack of proper coordination among various agencies in implementation of the programme (Laskar, 2010: 132–33). Therefore, small-scale industries based on local resources like agricultural products, bamboo and other forest products needs to be identified with special packages of incentive for educated youth to take those enterprises. Involvement of Non-Government Organisations (NGO) in providing loans in such sectors as floriculture, small-scale industries like development of weaving and knitting, horticulture, etc. and help in the marketing of those products, will ensure employment to a sizeable number of poor people. The NGOs can also form committees like Forest Protection Committee, Product Marketing Committee, Monitoring Committee, Development Committee and Awareness Committee, etc. This will ensure people's participation and help to make the people aware in minimising corruption and political interference at implementation level of all development initiatives.

The local self-government institutions in the hill areas of North-eastern states are highly restricted by the governmental interference and without financial power; they seems to be irrelevant local self governing institutions. The traditional institutions of the region are characterised by gender injustice, rule of the male elders, kinship and group solidarity (Haokip, 2009: 36). Therefore, strengthening of local self-government system by introducing Panchayati Raj Institutions (PRI) in the hill areas as per the Constitution (73rd Amendment) Act at the Village and District level with certain modifications in ensuring the existing traditional values will guarantee financial autonomy, reservation of women and the decision making power.

Concluding Remarks

There is no denying of the fact that regionalism has direct bearing on the economic backwardness. Economic development is one the most important aspects for countering this inherent problem in Northeast India. The Central

Government is often blamed for not giving funds and also for giving funds. It is often argued that development in the region never accorded the priority it merits and the Central Government maintains an exceptionally oppressive grasp over the entire region. On the other hand, the Central Government is often blamed for giving money without infrastructure and makes the people corrupt. The fact of the matter is that the massive development initiatives undertaken by the Central Government, so far benefitted only a small elite section of the society in the Northeast and the marginal section of the society is deprived, oppressed and exploited. As a result, when the time is mature, the oppressed demands for autonomy. When the so-called autonomy is achieved, the elite section will again benefit and the oppressed section still cries for autonomy.

Money as central assistance and funds are not considered as own which causes leakages and mass corruption. Projects and schemes of development are frequently prepared and submitted to the Central Government only to draw funding and not because they fit in a methodical and inclusive plan which promises to benefit the poor people. There is lack of genuine desire and endeavour on the part of the Central Government to check the misuses and leakages.

Therefore, initiating a suitable development perspective and identification of the nature of problems faced and infrastructural prerequisites, public and private sector investments, human resource development, etc. for Northeast region followed by strong political will with corruption-free responsive administration for proper direction of the plans is essential. Then only peace, progress and prosperity – the North-East Vision 2020 – will be achieved and the region will strengthen and be consolidated.

Notes

1. In 1987, Mizoram was given statehood which resolved the Mizo problem, yet some elements in Mizoram still harp on secession while others keep on crying for greater autonomy.
2. Section 4 of the NEC (Amendment) Act 2002 stated that the Council shall function as a regional planning body for the northeast area. While formulating the regional plans for the area, the Council shall give priority to schemes and projects which will benefit two or more states.
3. *Jhum* means slash and burn method of cultivation (shifting cultivation).

References

Bandyopadhyay, P.K. (2005) *The North East Saga*. New Delhi: Publications Division, Ministry of Information and Broadcasting.

Borkakoti, S.K. (2002) 'Perspective of Development' in Deb, J. Bimal (ed.) *Development Priorities in North East India*. New Delhi: Concept Publishing Company.

Bhattacharya, N.N. (2002) 'Formation of the Appropriate Development Paradigm of Northeast India' in Deb, J. Bimal (ed.) *Development Priorities in North East India*, New Delhi: Concept Publishing Company.

Chaube, S.K. (1999) *Hill Politics in North East India*. New Delhi: Orient Longman.

Doungel, J. (2010) 'An Analytical Study of the Socio-economic Status of the Sixth Schedule Area of Mizoram: Problems and Prospects', Paper Presented in the UGC Sponsored State Level Seminar, organised by Govt. J. Buana College, Lunglei, Mizoram on 22–23 October.

Ghai, K.K. (2008) *Indian Government and Politics*. New Delhi: Kalayani Publishers.

Government of India. (1971) North Eastern Council Act.

Government of India. (1980) Brahmaputra Board Act.

Government of India. (2007) NEC Vision 2020 Document.

Haokip, Thongkholal. (2011) 'India's Look East Policy: Prospects and Challenges for North East India' http:/www.indoburmanews.net, accessed on 2.6.2011.

Haokip, T.T. (2009) 'Traditional Self-governing Institutions and Democratic Governance in NE India'. *Local Government Quarterly*, July–September. http://www.marinews.com/mizoram, accessed on 2.6.2011

Kumar, B.B. (1995) 'North-East: Need for a Fresh Look' in P.S. Datta (ed.) *North-East and the Indian State*. New Delhi: Vikas Publishing House.

Laskar, B.I. (2010) 'Industrialisation of Mizoram: Need, Opportunities, Growth and Constraints of Small Scale Industries' in Laskar, B.I. (ed.) *Mizoram: The Emerging Issues of Development*. Guwahati: DVS Publishers.

Minamparampil, George M.C. (2007) 'Youth Problems and Prospects of Employment in North East India' in Shiela Bora and S.D. Goswami (eds.) *Youth at the Crossroads*. Guwahati: DVS Publishers.

Nag, Sajal. (1994) 'Withdrawal Syndrome: Secessionism in Modern North East India' in S. Milton Sangma (ed.) *Essays on North East India*. New Delhi: Indus Publishing Company.

NECCI(I). (1995) 'Abstract Report of General Secretaries of the 8th General Conference of Northeastern Congress (I) Coordination Committee' 22 June 1993 in P.S. Datta (ed.) *North-East and the Indian State*. New Delhi: Vikas Publishing House.

Sikri, S.L. (1994) *Indian Government and Politics* New Delhi: Kalayani Publishers.

Sinha, Harendra. (2006) 'The Role of Block Development Officer in the Rural Development of Mizoram with Special Reference to Lunglei District Blocks' PhD thesis, Gauhati University.

Taher, M.P. Ahmed. (1998) *Geography of North East India*. Guwahati: Mani Manik Prakash.

7

Crimes against Women in Northeast India

An Analysis from Gender Perspective

POLLY VAUQULINE

Nationality, ethnicity and gender have been the cornerstones of discrimination and violence between man and man. However, violence based on gender within the confines of the community and home is perhaps the most degrading of all other forms of violence. However, the increase in reported incidences of violence against women over the past several decades has firmly established the issue of concern for the women's movement globally. The need for protection of the rights of women gained global recognition during the International Decade of Women (1975–85) and was steadily gaining momentum since then. This recognition became international law in 1979, when the UN General Assembly adopted the Convention on the Elimination of All Forms of Discrimination against Women (CEDAW). India became signatory to the Convention in 1993 and ratified CEDAW and committed itself to work for the elimination of all types of discrimination against women. The most painful of discrimination of women is the physical, mental and psychological violence perpetrated on them. The threat of violence on women manifests right before their life begins (female infanticides, female feticides), continues to scar the early life (gender discrimination), follows in the married life as domestic violence, endangers them as victims of rape and worse still, in murders and engenders suicides in other cases.

There are several forms of violence that constitute clear violation of the rights of women to live with dignity and respect (Subrahmanian, 1995: 146). It is also clear that the generic 'gender-blind use of the term violence' obscures the gender specific forms of cruelty and attacks experienced by the woman alone. The definition of violence also includes all forms of mental torture and other acts that have the same effects as physical violence on women. Violence against women includes rape (including marital and custodial rape), domestic violence, 'widow burning' (*sati*), female infanticide and foeticide (amino-cintosis through ultra-sound techniques – that is legally a criminal offence in India now), trafficking of women and minors, sexual harassment and molestation and 'eve-teasing', witch-hunting, dowry death, (Krishnaraj, 1991: 4), and obvert assault on the dignity of women and other forms of social ostracism. It may also be aggression of an individual woman against herself, such as suicides, self-mutilation, negligence of ailments, sex determination tests, food denial and so on (Karlekar, 2008). Put simply, violence is an act of aggression, usually in interpersonal interaction or relation.

Although women maybe victims in any of the crimes, be it 'murder', 'robbery' or any other, the crimes in which women are the victims and which are directed specifically against women are denoted as 'Crimes Against Women'. They are broadly classified under two categories: crimes identified under the Indian Penal Code (IPC) and crimes identified under Special Laws (SLL) (National Crimes Record Bureau: Government of India, 1997).

Probing the Connection: Northeast India, Gender Perspective and Crimes against Women

Northeast Indian states, earlier know as the 'seven sisters' have supplemented one more state within its collective, Sikkim. In most of the occasions, programmes and references this whole region of 2,63,179 sq km, accounting 7.9 per cent of India's landmass, is given a single identity. There exist a special and a separate Ministry of Development of Northeastern Region, DONER, specifying the commitment of the Government of India for the socio-economic development of the region. The North-Eastern Council aims at securing a balanced development of the region through its programmes and projects. Again, North-Eastern Development Finance Co-orporation, NEDFi, carters to the financial requirements of the region. However, within this assumed singular identity of Northeast India, there are great variations be it physiographical, socio-cultural or economical characteristics of the states. There is variation in the social position of the women within the region too.

Northeast India comprises a mosaic of heterogeneous culture and diversified society. These diversities of customs and traditions accordingly construct the identity of the women and thereby her position within the society. Her position reflects her status and the privileges she enjoys and at the same time the disadvantages and discrimination she confronts. An integrative perspective in feminist sociology has been *social constructionism,* which argues that people create their social realities and identities through interactions with families, friends, and colleagues. In the 1970s, Suzanne J. Kessler and Wendy McKenna, building on Horold Garfinkel's ethnomethodological analysis of how a transsexual constructs conventional womanhood, argues that everyone constructs their gender. Candace West and Don Zimmerman have developed the widely used idea of 'doing gender' as how the social construction of gender builds up masculine dominance and feminine submissive (Code, 2000). Socially constructed gender and reproductive roles restrict a woman's identity and behaviour. As many radical feminists see it, sexuality is the crucial issue in feminism because 'aggression and the 'need' to dominate form a routine part of what is accepted as (normal) male sexuality' (Coveney et al., 1984). Male violence against women is normalised and legitimised in sexual practices through the assumption that when it comes to sex, men are by nature aggressive and dominant, whereas women are by nature passive and submissive (Tong, 1995).

Govind Kelkar situates violence against women 'in the socio-economic and political context of power relations'. Wider definition of violence finds resonance in the hierarchical society based on exploitative gender relations (Karlekar, 2008). Cultural norms and values prevalent in a society can influence the attitude towards women, their status in the society and ultimately, the types of behaviour towards women which may be considered acceptable or unacceptable irrespective of the fact what construes a crime or not, in the eyes of law. In the Indian society, dowry for example, is considered appropriate though is illegal in eyes of law, irrespective of religious beliefs. A divorce is perfectly acceptable behaviour among the Muslims, but unacceptable among the Hindus, though it is perfectly permissible under the law. Beating of wives or battery is a perfectly acceptable behaviour among the North Indians, though it may construe a crime in law. Among many tribes, divorce is perfectly acceptable, but wife-beating may be unheard of. Thus, it becomes necessary to understand the atrocities committed against women in the context of diverse ethnic and cultural backgrounds of women and their families (Vauquline, 2007). This approach of the study may provide an enhanced perceptive to the prevalence of violence against women and ways to confront these crimes.

Why the Study?

Northeast India has certain unique characteristics of its own. One such primary distinction is its diversity. It is the homeland of several ethnic groups, their values and beliefs. Superficial understanding of this part of India, along with their cultural values, customs and practices, maybe considered as restraint insight of the region. One such superficial apprehension is that the women status in this region is better and they enjoy greater mobility and visibility than the other regions of the country (Lalkima, 2009). However, there are varied gender inequalities that exist in certain pockets of the region which can be understood by an in-depth investigation into its regional variations. One such gender disparity is gender related crimes. There exist great variations in its occurrence. Regional analysis of the pattern of its occurrences can give an insight to the existence of crimes against women in Northeast India. Its temporal investigation over a period of time (ten years) can offer a pattern and trend of its existence and growth. Narratives of the experience of the battered women on the basis of their ethnic and cultural background can furnish a comprehensive and deeper understanding to this problem.

Data Base and Methodology

Data and information from both secondary and primary sources are obtained for this study. Library materials in the form of books, journals, publications, newspaper, etc. are consulted. Relevant e-books and websites are looked up. Another set of secondary data regarding the incidences of crimes against women in the seven states of Northeast India is collected from the records of National Crime Record Bureau, Government of India, New Delhi (2002–11). These secondary data is obtained to analyse the temporal growth of overall crimes against women in the seven states of the region. The regional variation of the occurrences of the violence committed in the domestic space, atrocities by husband and in-laws are also explored from this set of data.

The office of the Senior Superintendent of Police of each district compiles the records of crimes against women in the district level. This complied information is forwarded to the CID office of the state, at regular intervals, for the state level assemblage which are again sent to National Crime Record Bureau, Government of India, for the national level collection. Even though the records of the cases are well maintained in the Crime Branch of the Office of the Senior Superintendent of Police, it has certain limitations and many a times do not depict the real scenario of its existence. They are as follows:

(i) Those cases which are very serious in nature are the ones registered.

(ii) Police personnel are usually hesitant to register cases. Many a times the complaints of the victims are not openly welcomed by the police personnel. They try to settle the matter without registering the case, particularly the poorer sections of the people. When cases of domestic violence come up, they usually call the husband, warn him and let him go. The major limitation of the police registered cases is that more than 90 per cent of the crimes against women go unregistered. Instead of considering the registration of the case in the police station as a convenience, the victims consider it as a hassle (as stated by the victims). Therefore, though police record is a good source that indicates nature of crimes, it does not indicate the extent of the crimes committed against women.

To trounce these limitations, it was felt essential to collect primary data through interviews of victims of violence by the researcher. Primary data was collected from 60 victims of domestic violence, with the help of a questionnaire from Assam as it is one of the most crime prone area in respect of crimes against women in the region. However, it was contemplated to incorporate women from varied ethnic backgrounds. This primary data was collected through a purposive sample survey of individual victims of domestic violence in respect of their ethnic and cultural backgrounds as well as the interview-based surveys of housewives and adult women in the households to study the nature and types of domestic violence, attitude of women, causes and frequency of occurrences and possible solution put forth by the victims. To counter the reliance on survey methods, a growing number of researchers are calling for the use of qualitative methods to study domestic violence (Avery and Cavanaugh, 1995 and Williams, 1997). For which the narrated daily experiences of the abused women are denoted through in-depth interview technique of qualitative research methodology. The survey though was based on structured scheduled; the aim was to meet each victim a number of times to gain confidence and access truth, as far as possible from the victims' perspective without being either intrusive or judgemental. The study was conducted during 2010 and 2011.

Findings

Incidence of Crimes against Women in Northeast India

For this study, the data of crimes against women are analysed in varied ways. Firstly it is highlighted on the basis of total number of incidences of crimes against women (CAW) registered, recognised by the Indian Penal Code (IPC) and the Special Laws (SSL), according to the year. The study period spans over a phase of 10 years, 2002 to 2011. The yearly growth rates of CAW, which are projected in Table 1 are analyses according to the states (Table 1).

The data brings to light that there is prevalence of CAW in all the states of Northeast India. However, there are certain distinctive variations. Assam along with Tripura registered the highest number of incidences of CWA during the study period and in the state of Nagaland, CAW has been always low. Again, incidences of CAW in these two states (Assam and Tripura) have increased more than the double between 2002 to 2011. Another alarming indication is highlighted in the state of Meghalaya. Even though the number of incidences are less in the state, but there is a constant increase in the number of incidences of CAW during these 10 years.

Table 1

No of Incidence of Crimes against Women, 2002–2011

Year	*Arunachal Pradesh*	*Assam*	*Manipur*	*Meghalaya*	*Mizoram*	*Nagaland*	*Tripura*
2011	171	11,503	247	269	167	38	1,358
2010	190	11,555	190	261	170	41	1,678
2009	164	9,721	194	237	150	46	1,517
2008	175	8,122	211	208	162	47	1,416
2007	185	6,844	188	172	151	32	1,067
2006	168	6,801	171	176	125	43	964
2005	150	6,027	140	131	95	37	840
2004	148	5,700	134	113	91	30	670
2003	139	5,312	137	69	147	25	537
2002	159	5,092	170	71	154	26	536

Source: National Crime Record Bureau (2002–2012)

Figure 1

Incidences of Crimes against Women in Northeast India, 2002–2011

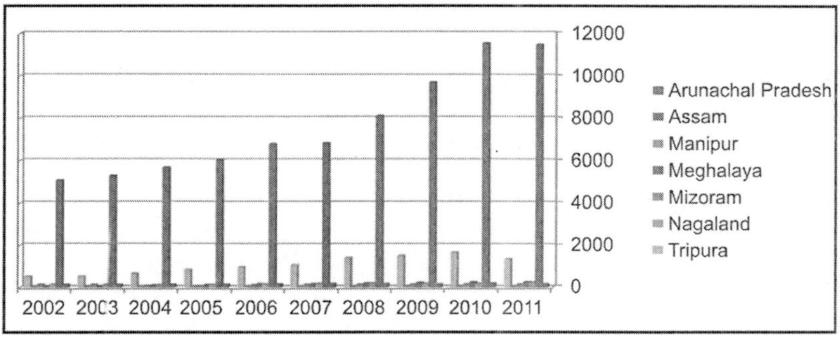

Source: As calculated by the author.

Growth Rate of Crimes against Women in Northeast India

There is great variation in the growth rate of CAW within the region. In the state of Assam, Tripura and surprisingly Meghalaya, there is a positive and steady growth of CAW during the period 2002–11. In the year 2010–11, in Assam and Tripura, the growth rate has plunged. In Meghalaya, during 2006–07, the growth has gone down. Otherwise there is a steady growth of CAW in the state, though in varied proportion.

Graphical representation of the growth rates of the three states (which are showing positive trend) offers further insight into the pattern of growth of CAW. Of these three states (Assam, Tripura and Meghalaya), the growth rate of Meghalaya is far higher than the other two states. It is followed by Tripura and Assam, respectively. It is observed that the growth rate has gone down in Tripura and Assam in the last year.

It is important to note here that the growth rate of Assam is showing a lower trend than the other two states because of the proportion of incidences of CAW registered. Since the number of incidences is high, the growth rate indicates a lower proportion of growth in Assam. It is vice versa for Meghalaya. Since the total number of cases of CAW is smaller it will indicate a larger growth with slight increase in the number of cases. As for Meghalaya, it is a matter of grave concern and calls for a deeper investigation as it is a matrilineal society.

On the other hand, there are certain states within the region which indicates negative growth of CAW in most of the span of the study period. Of these states, in Nagaland there were negative growths in five years of the 10 years of the study. Again, in Arunachal Pradesh, Manipur and Mizoram there were negative growth in four years of 10 years of the study.

Domestic Violence in Northeast India

To study the pattern of occurrence of domestic violence in the region, cases registered under the IPC 498A, which is cruelty by husband and relatives, are taken into consideration. The incidence of atrocities by husband and relatives is again highest in the state of Assam followed by Tripura. However, Manipur ranks third trailed by Meghalaya. Here again, it can be drawn to attention that Nagaland, followed by Mizoram, registers the lowest cases of atrocities by husband and relatives in the region. It is interesting to note that there is a close relationship between the pattern of occurrence of overall CAW and domestic violence in the region. On the basis of the analysis of these data it can be stated that there is a positive relationship between the two and vise versa.

Another factor which is brought to light is that, leaving aside Nagaland, the incidence of domestic violence has increased during the study period in the region. An exponentially growth is observed in the state of Tripura and Assam in these 10 years (almost five times). It is also observed that there is sharp increase of this incidence in Manipur and Meghalaya since 2005 and 2006, respectively. Arunachal Pradesh does not depict any distinctive pattern (Table 2).

Table 2

Incidences of Atrocities by Husband and Relatives in Northeast Region, 2002–11

Year	*Arunachal Pradesh*	*Assam*	*Manipur*	*Meghalaya*	*Mizoram*	*Nagaland*	*Tripura*
2011	18	5,246	39	21	9	1	702
2010	12	5,410	18	24	3	1	937
2009	13	4,398	25	24	4	0	815
2008	13	3,478	28	32	5	4	735
2007	20	3,000	15	19	2	0	545

Cont'd...

...Cont'd

2006	14	2,548	10	13	1	3	471
2005	9	2,206	20	3	0	0	439
2004	4	1,945	2	5	0	0	302
2003	14	1,808	4	4	3	0	247
2002	13	1,694	10	0	3	0	236

Source: National Crime Record Bureau (2002–12).

Rate of Atrocities by Husband and Relatives in Northeast India

The rate of occurrence of atrocities by husband and relatives is analysed on the basis of the national scenario. It is observed that it is highest in Tripura followed by Assam. At the same time, there is a great variation between these two states and the other states of the region. Manipur and Meghalaya are portraying a creeping growth of the pattern of its occurrences since last 10 years. Yet again there is very dawdling growth of the rate of occurrence in Mizoram since 2006, however, not a steady one. Nagaland, yet again, has the lowest rate of occurrence of domestic violence in the region (Table 3).

The graphical representation of the rate of atrocities (Figure 2) provides more insight into its pattern of occurrence. It highlights that there is a sharp increase in its rate in Tripura. Again the variation of it occurrence between Tripura and Assam gradually widen within these 10 years though there is a sharp dip in 2011 in case of Tripura. The proportion of occurrence of the rest of the states is squeezed in the periphery in respect of the variation within the region. The analysis of the data clearly represents large variation and a wide disparity of the pattern of occurrence of domestic violence in the region, as well.

Table 3

Rate of Atrocities by Husband and Relatives, 2002–11

Year	*Arunachal Pradesh*	*Assam*	*Manipur*	*Meghalaya*	*Mizoram*	*Nagaland*	*Tripura*
2011	1.3	16.8	1.4	0.7	0.8	0.1	19.1
2010	1	17.5	0.7	0.9	0.3	0	26
2009	1.1	14.4	0.9	0.9	0.4	0	22.8
2008	1.1	11.6	1.1	1.3	0.5	0.2	20.9
2007	1.7	10.1	0.6	0.8	0.2	0	15
2006	1.2	8.7	0.4	0.5	0.1	0.1	13.7
2005	0.8	7.7	0.8	0.1	0	0	12.9
2004	0.3	6.9	0.1	0.2	0	0	9
2003	1.2	6.5	0.2	0.2	0.3	0	7.5
2002	1.2	6.2	0.4	0	0.3	0	7.3

Source: National Crime Record Bureau (2002–2012).

Figure 2

Rate of Atrocities by Husband and Relatives in Northeast Region, 2002–11

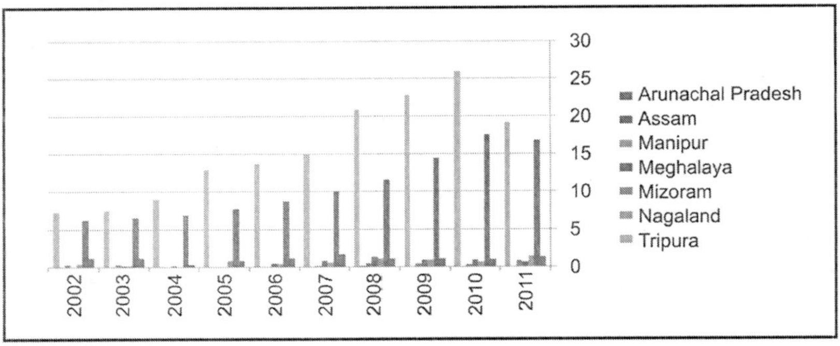

Source: As calculated by the author.

Domestic Violence and Ethnic Background of the Respondent

Culture is an acquired tread. It is noticed that the ethnic groups are governed by certain cultural ethos which may generate certain types of crimes at times and or may obliterate certain types of crimes to certain extent. Does culture and ethnicity facilitates certain types of gender specific crimes or do they have roots to crimes against women? Domestic violence on the basis of the ethnic background of the respondents is essential to be investigated and thereby probe into these queries.

To investigate this sensitive but essential arena on the basis of ethnic background of the respondents, 8.33 per cent of the respondents belonging to Scheduled Tribes (ST), 20 per cent to Scheduled Caste, 5 per cent from Other Backward Classes (OBC) and 66.66 per cent belonging to general caste were interviewed. There is variation in the proportion of representation of the groups. This variation and non-uniformity reflects the ground reality. Even though the study was based on purposive sampling method, during the fieldwork there were hardly any women belonging to ST and OBC caste who could be interviewed. On the other hand, there was easy accessibility of victims of domestic violence belonging to general and Scheduled Caste.

Caste/Community and Types of Crimes

Physical Violence by Husband

All forms of physical violence by husband exist among the Scheduled Caste. However, battery is the highest form of physical torture followed by attempt to murder which is 41.67 per cent, highest among all the communities. Physical disfiguring of all nature such as branding with hot objects, disfiguring due to excessive battery are common among majority of them, even though it exists also among the general caste women. Few of these women have lost their hearing ability and eyesight due to excessive battery.

Among the general caste, battery (82.5%) and physical disfiguring (27.5%) are high. Twenty per cent of them are attempt to murder. Acts of attempt to burn and other forms of crimes exist in lesser number among these women.

Among the Other Backward Classes, 66.67 per cent of the acts are that of battery and 33.33 per cent of them are attempt to murder. Besides these two crimes, the other forms of violence do not exist among the Other Backward Classes.

Among the Scheduled Tribes, physical violence by husband is considerably low even though 20 per cent of them are attempt to murder and 8.33 per cent are attempt to burn. It is important to note here that majority of these Scheduled Tribe women are married to spouses belonging to non-Scheduled Tribe community (Scheduled Caste and general caste). The high proportion of occurrence of these two crimes within this group can be attributed to this reason. It can be considered so because these crimes, though not very common, prevail to a certain extent within these communities.

When compared between the castes, it is observed that all forms of crimes are high among the Scheduled Caste. The Scheduled Caste belongs to the lower caste of the Hindu community. They are often seen to mimic the upper caste at their own level. Very often they are not able to imitate them totally due to their lack of adequate educational qualification and economic condition. These often act as factors of violence against them. On the contrary, physical violence by husband is low among the Scheduled Tribes. Usually among the Scheduled Tribes the status of the spouses are more or less equal. Both of them are engaged in physical labour and economic activities. The women also share a lot of responsibilities in the household activity and in the decision-making process both within and outside the home. As mentioned earlier, during the field study, very few Scheduled Tribe women were intercepted who were victims of domestic violence. And those interviewed had a common ground among them; they were married to non-Scheduled Tribe family. Existence of violent crimes against them such as attempt to murder and attempt to burn is maybe because of this cause.

Table 4

Physical Violence by Husband by Caste/Community

Caste/ Community	*Percentage*	*Battery*	*Physical disfiguring*	*Attempted to burn*	*Attempted to murder*	*Others*
ST	8.33	40.00	0.00	20.00	20.00	0.00
SC	20.00	83.33	33.33	8.33	41.67	8.33
OBC	5.00	66.67	0.00	0.00	33.33	0.00
General	66.66	82.50	27.50	2.50	20.00	10.00
Total	100	78.33	25.00	5.00	25.00	8.33

Source: Based on Field Work by Author.

Mental Violence by Husband

All forms of mental violence by husband exist among all the castes and communities, though in different proportions (Table 6). In this study, persistent quarrelling between the spouses which affects her psychologically is taken into consideration for this study. Quarrels and cursing/swearing are high among the Scheduled Caste whereas, emotional blackmailing is substantially high (60%) among the Scheduled Tribe women. Majority of them are emotionally blackmailed by their husband for dowry whenever they undergo financial problems. They are often threatened of breaching their nuptial relationship or leaving her at her own fate. Among the Other Backward Classes, all forms of mental violence are of equal proportion except emotional blackmailing, which is low (33.33%). Among the general caste cursing/swearing is high and emotional blackmailing is low.

When compared between the caste/community, it is noticed that all forms of mental violence by husband are substantially high among the Scheduled Caste, except threat of assault. The next community where almost all forms of mental violence are high is among the general caste. It is because the general caste in this study comprises women belonging to different linguistic groups and religions among whom the pattern of occurrence of atrocity are diverse.

Table 5

Mental Violence by Husband by Caste/Community

Caste/ Community	*Quarrels*	*Cursing/ swearing*	*Use abusive language*	*Emotionally blackmail*	*Threat of assault*	*Others*
ST	40.00	40.00	40.00	60.00	20.00	20.00
SC	91.67	91.67	83.33	50.00	50.00	16.67
OBC	66.67	66.67	66.67	33.33	66.67	0.00
General	77.50	80.00	72.50	45.00	62.50	17.50
Total	76.67	78.33	71.67	46.67	56.67	16.67

Source: Based on Field Work by Author.

Among the Scheduled Tribe respondents, mental violence by husband is lower when compared between the different communities. During the study, it was observed that the Scheduled Tribe victims usually remain dormant during the initial stage of their abusive life but often resisted aggressively as it prolongs. In fact, they are not passive and are reluctant to accept the harassment as a part of their married life unlike the victims belonging to general caste.

Sexual Violence by Husband

Sexual violence by husband exists only among the general caste. There are more cases of sexual abuse among them than sexual harassment. Other forms of sexual violence such as indulgence into prostitution and immoral trafficking of women exist among the general caste. These women are married and later on forced into sex work by their husbands, who otherwise can be considered pimp of the sex worker racketeer. However, all of these women were able to escape from the clutches of these men who are now either remarried or planning to remarry. Very interesting commonalities exist among all these women. They all belong to economically backward families and come from rural set-up. They do not have any male member in their family and happen to belong to a family where all of them are unmarried daughters staying with their widowed mother. They are married off within a very short notice. The study indicates that women with the above mentioned background become easy target for immoral trafficking and are more vulnerable.

There are certain deep rooted cultural significances of marriage in Indian society which can be attributed to the evolution of this type of situation. Not only is there something unnatural about a delay in or absence of marriage but that such a situation is considered full of danger and risk to the reputation of the family. Moreover, it is impossible for young girls to escape the value of the married state. Marriage signifies good fortune and a state of bliss, whereas unmarried women are excluded from the 'auspicious' activities of the 'fortunate' women in certain society and are made to feel that there is something wrong with them (Dube, 1988). These values associated with married women in Hindu family in the Indian society drags women to other adversities and negative situations too. Few of these women are hauled to false marriages, they are married for few months and after a short span of conjugal life, the husband disappears. These women feel sexually exploited in the name of marriage. Prolong sexual abstinence in the form sexual violence emerged in this study and is categorised as other forms of sexual violence.

Time of Occurrences

Among the Scheduled Tribe victims, there are instances where the husband is unemployed or has started a small business after marriage, more often with the wife's parental financial support. Instead of earning on their own and being financially independent, they often insist their wives to bring money from their parental homes whenever they undergo any financial constrains. On such occasions, the husband gets drunk and physically abuses the wife when she goes against his will. On other occasions, when the husband is not drunk, she is mentally abused on all occasions for not meeting their financial demands. In this study, these types of prerequisites are considered as dowry demand. This type of stipulation also exists among other communities. But it is a common phenomenon within the Scheduled Tribe victims where the husband belongs to some other community. The dowry demand in most of these cases did not take place in the form of negotiation during the pre-marriage settlement as it takes place in rest of India. Here the woman is rebuked on different occasions for not bringing adequate dowry along with her. More so, during financial constrains of her husband and in-laws, she is expected to seek financial assistance from her natal home. There are also certain cases among the Scheduled Tribes where the victim is abused whenever the husband is drunk or when the family undergoes some financial problem. It is observed that the intensity and nature of violence becomes brutal when the husband is in drunken state in all the communities.

Among the Scheduled Caste, 8.33 per cent (only when alone) of them are those victims who were sexually exploited by the 'short term' husband. Most of these victims were sexually exploited when they were alone at home before their marriage. They were lured into marriage later on by their husband when the victim resisted to their perpetrator's sexual desire. All of these victims were around 16 years of age. Later on they were deserted by their husband after few months of stay. Among the Scheduled Caste, a large proportion of the victims were harassed during financial problems or when they were drunk more so because majority of them belongs to lower economic group. And it has been observed that drinking is a common habit among them.

Among the Other Backward Classes, the victim is abused more whenever they go through financial constrains or when they go against the will of their husband or in-laws. It is expected from the women to meet to all the demands of the husband and in-laws.

The women belonging to general caste are abused on varied occasions. But the violence is more when they go against the will of the husband or in-laws (40%) but more so on all occasions (42.5%). It is narrated by these victims that the atrocity usually starts from any petty reason and on any occasion. Usually it starts from quarrel and subsequently it intensifies and at the end the women is battered or physically tortured. The majority of these victims is educationally qualified and they want to have a view of their own or have their own way of life. They have or want to pursue a job. When they go against the will, more so, of the in-laws, they are abused, very often mentally.

Table 6

Occurrence of Crimes against Women by Caste/Community

Caste/ Community	*Only when Alone*	*Husband away from Home*	*Financial Problem*	*Drunk*	*Go against Will*	*On all Occasions*	*Others*
ST	0.00	0.00	40.00	20.00	20.00	60.00	0.00
SC	8.33	0.00	58.33	41.67	25.00	25.00	25.00
OBC	0.00	33.33	66.67	33.33	66.67	33.33	33.33
General	2.50	2.50	15.00	22.50	40.00	42.50	25.00
Total	3.33	3.33	28.33	26.67	36.67	40.00	23.33

Source: Based on Field Work by Author.

When compared between the communities it is observed that atrocities on the victim belonging to Scheduled Caste and Other Backward Classes are more when the perpetrator is drunk and during their financial problems whereas among the Scheduled Tribes and the general caste, it is less on these occasions. On the contrary, among these two communities, violence is exerted more on all occasions because of dowry demands and other reasons like illicit relation of the husband (Table 6).

Causes of Crimes against Women

It is interesting to note that atrocity due to financial problems and dowry is high and exist in same proportion among the Scheduled Tribes. These women are abused due to dowry demand which erupts whenever they undergo financial problems. A majority of them demanded the wife's parental property as dowry. Though the violence is due to dowry demands in 40 per cent of the cases, it can be emphasised here that these dowry demands emerges from the financial problems that the family face. The greed for dowry is also an emerging factor of domestic violence in an otherwise dowry less Northeast India, more so in Assam (Vauquline, 2012). Few of these women have undergone abusive life due to other financial problems too. Bigamy is another cause of violence against these women among the Scheduled Tribe respondents. In these cases, the husband has gone for his second marriage without the consent of his wife or has married without her knowledge. At times, the husband wants his first wife to leave the house or is away with his second wife. These women suffer from psychological as well as physical atrocities when the husband wants her to leave or to accept his bigamous relationship.

Among the Scheduled Caste, the causes of violence against the victims are varied and more due to financial problem and bigamy. A large proportion of the victims' husbands are engaged in illicit relation, which is another cause of violence against the victim. Usually when the cause of violence is dowry or illicit relationship, atrocity is exerted on the victim on all the occasions among all the communities. They are often threatened of being thrown out of their house. In certain instances they are driven out from the house in the middle of the night and in other junctures too. Throwing the women out from the house for any reason is a common phenomena and cut across all economic groups and in all communities. Analysing the narratives of these women' it is realised that these women's worst fear is being dragged out from their home. They fell shelter less and exposed to a hostile and unsafe place. Those women who are from lower economic group in this community are often battered when they refuse to part their earning with the husband. Their husbands are either alcoholic or are engaged in illicit relations or both.

Alcoholism, dowry and financial problems are the cause of violence among the Other Backward Classes. Instances of illicit relation is high among all the communities but it is utterly common among the Other Backward Classes. In few of these cases the husband expects the wife and the children (if they happen to be girl child) to earn for the family. The atrocities intensify on the women if there are more or only daughters in the family. However, this type of attitude towards a girl child is more common among the lower economic group but is also prevalent among the other economic classes though in lower proportion.

There are different types of causes of violence against the victim among the general caste but dowry is one of the major causes (25%). It is high among them because it includes the Bengali community (both the Hindus and the Muslims) where this evil practice is prevalent and also the Assamese community where dowry demands after the marriage are emerging. For a few general caste respondents, the cause of violence is the suspicious nature of the husband and most of these husbands suffer from inferiority complex. In most of these instances, the wife is in better position economically as well as socially. Frustration is the cause of violence among all the community where the husband is unemployed or when he is not able to perform as per his expectations or excel in his workplace (among the middle income families). Atrocities due to stress and exertion are common among the general class communities.

When a comparative study is made between the communities, it is observed that violence because of alcoholism is high among the Other Backward Classes (33.33%) and the Scheduled Caste (25%) but it exists among the other castes/communities also. Violence due to dowry is high among the Scheduled Tribes (40%) and the Other Backward Classes (33.33%). Atrocities due to financial problem are high among the

Scheduled Tribes (80%) and the Scheduled Caste (50%) and it is also due to illicit relation of the husband. Either it is bigamy or illicit relation in whatever community, the victim is either expected to accept the relation or leave the house if she disagrees. However, in this regard (illicit relation) there is a complete contrast between the Scheduled Tribe communities and the other communities. Except the Scheduled Tribe community, illicit relation (which is classified as others) is one of the major causes of violence among the other communities. Among the Scheduled Tribes the women has greater liberty and it is acceptable for the women to break free from their marital engagement due to disagreement between spouses. They are never forced to marry against their will nor forced to stay within a disrupted married life (Mitra, 2007). These can be attributed to low rate of occurrence of crimes against women and more so domestic violence in the states on Nagaland, Mizoram, Arunachal Pradesh, Manipur and Meghalaya where the proportion of Scheduled Tribe population is much high. In contrast, Assam and Tripura, has low proportion of Scheduled Tribes population but has higher rates of crimes against women. In an early study, Furer-Haimendorf (1933) wrote in *Naked Nagas* about the Naga women in the Northeastern states, 'many women in most civilised parts of India may well envy the women of Naga Hills, their high status and their free happy life and if you measure the cultural level of the people by the social position and personal freedom of its women you will think twice before looking down on the Nagas as savages' (p. 101).

Perceived Solution to the Problem

A high proportion of the Scheduled Tribe victims feel that being economically independent will improve their situation to a great extent. Few of them have trained themselves in vocational training courses and have pursued higher education to stand on their own feet. This is a common view also among the general caste women. For many of them adequate educational qualification has built up their confidence to confront the abusive situation. Among the Scheduled Tribes, living with their parental family is also a perceived solution (40%). Their parental family strongly support and encourage them to come out from their abusive life and stay with them. This type of parental support is, however, lacking among the general caste and fails to exist among the Scheduled Caste and the Other Backward Classes. On the contrary, these women are asked by their parents to compromise with their situation. They are reluctant to bring back their married daughter home, fearing loss of social image in the society and even social ostracism. From the narratives it is disclosed that at this juncture the parental support of the victims is very essential because it gives them confidence to confront violence against them. It not only provides an alternative place of shelter but also a place to fall back upon for support at the time of distress. It is also observed in the study that severe forms of physical violence fail to prevail where the parental support is provided. However, the process of socialisation of a girl child of considering themselves as temporary member of their natal home is so strong among the Scheduled Caste and Other Backward Classes that these women are themselves reluctant to go back to their parental home. These women usually compromise with their situation in most instances. Few of these women haven't even disclosed their abusive life to their parents.

Among the Scheduled Caste, living a separate life is a solution to the problem of 66.67 per cent of the women. Most of these victims are employed and those who are unemployed, being economically independent is not a difficult task for them as they are willing to take up even low paid or odd jobs. It is for this reason they prefer to live on their own than to compromise with their abusive life.

Among the Other Backward Classes being economically independent and living on their own is their only perceived solution. They are victims of severe forms of violence. There are women in this group who are braded with hot objects by their husband, whose ears are chopped off and even physically handicapped (broken arms and legs) during the acts of violence perpetuated on them. They feel that their level of tolerance of abusive life has saturated and they want to come out from these abusive situation for themselves and also for the sake of their children. (However no follow-up study was carried out to study their ultimate decision).

Only a few general caste women want to come out from the joint family (7.5%) to lessen their atrocity. But a large proportion of them feel that being economically independent and living on their own will help them to be away from their abusive life. At the same time, the equal proportion of the general caste victims wants to compromise with their husband/in-laws. And majority of them are Bengali speaking Hindu as well as Muslim respondents who prefer to compromise with their husband/in-laws not for financial security but for physical, psychological and social security provided by the marriage. Few of these women compromise because of their children. They feel that their children's life will be at stake if they move out from their family and as they are not financially strong to provide adequate economic support. There are a few of them (general caste) who want to remarry or have remarried to come out from their abusive life. This is a common view and a solution more so among the qualified Muslim respondents.

Between the communities, a high proportion of 40 per cent of the respondents among the Scheduled Tribe victims prefer to come to a compromise with their husband/in-laws. They are those victims who are abused due to financial problems and alcoholism. The Scheduled Caste and the Other Backward Classes respondents feel that living a separated life is an easy exit from their atrocities of life. But majority of the victims from all the castes and communities feels strongly that being economically independent is their ultimate solution.

Narratives of the Victims

A narrative provides an in-depth understanding of the situation. It is a popular feminist researcher methodology which can also be considered as the 'voice of the women'. Feminist narratives' interpretation may create a context in which non-unitary subjectivity can be engaged as the grounding for the study of women's life and experiences (Bloom, 1998). These case studies in the form of narratives are essential as they give a detailed account of the nature, intensity, causes and consequences of the violence against women and helps in developing 'understanding' the issues involved. It also highlights the family backgrounds of both the victims and the perpetrators, which may influence the actual acts of violence against women. It also reveals the hidden factors and circumstances, which cannot be totally brought into light by statistical analysis alone. For purposes of keeping the identity of the victims confidential, the specific victims have been provided with pseudonyms, like Ms A, Ms B, and so on.

Narrative 1

Mrs A is 40 years old. She migrated to Guwahati from a small village after her marriage. She is married for more than 10 years but now she is staying on her own with her two daughters. She is an Assamese Hindu belonging to the Scheduled Caste community. She has not completed her metric level education and is employed in a private company. She got married into a middle class family. Her husband is a government employee. She was born into a middle class family, brought up by a step-mother.

She narrates, 'After my (arranged) marriage, I came to know that my husband is an alcoholic and spends all his earnings on drinks. This (his alcoholic addiction) was never revealed to me before our marriage. Moreover, I had disappointments over economic circumstances of my husband. Few months after our marriage, marital discord arose. He used to ask me to bring money from my parents as their economic condition was stronger than ours. Initially with great reluctance and out of fear I used to do whatever he asked me to do. Gradually it became a regular affair and I started to decline. If I refused, he used to slap me, pull my hair off and physically assault me. Consistent physical abuse led to my loosing a child in pregnancy. It was a daily affair for him, coming home drunk and assaulting me. I used to feel very humiliated in front of my daughters and our neighbour. I stopped going out from the house at all. My husband once even attempted to murder me by burning me alive! Since my existence became impossible with constant physical violence and torture, I parted ways, with a legal separation. It took a lot of courage to do so because I was all alone with two young daughters and no source of earning. My parents sympathised with me but I felt they that still wanted me to stay with my husband. I tolerated all his abuses for more than 10 years and for how long could I? I had to do this for my daughters. They used to shiver with fear when they would see their father all drunk and beating me up. Subsequently, I managed to get a job and gain economic independence to look after myself and my daughters. I want them to live in a better and safe environment'.

The narrative illustrates that Mrs A compromised with her situation till she could and she decided to come out from these situations not for herself but for her daughters. An Indian woman is always brought up to think for others first; serve her husband, her in-laws and children. She is expected to sacrifice for her family and consider her husband less as a partner and more as someone superior to her. It was these types of 'sanskritisation' which had an impact on her decision to come out from her marital code even though it went on for long 10 years.

Narrative 2

Mrs B is 30 years old. She belongs to general caste. She stayed with her husband for less than three years after her marriage and is now staying with her own parents. She is a Bengali Hindu. She is a graduate and was staying in a joint family (seven members) after her marriage. They were a middle class family and all of them were literate. Except Mrs B and her mother-in-law, all of them were employed.

Mrs B narrates, 'From the very day of my marriage conflict between the families started. My in-laws and their relatives were not satisfied with the food provided and the hospitality extended to the groom's side on our wedding day. In my in-laws house, I was beaten up a number of times by my mother-in-law and sisters-in-law and sometimes even by my husband. They used to scold and curse me and say rude things about my parents for not bringing sufficient dowry. This used to be a frequent affair but more when her husband was not at home. I was called 'evil' and cursed all the time. They demanded refrigerator, scooter and television in dowry, even though they had all of these in their house. I suspected all these were meant for the dowry of my sister-in-law who was yet to get married. My mother-in-law took away all my jewellery from me on the very next day of my marriage. My parents were aware of my abusive life but they could do little as my father was a retired person and two of my younger sisters were yet to be married off. They too were ill treated whenever they came to visit me. Incidentally, one day, my husband left me in my parental house. When days passed by and when there was no communication from my in-laws side my father gave a courtesy call. It was then my mother-in-law asked my father not to bring me back and refused to accept me as their daughter-in-law and informed that they were preparing for my husband's second marriage. My father insisted to take me but my mother refused to send me back, fearing they would kill me. My parents have filed a case against my husband and my in-laws for injustice done to me. Since then I am with my parents but I feel guilty of being a burden on them. I wish I could again go back and live with my husband but not again in a joint family. I fear that my broken marriage will lower my reputation in the society. I lack confidence in myself even though I am educated, maybe because I am not economically independent and was never outgoing since my childhood. Since we were all daughters, our parents brought us up with many restrictions'.

This is a case of atrocities due to dowry. It also illustrated the power relationship that exists in Indian joint family set-up. She belongs more to the family (joint) than to the husband. Mrs B felt that if she breaks free from this 'position of common ownership' her conjugal life would be better. For which, even after her harassment, she still wants to go back to her husband and start a new living with him in a nuclear family. As very rightly said, 'the traditional patrifocal family is based upon age and gender hierarchies of authorities: older members have authority over younger ones and males have authorities over females. Since these two hierarchies cross-cut each other, both men and women have authority in some context but are subordinate in other contexts'. Ideally, these relationships of dominance-subordination should take precedence over relationships based upon emotional bonds, between a husband and a wife (Seymour, 1999: 272).

Narrative 3

Mrs C is 20 years old. She is married for less than three years. She is now staying with her mother. She is a Hindu belonging to the Scheduled Tribe (Bodo) community. She is under-graduate and is working for a private company. She is now earning enough to meet her needs. She is the youngest of the three daughters of her widowed mother.

Mrs C states, 'I got married when I was only 17 years old. It was a love marriage. Both of us belonged to middle class families and were living in a nuclear family. Since my husband was unemployed, my mother assisted him financially to start a business. Marital disputes began hardly after one month of our marriage. He used to ask me to bring money from my mother and if I refused I was always beaten up. He was not interested in his business and so always faced financial constrains in his work, expecting my mother to help him all the time. He frequently started demanding money from my mother whenever we had any financial problem. I used to get petrified and never dared to disagree. My mother-in-law, whenever she visited us, also used to accuse me for not bringing any dowry. Subsequently, one day he demanded my parental property to be transferred in his name which I refused to convey to my mother at any cost. He felt that he has right to ask so because he was the eldest son-in-law and that I did not have any brother. He wanted this property (as dowry) as I did not bring anything along with me at the time of my wedding. I was kicked, beaten up, slapped and all sort of physical assault and mental abuse was exerted on me for more than two years over this issue. I never uttered a word about my torture to any of my family members. On one instance, my mother happened to visit me while I was battered and was horrified seeing the aggressive nature of my husband. Fearing that he might murder me in some instance she brought me home. Later on, on the insistence of my mother and other family members, I registered a case against him and my mother-in-law for atrocity for dowry and have asked for legal separation. As of now, I want to stay with my mother and take care of her as I am economically independent. But later on I may remarry if I meet a better person'.

This type of support from the paternal home to a married girl child is a common feature within the Scheduled Tribe community. There aren't distinctions between a male and a female child. Both are expected to work and support the family. Neither is it a shame to break free from a disturbed married life (both for a boy and a girl). Mrs C's mother did not hesitate to bring back her daughter home because she expected Mrs C to earn for herself and thereby Mrs C never considered herself as a burden on her mother. She felt that she belonged to her natal home because of this attitude of her mother and the type of society where she socialised. All these to a great extent contribute towards low rate of domestic violence among the Scheduled Tribe community. There is existence of greater mutual understanding and respect amongst Scheduled Tribe community.

Narrative 4

Mrs D is 40 years old. She was married for more than 10 years but is separated and is staying on her own now. She is Assamese Hindu belonging to general caste. She is a government employee. They were staying in a nuclear family. They have a son.

Mrs D states, 'Both of us were working in the same department (Police) and were staying in the quarter. During the first few years of our marriage everything was sailing smoothly. Later on my husband indulged into alcoholism. I was frequently battered from then onwards in his drunken state. Later, as it was happening very frequently, I too used to hit back but was always overpowered by him. Once he kicked me so hard that my ribs were fractured. The harassment stopped for a period when he was posted in some other place. Few months after his transfer one of my colleagues, who was posted in the same place, informed me of my husband having an illicit relation with a girl of that locality. I refused to believe her in the first instance. Later on, when few more of my colleagues conveyed the same thing about my husband, I decided to visit my husband without informing him. When I visited him, I came to know that they had even secretly got married in a temple and the other lady was expecting his child. At that moment I felt devastated thinking about my future and our only son. I felt shattered. When I returned back to my workplace, my colleagues advised me that I should file a case against him and seek for legal separation. I did so as I had nothing to fear. I have a job to live on my own. Now we are legally separated and my husband is compelled by the court to provide maintenance to our son and the property right to our son. Being in the Police Department helped me a lot and gave me confidence. I was able to get what I wanted because I was aware of the laws and the procedures to procure them'.

This case indicates various aspects. Mrs D is courageous and bold. This attribute of her has to do with her job, which is a secured one. This makes her feel empowered and at the same time secured even without a partner. She felt shattered initially but with the support that she received from her peers changed her attitude to her situation completely. Later on, she went beyond and sought justice for her son too. This case clearly illustrates the sense of empowerment that women possess through her job and the exposures and experiences that she achieves along with it.

Conclusion

The position and identity of women in the Northeast India is unique and diverse indeed. The region encompasses two states with the highest number of instances of crime against women in the country (Tripura and Assam) and on the other hand, the least crimes against women states too (Nagaland, Mizoram Arunachal Pradesh). These least CAW areas are the Scheduled tribe dominated states and the CAW prone areas have least proportion of Scheduled tribe population of the region. It is amply clear that in communities where women's work participation is nearly equal to men; there is little spousal discord, i.e. the families in Scheduled Tribes, where wife beating is rare, and interference of in-laws totally absent. It is also for the fact, it indicates a truly shared life between the spouses, both working together to make that life possible. If, it does not work, then the exit is simple and without much fanfare. When one looks at the general population irrespective of caste or religion, the husband sits on a moral high ground being the 'provider' in the family, thus, the one to be heeded on all counts, reasonable or otherwise. Second, the exit out of a messy married life is awfully difficult and becomes a public nuisance for the women; many dread it and prefer to live a life without much interest. The tribal model is simple: men and women work equally; the marital entry is easy, so is the exit, there is no burden, there is no dependence of one on the other.

The causes of violence against women in the most crime prone area are also distinctive (alcoholism and illicit relationship). Stress, anxiety and financial constrains, the ill-effects of modernisation, contributes towards gender violence to a great extent. Alcoholism is the driving force to brutality in most cases. Atrocities due to dowry do occur in the study area and is a growing threat though it is assumed never to be a part of marital ritual and custom of this region (Vauquline, 2012). The major concern that emerges from this study is that crimes against women are on rise in the states of Assam, Tripura and Meghalaya even after the enactment of several legal provisions for protection of women more so against domestic violence. At the same time the study reveals that of the 60 women interviewed for this study only 6 of them registered their cases in the police stations. Of these six cases only three were registered by the victim themselves, rest by their relatives, parents and neighbour. Thereby it can be emphasised here that the ground reality regarding the number of incidences of crimes against women is far higher than what is depicted by official statistics.

As is clear from the study, when women are in some form of employment or are earning and have independent incomes, they are more than willing to break out of an abusive family life either to live on their own or start life all over again. A large section of these women are more than willing to pursue their education or undergo vocational courses. 'Gainful employment' of women can correct this situation too as in declining sex ratio. It can serve as a means of making a living on which women can rely, making them less vulnerable (Sen, 1990). So, the crux of the solution to the problem to a great extent lies with women's education and independent economic standing, which will not be forthcoming without education. Education also creates awareness about rights of the women and the general role they play and the responsibilities of the state towards the citizens; thus, it makes them confront unreasonable spouses or intimidating in-laws by making them self-confident. It, no doubt, has acted as solution to these women. However, the ultimate solution lies on how a woman is perceived and acquires her identity in the society. Are women perceived as equal human beings and get their due unconditionally? Why do they have to owe the privileges only after performing the roles as defined by the society? Why it is an accepted behaviour of a man to be violent and women to be submissive and sacrificing? Why are there these different sets of codes of conduct for men and women? Is it necessary to have different processes of socialisation for men and women? Why is it there power politics within the family? Once we ponder over these queries we can obtain certain concrete solutions to violence against women. The existing legal provisions should have by now reduced the rate of crimes against women in the country. On the contrary, it is on rise because the general mindset towards women has remained the same in the Indian society as it was in the yester years. The women of modern India have definitely taken strides towards development but the general attitude towards women is still rigid, orthodox, conservative, insensitive and unprogressive. Once these barriers are overcome, women will definitely have safer homes to live in.

References

Acker, J. (1990) 'Hierarchies, Jobs, Bodies: A Theory of Gendered Organizations'. *Gender & Society* 4(2). pp. 139–58.

Adkins, L. (1992) 'Sexual Work and the Employment of Women in the Service Industries' in M. Savage and A. Witz (eds) *Gender and Bureaucracy.* Oxford: Blackwell. pp. 207–28.

Arvey, R.D. and M.A. Cavanaugh. (1995) 'Using Surveys to Assess the Prevalence of Sexual Harassment: Some Methodological Problems'. *J. Soc.* 51(1). pp. 39–52.

Bloom, L.R. (1998) *Under the Sign of Hope: Feminist Research Methodology and Narrative Interpretation*. Albany: State University of New York Press.

Code, L. (2000) *Encyclopedia of Feminist Theories.* London and New York: Routledge Taylor & Francis Group.

Coveney, L. and et al. (1984) *The Sexuality Papers: Male Sexuality and the Social Control of Women.* London: Hutchinson.

Dube, L. (1988) 'On the Construction of Gender Hindu Girls in Patrilineal India'. *Economic and Political Weekly,* Vol. 23, No. 18, 30 April, pp WS 11-WS 15. Retrieved from http://www.jstor.org/stable/4378429.

Garfinkel, H. (1967) *Studies in Ethnomethodological,* Englewood Cliffs, NJ: Prentice Hall.

Hutton, J.H. (1921) *The Sema Nagas.* New Delhi: Oxford University Press.

Karlekar, M. (2008) 'Domestic Violence' in Mary E. John (ed.) *Women Studies in India,* London: Penguin Books. p. 241.

Kelkar, G. (1991) *Violence against Women in India: Perspectives and Strategies.* Bangkok: Asian Institute of Technology.

Kessler, S.J. and Wendy Mc Kenna. (1978) *Gender: An Ethnomethodological Approach.* New York: Wiley.

Krishnaraj, M. (1991) *Women and Violence: A Country Report.* Bombay SNDT Women's University. Bombay: Research Centre for Women's Studies. pp. 11–16.

Lalkima, C. (2009) *Changing Status of Women in North-Eastern States.* Mittal Publications: New Delhi.

Maharatna, A. (1998) *On Tribal Fertility in the Late Nineteenth and Early Twentieth Century India.* Working Paper Series No. 98.0. Harvard: Harvard Center for Population and Development Studies, Harvard University.

Mitra, A. (2007) 'The Status of Women among the Scheduled Tribes in India'. *The Journal of Socio-Economics.* doi: 10.1016/j.socec.2006.12.077.

National Crimes Record Bureau. (2002–2012) Ministry of Home Affairs, Govt. of India, N. Delhi.

Savage, M. and A. Witz. (1992) *Gender and Bureaucracy.* Oxford: Blackwell.

Sen, A. (1999) More than 100 Million Women are Missing. *The New York Review of Books,* Vol 37, Dec 20, 1999. Retrieved from http://ucatlas.ucsc.edu/gender/Sen100M.html.

Seymour, S.C. (1999) *Women, Family and Child Care in India: A World in Transitional.* Cambridge: Cambridge University Press.

Subrahmanian, R. (1995) 'Combating Violence Against Women: Finding Ways Forward'. *The Administrator,* Vol. XI, July–September. pp. 145–159.

Tong, M. (1995) *Feminist Thought a Comprehensive Introduction.* London: Routledge.

Vauquline, P. (2007) *Gender Related Crimes in Greater Guwahati Urban Area* (Unpublished Ph.D thesis). Shillong: North Eastern Hills University.

Vauquline, P. (2012) 'Growing Incidences of Gender Crimes and Dowry Deaths: An Evolving Threat to Assamese Society'. *Asian Journal of Research in Social Sciences and Humanities,* Vol. 2, October 2012.

Von Furer-Haimendorf, C. (1933) *Naked Nagas.* Calcutta: Thacker, Spink and Co.

Williams, C. (1997) 'Sexual Harassment in Organizations: A Critique of Current Research and Policy'. *Sexuality Culture* 1. pp. 19–43.

West, C. and D. Zimmerman. (1987) 'Doing Gender'. *Gender and Society* 1: 121–151. Retrieved from doi: 10.1177/0891243287001002002, http://gas.sagepub.com/content/1/2/125.

8

Tribal History and Identity

Challenges of Northeast India

WALTER FERNANDES

Amid a general feeling that the Northeast is a zone of conflicts in which some efforts are made for peace, one needs to ask, 'Where do the tribal communities of the region stand today? Why do the conflicts arise?' An answer to this question requires an understanding of their past history and present situation in order to move towards the future. One sees in the past of the region, tribal traditions followed by change of religion, i.e. their Christianisation or Hinduisation, modern inputs like education and commercial forces, the political processes, laws and other components impacting their everyday life and the value system guiding them. This paper will reflect on some of them.

History and Identity to the Fore

Since one cannot understand the present without a glimpse of the past this section will attempt to take a look at the tribal traditions of the Northeast to see their relevance for the present. More than 200 tribes of the Northeast do not have a single tradition but have some commonalities amid diversity. One can, therefore, only identify some salient features of commonality in their traditions.

Community, Resource Management and Equity

Amid the diversity of tribal traditions of the region, one can identify three common traits. The first is the sustainable use of the natural resources composed of forests, land and water sources. They were managed as renewable according to human needs and environmental imperatives because they were the sustenance of their communities. The community dimension was stronger among the tribes practising *jhum* (shifting cultivation) than among those with a strong individual orientation. The former did not reject individual ownership totally. Only a few like the CPR dependent Aka of Arunachal Pradesh lacked the very concept of individual ownership and had only usufruct rights. In the *jhum* season, every family cultivated as much land as it required for its sustenance. After the harvest or the three-year cycle that plot reverted to the community (Fernandes, Pereira and Khatso, 2007: 8–9). Most other tribes like the Angami of Nagaland, the Khasi of Meghalaya and the Dimasa of Assam combined individual with clan or village ownership. But the families with individual assets managed them too within a community ethos, according to their customary law (Nongkynrih, 2009).

Secondly, the community was partially exclusive. It was exclusive in the sense that resource management was geared to the needs of one tribe but it was inclusive in the sense that the equity it practised was inter-generational. Their resource management included not merely the present but also the past and the future generations. Their customary laws ensured that they treated the resources as a livelihood that had come down from the past to be used according to present needs and environmental imperatives and preserved for posterity. Thus, the tradition of most tribes in the Northeast combined present sharing with future security, i.e. intra and inter-generational equity (Roy, 2005: 10–11). But both sharing and equity that were intrinsic to the system were within the tribe. Each tribe exercised exclusive control over its area in which it lived and the customary law was specific to it. Every member of the tribe was equal but equality and sharing did not extend to other tribes (Chakraborty, 2006: 69–72). Thus, the tribe had a value system of equity and sharing but with limitations.

Linked to the community was the third feature of the relatively high status of women compared to their counterparts in caste societies. No tribe treated women as equal to men. All the tribes, even the matrilineal ones, were patriarchal. But as long the resource is community managed, women exercised partial control over it because of the gender-based division of power between the family and social spheres. In most tribes, the village council, made up of men alone controlled the common property resources (CPR). But unlike in caste societies and in settled agriculture, where the man controls both the family and social spheres, in the tradition of most tribes, the woman controlled the family economy and production. The man represented it in his society (Menon, 1995: 101–102).

An example of the gendered division of work is *jhum* on which some 25 per cent of the tribals in India as a whole and 90 per cent in the Northeast have traditionally sustained themselves (Roy Burman, 1993: 176–177). Decision-making and work in this form of cultivation symbolised all three features given above. Traditionally the village council decided which plot to cultivate in a given year, determined the amount of land to be allotted to each family according to the number of mouths to feed and decided which family with excess adults would assist which one with a deficit of workers. After it the man of the house chose the plot his family would cultivate that year and performed religious rites to mark the beginning of cultivation. The woman then took charge of it and organised work (Gangwar and Ramakrishnan, 1992). As a result, work division was more equitable from a gender perspective in *jhum* than in settled agriculture. In *jhum* men control the resource and women are in charge of production. In settled agriculture, the man owns land, takes decisions on the crops to grow and determines the division of work. Men do work like ploughing that is considered difficult and allot to women tasks that involve standing in wet fields and bending for a long time (Misra, 2000: 74–77).

Resource, Customary Law and Identity

Basic to this division of work and the relatively high status of women is the separation of the family and social spheres. Women were the decision-makers in the family economy and production and men controlled the resource and social institutions. Since the resources were their sustenance, i.e. the centre of their culture, economy, social systems and identity men managed them equitably. Their customary law that was linked to resource management bound these components and controlled their behaviour, male-female relations, marriage, child upbringing, inheritance and division of political and social power. The village council made up of men alone controlled the CPRs. Men also interpreted the customary law. This combination of economic and political power symbolised the control they exercised over their societies and their patriarchal nature of the tribe.

Inheritance too was largely on male lines but its norms differed from tribe to tribe. The Angami woman cannot inherit clan property but her parents can gift her acquired land. If the man dies without a son his inheritance goes to his closest male relative (Fernandes and Barbora, 2002: 115–116). Among the Dimasa, the daughter can inherit her father's property if he dies without a son (Barpujari, 1997). In the Gallong tribe of Arunachal Pradesh, the girl enjoys some rights in her parental home till she becomes a mother. But among them (Norbu, 1997: 113–114) as well as the Minyong (Mitkong, 1997: 136–139) sons inherit land. The Mizo too are patrilineal but in the absence of male relatives, a woman inherits to the exclusion of distant kinsmen [Rule 109 (2)]. 'In the case of more than one daughter the youngest daughter will be given first preference as in the case of sons' [Rule 109 (10)] (Das, 1990: 167–170). The Khasi, Jaintia and Garo of Meghalaya are matrilineal. One of the daughters is the heiress but she does not have as much power as female inheritance would indicate.

Some of her male relatives control her property. She needs their consent to part with it (Syiem, 1992: 24). Heavy responsibilities are laid on her to ensure the welfare of the family. She looks after her aged parents but men manage most of the wealth and their society (Gassah, 1992: 42–43). Thus, equity was conditional. A family was ensured its material needs but power was hierarchical and male-centred.

Legitimising the Value System

Within these limitations, the tribes legitimised their value system through myths of origin and divine intervention. But there was a major difference between the tribes of Central India and those of the Northeast. The sacred groves and myths of origin belonged mostly to Central India. Their myths centred round the origin of the tribe or clan from an animal or a plant that they venerated and protected. They had sacred groves to which they accorded protection. Among them were the *sasan* or burial ground of their ancestors, the *sarna* where the teenagers were trained into adulthood and the *akhara* or the dancing ground where young men and women met and formed alliances. These three sacred groves symbolised the past, the present and the future of the tribe. No axe or sickle could be used in the groves that symbolised their past, present and future (Sachchidananda, 2004: 141–143).

The Khasi are probably the only tribe of the Northeast to have both sacred groves and a myth of origin. They claim to have originated from the seven huts that broke away from the16 huts in heaven after a conflict and landed in the Khasi Hills. Thus, their sacred groves symbolise their origin and continuity within the region in (Bhattacharyya, 1995: 22–23). A few other tribes have sacred groves but not myths of origin mainly because of the difference in the origin of the tribes. The Central Indian tribes seem to have originated in the region of their present habitat and found an identity around the land and other resources that were their sustenance. Most Northeastern tribes, on the contrary, are relatively recent immigrants to the region and had formed their clan or tribe identity before coming to the Northeast. Since they could not create a new clan or tribe identity after their arrival their myths are linked to the origin of the village, not of the tribe or clan. The village became central to it and most of their oral histories are centred round the spirits of the village and of the forest (Khekhrieseno, 2002: 179–180). Another part of their oral tradition refers to the divine origin of their customary law to which their identity is linked. This law also imposes some restrictions on cutting forests and fixes norms for resource management (Fernandes, Pereira and Khatso, 2007: 24–25).

Thus, though both the Central Indian and Northeastern tribal traditions had resource management as well as customary laws, their role in their identity formation differed. The Central Indian tribal identity was linked to the resources that are their sustenance. Their customary laws were meant to ensure their equitable and sustainable management. In the absence of an identity linked to their sustenance most Northeastern tribes linked it to their customary law which too ensured sustainable management of their resources. But central to their identity was not the clan or the sacred groves but the village, its spirits and the customary law linked to it.

The Tribal Value System

Equality was in an embryonic state in this equity based sustainable resource management and relatively high women's status. The traditions of the region also contain seeds of an environmental ideology in the sense that they viewed their sustenance as a gift of the divine that is protected by the spirits. This view legitimised their understanding of the resources as renewable. That view has to be updated to suit present needs and the present state of the resources and to move towards total class and gender equality. The culture of sharing has to be taken beyond the tribe to all those who need them. This section will take a look at their history in order to see whether some such steps have been taken and if not, whether a movement towards equality is possible. The context of this questioning is new inputs such as education, the commercial forces, religious change and the interface with the formal law. These inputs have on one side built on their past and on the other changed some of their traditions. They have thus forced them into an interface with the formal system with which they are not always familiar. A study of this process can give one an understanding of the main changes that they have experienced and can help one to deal with present needs.

Change and Modernity

A major change that the tribes have experienced is religious conversion to Christianity or Hinduism or Buddhism. That has also been a catalyst of many other changes among the tribes of the region and adds to diversity among them. It introduces some new values among them but also builds on the past. In other words, though tribal religions are on the decline, most tribes combine the macro-religious practices with their traditional customs and beliefs. Tribal beliefs have also influenced Buddhism, Christianity and Hinduism and have in their turn been influenced by these religions (Fernandes and Barbora, 2002: 186–189). Kumar Suresh Singh (1985: 17) says that the Christianisation of the tribes of Jharkhand has on one side given them a sense of history, self-respect and identity. On the other, it gave them an individual-based morality and an exclusive outlook. So he pleads for a good understanding of their past in order to build on its positive traits and remedy the negative ones. That analysis can be also applied to other macro-religions.

The same can be said about the tribes of the Northeast. Their conversion was by and large a social process. A majority of the hill tribes were converted to Christianity at a time when interventions of the colonial regime and of their dominant class Indian collaborators disrupted their economy and culture and caused an identity and social crisis in their societies. Amid this disruption, religious change helped the tribes to acquire a new identity (Ruivah, 2002: 127). By accepting Christianity the Hill tribes and, through Brahmo Samaj, the Boro in the Assam Plains could modernise themselves without losing their past completely. Thus, change of religion to Christianity in the hills to Brahmo Samaj by the Bodos is linked closely to a new history, a new identity and the possibility of joining the modern world with the hope of a better future. For example, in response to the destabilisation of their society by colonial inputs and the new economy and culture over which they had no control a somewhat big number of the Bodos had converted to Christianity in the 1920s in search of a new identity. That is when Kallicharan Brahma came in contact with the reformist Hindu sect of Brahmo Samaj at Calcutta and felt that his people could get a new identity without giving up their past (Roy, 1995: 30–31). A section of them, therefore, joined this reformist Hindu sect.

The situation is different when a new religion becomes a process of domination. For example, the Dimasa of Assam who were Hinduised by the Bengali railway and clerical workers who accompanied the British officials feel that the religion was imposed on them. They are reacting to it by trying to regain their past identity (Fernandes and Barbora, 2002: 198–199). The Adivasi of Assam identified themselves through their tribal indigenous faith of a *sarna* religion as late as the 1920s. But today, about 12 per cent of them are Christians and the rest are Hindus. Their religious change seems to have occurred through osmosis and not through either a social process or imposition (Fernandes, 2004: 116–117). A change through osmosis or imposition can be an attack on their identity and self-image and may not help them to combine their past with the present as it did to the Bodos.

Also religious change during a conflict can become a way of establishing a new identity. For example, the Thadou of Manipur who were converted to the Presbyterian Church in the early 20th century used the fact of being the first Christians to establish their control over the community structures formed by the 21 tribes belonging to the Kuki family. Though all of them contributed to the office of the Kuki Company (federation) at Imphal, its minutes and notices continued to be recorded in the Thadou dialect and most of its officials were Thadou. The resentment of the rest became the basis of the Kuki-Paite conflict. They rejected the domination of one tribe and found a new identity by joining the Baptist Church and some of them aligned themselves with the Nagas (Haokip,

2008: 189–191). Such a change linked to a conflict can perpetuate tensions rather than rebuild the tribe.

Religion, Education and the Gender Issue

Change of religion has implications for the gender issue because both Hinduism and Christianity are male dominated. But Christianity is somewhat ambiguous on this issue because though male-dominated the Churches also opened schools. The Hindus could not do it since they lacked a formal structure of the type that the Churches had. The Church-run schools were open to both boys and girls. As such in theory they could counter their patriarchal structure. But these institutions had to interact also with the patriarchal tribal societies. So whether girls gained access to schools or not depended not only on their religious conversion but also on political and other processes. When such an input supplemented the Church inputs they ensured that all classes and women availed of the opportunity to send girls to school.

Among its examples are Nagaland and Mizoram. The latter has overtaken all the states of India except Kerala in literacy. The Mizos seem to have also taken partial control of their economy. It can be attributed mainly to their nationalist struggle that built on the sense of history that they had gained for themselves (Joshi, 2005: 108–110). Also, the Angami were in the forefront of the Naga Nationalist struggle so many of their young men were underground or in hiding in the early 1970s when new Church-run high schools came to their area. The absence of men from the village left women in charge of the family and society and gave girls access to the schools. Its result is visible in a study done in 2001. Two-third of the graduates in the 189 families who studied in the southern Angami area were women. The matrilineal Garo of Meghalaya, on the contrary, did not pass through either the Angami or Mizo type of political process. So their educational status is lower than that of the Angami and fewer women among them are educated (Fernandes and Barbora, 2002: 88–90).

Modernisation and the Community Ethos

One has, however, to remember that those who introduce the inputs do not necessarily intend change in the form it impacts a community. The change comes about as a result of the reaction of a community to the inputs as such it is often different from the original intention of the inputs. Many missionary interventions that had positive effects on the tribes were made for evangelical purposes but the tribes that were searching for a new identity reacted to them according to their need. For example, at a time when the tribes were on the verge of breaking up because of the disruption caused by the colonial and dominant class Indian inputs, the missionary brought the tribal Christians together for Sunday worship. It was a religious action but it happened at a time when the community was breaking up. So the tribes turned the Sunday gathering for worship into a social tool of rebuilding their community. Similarly, the churches opened schools that brought children of warring tribes together under one roof. The schools played two social roles. First, they created new leaders different from the traditional chiefs. Secondly, children from hitherto warring tribes were forced to interact with each other on a day-to-day basis. Such interaction helped them to develop a belief in their common origin. Many tribes that were till then at war with each other began to view themselves as one people and developed a common identity. For example, 17 tribes inhabiting the Naga Hills slowly developed a Naga identity and in 1918 founded the Naga Club that later became the Naga National Union and eventually became a political base of Naga nationalism (Sanyu, 1996: 115–116).

In contrast, the individual morality of the churches and the pedagogy of the schools upheld the individual and devalued the community. Without either the missionary or the educationist intending it, this approach helped the commercial forces that entered their region in the colonial age and treated land and the rest of their sustenance only as a commodity. That introduced a new outlook in their relationship with nature. The commercial elements had to introduce this outlook because land was central to the colonial enterprise. Though it was legitimised in the name of the civilising mission of Europe the objective of colonialism was to change its economy and turn the colony into a supplier of capital and raw material for the industrial revolution and a captive market for its finished products (Rothermund, 1981: 2–4). Monopoly over land was basic to achieving this objective because it was required for schemes like the railways, roads, coalmines and plantations. In order to change the economy to suit its purpose of exploiting the resources of the colony of its own benefit, the colonial regime enacted new land laws meant to facilitate land transfer to the capitalist owners. The process began with the Permanent Settlement 1793 meant to ensure capital flow through land tax. It continued in other land laws of the 19th century and culminated in the Land Acquisition Act 1894 (Upadhyay and Raman, 1998).

The Formal Laws and Community Resources

These laws continue to be in force even today. Basic to them is the principle of the eminent domain of the state and their individual orientation. All biodiversity and land without individual titles were thus turned into state property. By not recognising the CPRs as the sustenance of their dependants in practice, the formal laws turned tribal community lands, biodiversity, forests and water sources into state property. Their dependants, thus, became encroachers in their own habitat where they had lived for centuries before the laws were enacted. This law also authorised the state to appropriate the CPRs without even paying compensation to their dependants. By, thus, denying them rights over the resource the law created a disjunction between them and their sustenance. The laws also authorised the state to acquire individual land without the owner's consent by paying some compensation (Ramanathan, 2008: 28–30).

However, the colonial regime did not touch the hill areas of the region as much as it did the plains. The regime needed the hills more for taxes and handicrafts than for land and Assam for tea gardens at first and later for petroleum. So they enacted the Assam Waste Land Settlement Rules 1838 to make its acquisition at a low price easy. It resulted in massive land alienation among various communities of Assam (Bora, 1986: 46–49). They turned the Imphal Valley into a princely State controlled by a British resident but kept the hill areas of Manipur directly under the British Crown since they needed them only for taxes (Guite, 2000). Thus the regime enacted laws in the plains and in the mining rich areas in order to acquire land but left most tribal areas out of their purview.

That changed after 1947 when the State wanted tribal land for development projects and the dominant classes had an eye on their resources. As a result, many of these laws have been extended to the tribal areas or new laws have been enacted in order to make land alienation easy. For example The Assam Land and Revenue Regulations 1886 (AL&RR) has been used as the model for new laws promulgated in Manipur as the Manipur Land Reforms and Land Revenue Act 1960 and in Tripura as the Tripura Land Reforms and Land Revenue Act 1960 (Das, 1968: 13). Like the colonial laws they too recognise only individual ownership. The result of these measures is massive tribal land alienation. For example, most Tripura tribes are CPR dependants but the Tripura Land Reforms and Land Revenue Act, 1960 was enacted at a time when Hindu Bangladeshi migrants were encroaching on tribal land. As a result, the tribal proportion of Tripura has declined from 58 per cent in 1951 to 31 per cent in 2001. It has deprived the tribes of all protection and taken away not less than 72,000 acres of their community land in the name of refugee rehabilitation and more for other schemes. As a result, though the tribal proportion has been reduced to 31 per cent of the population, more than two-third of the 1,80,000 DP-PAPs are tribal (Fernandes and Bharali, 2010: 77). After they had lost 20 to 40 per cent of their land to the East Pakistan immigrants in the 1960s, the state took over 32,000 acres of their CPRs for the Dumbur dam. They protested but the state did not heed their voice. The project authorities counted only 2,634 individual *patta* holding families as displaced and treated around 6,000 CPR dependent families as encroachers and evicted them without even compensating them. That was the beginning of tribal insurgency in Tripura (Bhaumik, 2003: 85).

There have been land-centred conflicts in other states too. Manipur has experienced the Naga-Meitei tension around the Sixth Schedule and the Kuki have been demanding a district of their own. These demands have resulted in blockades and other conflicts. In Assam, the number of tribal blocks where land is protected have come down from 35 in 1947 to 25 in 2000 and the size of the rest has been reduced. That too has resulted in much land alienation (Shimray, 2006: 6). It is seen also in land loss to development projects. Since community land is considered state property, those losing it to the projects are often not even counted among the displaced. For example, by official count development projects used 3,91,772.9 acres in Assam 1947–2000 and displaced 4,23,262 persons. The reality is not less than 14,01,184.8 used acres and 19,18,368 persons deprives of their livelihood (Fernandes and Bharali, 2011: 216 and 220). The 15.5 lakh persons who were not counted inhabited in the official files inhabited the 10 lakh acres of tribal commons. The law considers it state property though it was their sustenance. So they become encroachers in their own habitat.

Modernisation, Equality and Conflicts

The data given till now shows the problems linked to modernisation without involving the communities affected by it. In theory modern inputs uphold the value of equality but they tend to strengthen the tradition of a community when they are imposed on it without adequate preparation. The gender issue in the tribal societies belongs to this category. In theory, the modern educational and other systems are gender neutral. In practice they interact with the tradition of the communities. An example is the impact of education on Angami women that has been mentioned above. Two-third of the graduates and post-graduates in the families studied are women but their community and the state continue to perceive men alone as breadwinners. As a result, men are two-third of the 168 persons having salaried jobs, most of them in the administration (Fernandes and Barbora, 2002: 108–112).

Similarly, men continue to interpret the customary law that treats women as unequal. Individualism that is linked to modernisation results in class formation. But the tribal male elite tend to interpret the customary law in their own favour. For example, they interpret the land laws in favour of those who monopolise land. Similarly, while women gain access to higher education, men keep to their tradition that the husband should be at least as educated as the wife, if not more. As a result, a large number of women remain unmarried or marry outside their community. Many migrate away from their region in search of jobs because of preference given to men in employment (Fernandes, Pereira and Khatso, 2007: 63–64). Both the gender issue and equity are thus re-interpreted and modified and they go against equality that are intrinsic to tribal tradition. This interaction between their tradition and modernity weakens their spirit of mutual assistance, solidarity and sharing. Class formation becomes part of their societies that were egalitarian. With the weakening of the spirit of mutual assistance competition begins for the limited resources. The culture of sharing the resource according to each one's need gives way to individualism.

While the individual orientation of the land laws results in its alienation to outsiders, its acceptance by the tribal elite weakens their communities and leads to land alienation within the tribe. But the elite reinterprets the customary law in favour of this change by first monopolising community land. For example, in some Khasi villages, men who control the *durbar* (village council) have misused their position to transfer community that was under women's control to their own name. That goes both against women and the community (Mukhim, 2009: 000). It continues with alienation of individual land. For example, some Aka leaders in Arunachal Pradesh are appropriating wetlands on the riverbanks and are treating them as their own property without a *patta,* thus denying access to others who need it (Fernandes, Pereira and Khatso, 2007: 8). The Dimasa elite want individual *pattas*. One of their leaders has appropriated 200 acres by depriving others of their due (Barbora, 2002). A major cause of internal land alienation is education and health emergencies. Many families sell their individual land to some members of the elite in order to earn money to send their children out to colleges in big cities or for treatment in the health centres since their infrastructure has not been developed in villages and small towns (Khekhrieseno, 2007).

The new value system also has implications for the relations between the tribes. Many ethnic conflicts arise from the shortage of jobs and land that result from the interface between the modern and traditional systems. Because of the close link with land, many tribes of the region view the shortages as attacks on their culture and identity and interpret conflicts as modes of protecting them. They legitimise these conflicts by rewriting their history. The communities of the Northeast have given to the indigenous issue an interpretation that is different from that in mainland India. They speak of peoples who are indigenous to the Northeast as different from the mainland concept of those who are indigenous to the country as a whole (Fernandes, Bharali and Kezo, 2008: 37–40). The indigenous issue spills over to the ethnic conflicts. All the ethnic communities rewrite their history in order to show that they are the original inhabitants of a given area in the Northeast. Based on it they lay exclusive claims to its resources to the exclusion of all others. For example, alienation of land, culture and identity and the resultant indigenous claims are the bases of the Naga-Kuki conflict in Manipur (Fernandes and Bharali,

2002: 52–55), the Bodo-Santhal and Dimasa-Hmar tension in Assam (*The Telegraph,* 23 April 2003) and the Tripura tribal demand for a homeland (Bhaumik, 2003: 84).

Modernisation and Gender Equality

The formal-customary law interface also has implications for gender relations. For example, the Nagaland tribes consider all elective offices men's reserves and even women do not vote for female candidates (Changkija, 2004). The only woman to become a legislator since the formation of Nagaland is Rano Shaiza who was elected to the Union Parliament in the 1970s. The tradition exists in other states too. Manipur has three women among the 60 MLAs elected in 2011 and Meghalaya, where all three major tribes are matrilineal, has one woman against three in the previous legislature. These are examples modernising the customary law according to which the social sphere belongs to men.

During 2012 Nagaland witnessed the controversy around the Municipal and Town Council elections. In early March 2012, the Governor of Nagaland issued a notification for elections with 33 per cent reservations for women. Tribal leaders of the state protested against it immediately. The Gaonburah Association passed a resolution opposing this move as being against their tradition because their customary laws do not allow women to get elected to any political body (*The Nagaland Post,* 13 March 2012). The apex body of the Naga Ho-Ho did the same. A minister of Nagaland argued that the reservations are against Article 371A of the Constitution that confers on the state the power to run its civilian affairs according to the customary law (News item, *The Eastern Chronicle,* 5 April 2012). Other leaders (e.g. Angami, 2012) challenged women to prove that they are equal to men. Because of the controversy the state government filed a miscellaneous petition in the Kohima bench of the Gauhati High Court seeking postponement of the civic polls by six months till the select committee submits its report and the issue of 33 per cent reservations is resolved. The Court rejected the plea so the Government has approached a Division Bench (*The Assam Tribune,* 30 April 2012). The tradition is thus being used to prevent a move towards gender equality. Though not stated in such strong terms, the feeling that men alone should rule has been strong not merely in Nagaland but also in other parts of the region.

Search for Alternatives

The preceding sections show that most changes that the tribes of the Northeast have experienced result from an interface of their community-based system with the individual-based formal system without adequate preparation. Their traditions and the modern systems are based on different even contradictory worldviews. Through this interaction, the individual-based formal system is often imposed on their community-based tradition. That is the basis of class formation in their egalitarian societies. It is also the starting point of the search for alternatives that can combine an egalitarian value system with the equality that modernity proclaims but rarely upholds in practice.

The Sources of Change

Identifying the causes of the changes is the first step in finding a solution. One is often tempted to attribute the disjunction between their tradition and modernity or the strengthening of patriarchy only to education or to religion and their male-dominated structures. All of them have certainly contributed to the changes in different forms. For example, it is possible that through their exclusive approach, many churches reinforce the tribal sense of exclusive rights over an area. While internal sharing was basic to tribal culture, their relations with other tribes were based on the need to protect their resources from attackers. So they claimed exclusive rights over an area (Chakraborty, 2006: 69–72). That claim is reinforced when the tribes feel a threat to their livelihood. So they legitimise their claim to the resources by reinforcing their exclusive claims. That is further reinforced by the value of individualism which comes mainly from the commercial forces and education.

The administration adds to this situation through its individual approach. For example, many administrators treat the *gaonburah* (village leader) as the owner of all land, not as its trustee on behalf of the village. They follow this approach because it is easier to motivate an individual than a community to transfer that land for another purpose. Most incentives in development are individual and male-centred. For example, in the N.C. Hills the Coffee Board gives subsidies and loans only to individuals. In the 1990s, in the East Garo Hills, the Rubber Board gave subsidies to individual owners and 'heads of families' understood as men in this matrilineal tribe. A study done two decades later showed that around a third of the Garos in this area were landless. It was not the case in West Garo (Fernandes, Pereira and Khatso, 2007: 75). Similarly, much of the environmental degradation is caused by the commercial need to supply raw material to forest-based industries. However, one can say that change of religion has contributed indirectly to this aspect by weakening the sense of the sacred that their tradition had attached to the natural resources (Ruivah, 2002: 129–130).

Coping with Change

An understanding of these processes can be a starting point of the search for alternatives. Its first step is to recognise the fact that shortages have to be dealt with by the community but that other issues cannot be ignored.

For example, as stated earlier, individual ownership reduces the little power women enjoyed traditionally over the CPRs. Thus, gender relations become an area of concern. To deal with these issues one can suggest many solutions in the form of development initiatives. They are important if they contribute to maximising land productivity and employment generation but class and gender equality have to be basic to all of them. An approach that combines these components can be a good step in the direction of a solution. However, the value system cannot be ignored in this search because that is basic to the effort to rebuild their communities. In other words, not merely new technologies but also new ideologies are required for the tribal communities to go beyond the modern values to build a new system based on the combination of their tradition and what modernity can contribute.

The first step in this search is great respect for tradition but not the fundamentalist approach of trying to find all answers in it. One can go back to the values mentioned above of the community, gender and the environment. The environment is probably the best starting point because equity, community and women's status were built around the natural resources which were considered sacred. But that has been weakened by religious change. For a new ideology to evolve one needs to re-introduce the sense of the sacred possibly by re-interpreting nature as God's gift to a community. That goes beyond the western environmental concept of God's creation as nature alone that has to be protected as God's creation often from human communities whose sustenance it is. The approach in the Northeast would have to be the tribal concept of the environment as the ecosystem with human communities at its centre. Their environmental management was founded on the belief that God created them and put them at the service of human communities. That view got them to treat both nature and the human community as sacred. That sense of the sacred can replace individualism and selfishness. From this sense of the sacred is to be rebuilt an ideology of sharing that goes beyond one tribe or clan to every community that needs the resource and help their communities to rebuild their economy while maintaining the renewable nature of their natural resources.

In this value system equality goes beyond equity that is intrinsic to the tribal traditions. One may begin with it and move towards gender and class equality as well as sharing of the resources with other communities. In other words, a value system needs to be evolved that lays the foundation of cooperation in the place of conflicts. These three values can provide the foundation of this ideology from which their history has alienated them. But one has to go beyond their tradition of equity to equality and take steps towards cooperation with other communities. It would also involve taking a new look at the history that included both cooperation and division. That can take place of the present history that focuses on conflicts and divides different groups. The value system that legitimises conflicts has to be overcome through cooperation with other communities.

This long process requires the cooperation of many groups such as tribal leaders, intellectuals, youth and religious leaders. They would have to work hand in hand with the tribal community and women leaders to reflect together on the future of their communities. They can, thus, develop a new ideology meant to assist them in the task of combining their tradition with modernisation, with the values of gender and class equality and sustainable use of the natural resources.

Conclusion

An attempt has been made in this paper to look at the tribal tradition and history of the Northeast and the changes that have overtaken them. That has given one indication of areas that have been renewed and have also caused problems for the tribes today. One has also seen in this history the need for a new ideology and environmental management that can reassert the role of women in the life of the tribe. This ideology can be developed through cooperation between various male and women leaders and through an inter-disciplinary approach to analysis.

References

Angami, T.N. (2012) 'Few Questions and Guidelines on Women Reservation,' *The Morung Express,* March 16.

Barbora, Sanjay (2002) 'Ethnic Politics and Land Use: Genesis of Conflicts in India's Northeast'. *Economic and Political Weekly,* 37 (n. 13 March – 30 April 5). pp. 1285–1292.

Barpujari, S.K. (1997) *History of the Dimasas.* N.C. Hills: District Autonomous Council.

Bhattacharyya, N.N. (1995) *Religions of Northeastern India.* New Delhi: Manohar Publications.

Bhaumik, Subir. (2003) 'Tripura's Gumti Dam Must Go'. *The Ecologist Asia* 11 (n. 1, January–March). pp. 84–89.

Bora, Ajit Kumar. (1986) *Pattern of Land Utilization in Assam.* Delhi: Manas Publications.

Chakraborty, Gorky. (2006) 'Conflict of Contours: The Changing Power Structure in Traditional Tribal Societies of Northeast India,' in Basudeb Datta Ray and Asok Kumar Ray (eds) *Dynamics of Power Relations in Tribal societies of North-East India.* New Delhi: Om Publications. pp. 67–90.

Changkija, Monalisa. (2004) 'Right to Choose One's Destiny,' *The Telegraph*, 19 March.

Das, J.N. (1968) *An Introduction to the Land-Laws of Assam.* Guwahati: Panbazar (reprint 2005).

Das, J.N. (1990) *A Study of the Land System of Mizoram.* Guwahati: Law Research Institute, Eastern Region, Gauhati High Court.

Fernandes, Walter. (2004) 'The Assam Adivasis: Identity Issues and Liberation'. *Vidyajyoti JTR,* 68 (n. 2, February). pp. 110–122.

Fernandes, Walter and Sanjay Barbora. (2002) *Modernisation and Women's Status in North Eastern India: A Comparative Study of Six Tribes.* Guwahati: North Eastern Social Research Centre.

Fernandes, Walter, Melville Pereira and Vizalenu Khatso. (2007) *Customary Laws in North East India: Impact on Women.* New Delhi: National Commission for Women.

Fernandes, Walter, Gita Bharali and Vemedo Kezo. (2008) The UN Indigenous Decade in Northeast India. Guwahati: North Eastern Social Research Centre.

Fernandes, Walter and Gita Bharali. (2010) *Development-Induced Displacement 1947–2000 in Meghalaya, Mizoram and Tripura: A Quantitative and Qualitative Database on Its Extent and Impact.* Guwahati: North Eastern Social Research Centre (mimeo).

Fernandes, Walter and Gita Bharali. (2011) *Uprooted for Whose Benefit? Development-Induced Displacement in Assam 1947–2000.* Guwahati: North Eastern Social Research Centre.

Gangwar, A.K. and P.S. Ramakrishnan. (1992) 'Agriculture and Animal husbandry among the Sulungs and Nishis of Arunachal Pradesh,' in Walter Fernandes (ed.). *National Development and Tribal Deprivation.* New Delhi: Indian Social Institute. pp. 100–130.

Gassah. L.S. (1992) 'Status of Women in Jaintia Culture,' in Soumen Sen (ed.). *Women in Meghalaya.* New Delhi: Daya Publishing House. pp. 36–45.

Guite, K.C. (2000) 'MLR & LR Act, 1960 and Sixth Schedule in Relation to Hill Area' in M. Horam (ed.) *The Rising Manipur*. New Delhi: Manas Publications.

Haokip, Rebecca C. (2007b) 'The Kuki-Paite Conflict in the Churachandpur District of Manipur' in Lazar Jeyaseelan (ed.) *Conflict Mapping And Peace Processes in North East India*. Guwahati: North Eastern Social Research Centre. pp. 185–208.

Joshi, H.G. (2005) *Mizoram Past and Present.* New Delhi: Mittal Publications.

Khekrieseno, Christina. (2002) 'Changing Property Rights and Women's Control Over Livelihood in Nagaland' in Walter Fernandes and Sanjay

Barbora (ed.). *Changing Women's Status in India: Focus on the Northeast.* Guwahati: North Eastern Social Research Centre. pp. 183–192.

Khekhrieseno, Christina. (2007) 'Changing Land Relations in Angami Society,' Paper presented at the Seminar on *The Angami Society at the Beginning of 21st Century.* Kigwema: Japfu Christian College, 28–29 November.

Menon, Geeta. (1995) 'The Impact of Migration on the Work and Tribal Women's Status,' in Loes Schenken-Sandbergen (ed.). *Women and Seasonal Labour Migration.* New Delhi: Sage. pp. 79–154.

Misra, Bhawna. (2000) *Peasantry Movement in India.* New Delhi: Mohit Publications.

Mitkong. N. (1997) 'Status of Women: Padam-Miniong,' in B.B. Pandey, N. Sarkar and D.K. Duarah (eds.) *Status of Women in Tribal Society: Arunachal Pradesh,* Itanagar: Directorate of Research, Government of Arunachal Pradesh and Himalayan Publishers. pp. 133–162.

Mukhim, Patricia. (2009) 'Land Ownership Among the Khasis of Meghalaya: A Gender Perspective' in Walter Fernandes and Sanjay Barbora (ed.) *Land, People and Politics Contest over Tribal Land in Northeast India.* Guwahati: North Eastern Social Research Centre and IWGIA. pp. 37–50.

Nongkynrih, A.K. (2009) 'Privatisation of Communal Land of the Tribes of North East India: A Sociological Viewpoint' in Walter Fernandes and Sanjay Barbora (ed.). *Modernisation and Women's Status in North Eastern India.* pp. 16–36.

Norbu. T. (1997) 'Status of Women: Monpas,' in B.B. Pandey, N. Sarkar and D.K. Duarah (ed.) op. cit. pp.

Ramanathan, Usha. (2008) "The Land Acquisition Act 1894: Displacement and State Power,' in Hari Mohan Mathur (ed.) *India: Social Development Report 2008: Development and Displacement.* Council for Social Development and Oxford University Press. pp. 27–38.

Rothermund, Dietmar. (1981) *Asian Trade and European Expansion in the Age of Mercantilism.* Delhi: Manohar.

Roy, Ajay. (1995) *The Boro Imbroglio.* Guwahati: Spectrum Publishers.

Roy, Raja Devasish. (2005) *Traditional Customary Laws and Indigenous Peoples in Asia.* London: Minority Rights Group International.

Roy Burman, B.K. (1993) 'Tribal Population: Interface of Historical Ecology and Political Economy' in Mrinal Miri (ed.) *Continuity and Change in Tribal Society.* Shimla: Indian Institute of Advanced Study. pp. 175–216.

Ruivah, Khashim. (2002) 'Christianity and Social Change among the Tangkhuls of Manipur,' in S.M. Channa (ed.) *The Christian Mission: Christianity and Tribal Religion.* New Delhi: Cosmo Publications. pp. 123–140.

Sachichidananda. (2004) *Man, Forest and the State in Middle India.* New Delhi: Serials Publications.

Sanyu, Visier. (1996) *A History of Nagas and Nagaland: Dynamics of Traditional Village Formation.* New Delhi: Commonwealth Publishers.

Shimray, U.A. (2006) *Tribal Land Alienation in North East India: Laws and Land Relations.* Guwahati: North Eastern Social Research Centre and Indigenous Women's Forum of Northeast India.

Singh, K.S. (1985) *Tribal Society in India.* Delhi: Manohar Publications.

Syiem, I.M. (1992) 'Women in Khasi society' in Soumen Sen (ed.) op. cit. pp. 22–35.

Upadhyay, Sanjay and Raman Bhavani. (1998) *Land Acquisition and Public Purpose.* New Delhi: The Other Media.

9

How Safe are the Public Spaces for Women of Northeast India?

Need for a Safety Audit

RITUPARNA BHATTACHARYYA

1. Manipur girl raped in Delhi: 48 hours on, no breakthrough; North East community angry, NDTV, 20 January 2012, available at: http://www.ndtv.com/article/cities/manipur-girl-raped-in-delhi-48-hours-on-no-breakthrough-north-east-community-angry-169060> (accessed 29 October 2012).
2. Let's stop pretending there's no racism in India, *The Hindu*, 29 May 2012, available at: <http://www.thehindu.com/opinion/op-ed/lets-stop-pretending-theres-no-racism-in-india/article3466554.ece> (accessed 29 October 2012).
3. Northeastern woman molested near Delhi University (DU), NDTV, 18 October 2011, available at: <http://www.ndtv.com/article/cities/north-eastern-woman- molested-near-du-142162> (accessed 29 October 2012).
4. NE girls battle racial slurs, feel like aliens *The Times of India*, 26 November 2010, available at: http://articles.timesofindia.india times.com/2010-11-26/delhi/28214579_1_young-women-study-po ints-northeast (accessed 29 October 2012).

These are some of the headlines, which we often read and heard in the media: there is a strong consensus that the metropolitan cities of India, especially New Delhi and Bangalore are the most unsafe cities for women of Northeast India. In these cities, women from Northeast India are often intimidated and suffer greatly from varied prejudices, cultural stereotyping and racial discrimination. As one of the editorials of *The Hindu* titled 'The Insensitive Indian' put it:

> The prejudice is driven by racism, no less, and there is no point mincing words or being coy about this. This racism manifests itself on the Indian street in rude comments, stares, and facile judgments about the lifestyle and morals of people from the Northeast. Such attitudes put women from the region at particular risk of sexual harassment and worse, as several incidents over the past few years have sadly demonstrated.
>
> The Insensitive Indian, *The Hindu*, 07 May 2012, available at: <http://www.thehindu.com/opinion/editorial/article3391080.ece> (accessed 30 October 2012).

While, it is undeniable that women from Northeast India suffer from collective prejudices in the metropolitan cities of India and the issue remains a bitter pervasive truth, I question as to how safe are our women folks in our own public spaces of Northeast India? Can they move about freely in the public spaces to fulfil their varied needs and aspirations of their everyday practices, while trying to maintain dignity, safety and self-respect? Of late, the media have been full of reports on the insecure, unsafe and timid lives of women, young, old and vulnerable in the public spaces of Northeast India. For instances: 1. On 21 March 2012, four persons, including two soldiers of the India Reserve Battalion (IRB), the protectors of our soil, allegedly gang-raped a Manipuri woman, who went to Imphal from Tamenglong district to sell vegetables.[1] 2. The squalid incident of sexual assault by a mob of men against a young woman that occurred on 9 July 2012 in the Guwahati-Shillong (GS) road shocked not only India but went viral across the living planet (Pidd, 2012).[2] However, the outrage and the widespread resentment over this incident fails to stop (or reduce) the flow of similar incidents being reported from different parts of NE India. 3. On 30 September 2012, a young woman, a mother of three young girls, all four were returning home from a science exhibition, where the mother was gang-raped at a remote tribal hamlet in Gandacherra sub-division of Tripura.[3] Contemporary Northeast, India, despite of its varied political instability, was known for its relatively polite public culture, especially while dealing with women. Shamefully, Northeast India has become a hub for crime against women: the latest figures compiled until 2011 and published by the National Crime Records Bureau (NCRB), India, reveals that Tripura occupies the top rank in the entire country for committing the highest rate of cognizable crime against women followed by Assam. The figure for Tripura stands at 37 per cent as compared to 18.9 per cent crime rate at the national level, while for Assam it is 36.9 per cent. Interestingly, although Tripura's position remains marginally higher and Assam records the second-most vulnerable place in

India with respect to the rate of cognizable crime committed against women, the numbers of incidences for Assam are much higher when compared to Tripura. According to the statistics published by the NCRB, 2011, there were 11,503 incidents of crime against women registered in Assam, while Tripura registered 1,358 cases. Yet sadly, for the period 1 January – 31 July 2012, the state of Tripura registers 119 rape cases, 426 cases of domestic violence and 171 cases of molestation against women.[4] Surprisingly, Nagaland registers the lowest rate of crime against women among the Northeastern states. In the years 2011, 2010 and 2009, the rate of cognizable crime against women in Nagaland stands, respectively, at 1.9 per cent, 1.8 per cent and 2.1 per cent. Notwithstanding, the media reports unpacks that almost every month, at least one form of crime is committed against women in public spaces in the state of Nagaland, particularly in the town of Dimapur.[5] Contrary to the popular belief that women of Northeast India have generally enjoyed greater freedom in their daily lives compared with Indian women as a whole (Bhattacharyya, 2009; Behal, 2002), such disquieting development signals that Northeast India has emerged as the dubious region of being one of the most dangerous places in India for women. So far, however, there has been little research, which has discussed on women's safety in public spaces of Northeast India. Driving this research, therefore, is a concern to tackle the question of the gendered dimensions of fear, which affect women's access to public spaces including their mobility; how and where women feel (un)safe (in their usage of public space) or how they negotiate with these spaces in their everyday practices. First, though, I discuss the key intersections of public space, gender, women and fear and safety that produces social actions through the notion of a sense of place, (in this research public spaces of Northeast India) to shape women's everyday mobility.

Mapping the Intersection of Public Space, Gender, Women and Fear in Everyday Lives

Feminists scholars have addressed the intersectionality of geographies of place, space, time, gender and fear (inclusive of the fear of crime, harassment, violence), which have previously been observed to be gender-blind, positivistic, and sometimes even stereotyped as racialised (Starkweather, 2007; Pain, 1991; Pain, 1997a, b, c). In this research, public space is connected to the discursive and the highly contested notion of public sphere, albeit public sphere and public space are not always interchangeable (Staeheli, 1996; Németh, 2009). The research locates the discourse of women's safety and security within a broader framework – it includes all sections of women of Northeast India, although experience may vary from woman to woman. I consciously use the notion of everyday practices as 'practiced places', (de Certeau, 1984: 117) intimately connected to the hierarchy of private and public spaces. The language of everyday life refers to 'the ways of frequenting or dwelling in a place, on the complex processes' through which diverse acts are carried out such as those of aspiring for something, reading, talking, walking, cooking, caring and so on (de Certeau, 1984: xxii). The practices entailed are active (though not always pre-conscious) ways of going about daily life; 'ways of operating' that embrace trivial as well as sophisticated 'background social activity'. Notwithstanding, increased urbanisation and neoliberal economic reforms remain pivotal to the transformations and growing complexities found in the everyday practices of people, families and households (in both private and public spaces). The research is an attempt to unfold the intersectionality of everyday life and the integrative analysis of geographies of routine mobility of women in public, fear, harassment; the strategies the women adopt to remain safe in the locales produces social action through the notion of a sense of place to shape these women's lives.

Public spaces are those spaces where all citizens, irrespective of gender, caste, class, sexuality, disability or any other social identity have a right to access. In this research, public space embraces those spaces used by all sections of women to commute to and fulfil their needs of everyday lives. Such spaces include streets (neighbourhood streets, lanes, alleys, streets leading to the main roads), modes of public transport (which may include city buses, inter-city coaches, trekkers', auto-rickshaws and rickshaws) as well as sites like bus stops and market streets (including bazaars and shopping malls). In his 1974 book, *The Production of Space*, Henri Lefebvre, the French Marxist, illustrated the explicit Marxist analogy of production of space to testify to the manner in which a particular space is created, coded and used through the processes of social, political and everyday practices (Lefebvre, 2004). According to Lefebvre (1991, 2004), social space is a by-product of social practices. He analysed the production of space through three key routes: first, he worked with the Marxist notion of dialectic; second, he (re)worked on Marxist political economy to experiment the everyday life of home and city and third, he discussed the sociology of rural and urban. In doing so, he argued that there are three ways to understand social space – as perceived, conceived and lived. He related his notion of space to three other moments: *spatial practices*, which is not only subjective but embraces concrete, material and physical space, *representations of space*, conceived commonly by planners, scientists, urbanists and embodies the space of abstract plans and mental map. Lefebvre (1991) claimed that both the spaces be linked together through dialectical relation and be termed as spaces of representation. *Spaces of representation* address the ways through which to reconcile between mental space and real space: a space, tangent upon the physical and social spheres of an individual or a group of people, through which social relations is reproduced. This research paints the unique experience of understanding the routine journey/mobility of women as lived, experienced and recorded (Lefebvre, 1991, 2004).

Straddling the intersection of public space, gender, women and fear signals that public spaces of Northeast India are a male domain and suffer greatly from hegemonic patriarchal culture and power. That said, although following India's Independence, the Constitution guaranteed equality between sexes (Chandra et al., 2000), historically however, women are expected to provide the inner world (the private space) with household chores and childcare whereas the outer world (public space) of 'material interests' is constructed by and for men (Bhattacharyya, 2009; in press). Scholars including feminists have argued that spaces are gendered (McDowell, 1983; Rose, 1993; Schwanena et al., 2008). The hidden politics of public/private dichotomy reside within the notion of power, which could be understood as a dynamic and multivalent set of practices and situations (Fennell, 1999). Allen (2003) points to the inherent spatiality of power. Reviewing the contributions of different social scientists, such as Michel Foucault, Max Weber, Hannah Arendt, Michael Mann and Gilles Deleuze, Allen shows how space determines the role of power largely. Contextualising the diverse vocabularies and constitutions of power (drawing on the reasoning of Weber and Arendt) such as those of domination, authority, seduction, manipulation, coercion and the like, he argues that these modes of power are far from identical; each hold 'their own relational peculiarities' and are 'always power of a particular kind' (Allen, 2003: 2). He puts forward his argument by stating that 'people are placed by power, but they experience it at first hand through the rhythms and relationships of particular places' (such as the home, the classroom, the street, market place) and the varied ways through which the actual registration of power is being shifted: proximity and reach, distance and mobility and of course, place and presence. The geography of power, thus, underpins the dynamic of everyday practices and the social and political organisation of a whole host of institutions disseminated across the contemporary geographical space (Allen, 2003). This research demonstrates as to how the male power operates in the public spaces of Northeast India and that in this way women become victims of unwanted assaults and anti-social behaviour. The following section discusses the methods that underpin this research.

The Method

The findings of this research are based on two tiers. Since, the research concentrates on women's safety audits, most of the participants are women. Using an on-line survey[6], in the first tier, the research was conducted through e-mails and via social networking sites, namely Facebook and LinkedIn, among the different sections of women of all ages of Northeast

India. By using the 'snowballing' method, the initial respondents of the e-mails were either requested to forward the link of the survey to their friends or share it in the social networking sites. Total response received in the survey is 102 (58% female and 42% male). In the next tier, the survey was supplemented by in-depth telephonic interviews conducted with 20 women. Most of the interviews were conducted in either Hindi or Assamese, and then, transcribed and translated into English by the author. The author being an insider into the research process also entailed a conscientious and diligent observation of the public spaces of Northeast India. Notwithstanding, as majority of the women were victims of some form of assaults in the public spaces, the nature of the research involves an issue of sensitivity (Hopkins, 2007). I felt that this sensitivity is to be respected and hence, the research 'required a tactful approach' (Hopkins, 2007: 532). During the process of telephonic interviewing, being a woman myself and from Northeast India, I followed the suggestions of Oakley (1981) and shared my own experience of being molested some years ago in public transport and streets and thereby, allowed myself to be gradually involved with the interviewees during the process of conversation. These interviews were more or less like informal talks, that is, 'conversations with a purpose' (Eyles, 1988) rather than formal discussion or what Kvale (1996: 5) refers to as 'professional conversations'. The questions were obviously open-ended and semi-structured, and most of the discussions were two way. In addition, there were full opportunities for the interviewees to raise questions and issues not thought of previously by me (Silverman, 1993), that is, there was an element of 'reciprocal interviewing'. Hence, I also prepared myself to answer the raised questions or issues on the topic of research. Pseudonyms are used for the interviewees and the details that may reveal their identity are not presented. Before discussing the findings, the legal provisions related to sexual assaults of women are discussed in the following section.

Legal Provisions Linked to Sexual Assaults

Sections 292, 292A, 294, 354, 375, 376 and 509 of the Indian Penal Code (IPC) are the comprehensive criminal codes intended to protect mainly a woman against any types of sexual assaults/abuses against her. Subtle reading of these sections, however, demonstrates that the procedural rule of laws connected to it are very complex to prove the assailant as guilty and it is very likely that the perpetrator can go scot-free. In actuality, the definitions of sexual harassment remain ambiguous and imprecise, which suggests these legal provisions as futile and inherently flawed. Even in cases where a perpetrator could be inflicted and penalised, penalties remain minimal, and victims receive very little or no support whether legal, financial, social, emotional or psychological. The above sections of the IPCs are defined in Box I. Sadly, in most cases the victims of sexual assaults such as groping, bottom slapping, inappropriate touching, lewd remarks in public places are seemingly considered as trivial, and therefore, the legal provisions fail to provide adequate support and assistance to the victims, despite the fact that the victims might face traumatic experiences (Bhattacharyya, in press).

Box 1

The section 292 states that a book, pamphlet, paper, writing, drawing, painting, representation, figure or any other object containing pornographic or obscene pictures/images and showing it purposely to a woman or girl with lewd intention shall be deemed as lascivious and will draw a fine of ₹ 2,000 with two years of rigorous imprisonment for first offence. In case of repeated offence, if and when proved, the offender will be penalised a fine of ₹ 5,000 with five years of rigorous imprisonment.

Section 292A states that whoever prints or disseminates grossly dirty or indecent pictures/images with an intention to blackmail shall receive a punishment with imprisonment for a term, which shall not be less than six months, however not more than two years.

According to Section 294, Chapter XIV: Of Offences Affecting The Public Health, Safety, Convenience, Decency and Morals holds that 'whoever, to the annoyance of others, (a) does any obscene act in any public place, or (b) sings, recites and utters any obscene songs, ballads or words, in or near any public space, shall be punished with imprisonment of either description for a term that may extend to three months, or with fine, or with both.'

Section 354, Chapter XVI: Of Offences Affecting The Human Body states that 'whoever assaults or uses criminal force on any woman, intending to outrage her modesty or knowing it likely that he will thereby outrage her modesty, shall be punished with imprisonment for a term which may extend to two years, or with fine, or with both.'

Section 375 is linked to the sexual offences of rape by a man against a woman. 'A man is said to commit 'rape' who, except in the case hereinafter excepted, has sexual intercourse with a woman under circumstances falling under any of the six following descriptions: First – Against her will; Secondly – Without her consent; Thirdly – With her consent, when her consent has been obtained by putting her or any person in whom she is interested in fear of death or of hurt. Fourthly – With her consent, when the man knows that he is not her husband, and that her consent is given because she believes that he is another man to whom she is or believes herself to be lawfully married. Fifthly – With her consent, when, at the time of giving such consent, by reason of unsoundness of mind or intoxication or the administration by him personally or through another of any stupefying or unwholesome substance, she is unable to understand the nature and consequences of that to which she gives consent. Sixthly – With or without her consent, when she is under sixteen years of age. Explanation – Penetration is sufficient to constitute the sexual intercourse necessary to the offence of rape.

Exception – Sexual intercourse by a man with his own wife, the wife not being under fifteen years of age, is not rape.' (Indian Penal Code, available at: http://www.childlineindia.org.in/CP-CR-Downloads/Indian%20penal%20code%201860.pdf accessed 25 November 2012)

Section 376 is connected to section 375 and states that whoever is guilty of committing a rape against a woman be it a police officer, public servant, gang rape or an individual shall be liable to rigorous punishment with sentence ranging from seven years to life imprisonment.

Section 509 of the IPC, Chapter XXII: Of Criminal Intimidation, Insult and Annoyance (Word, gesture or act intended to insult the modesty of a woman) and is cognisable, bailable and triable by any magistrate. It holds that: 'Whoever, intending to insult the modesty of a woman, utters any word, makes any sound or gesture, or exhibits any object, intending that such word or sound shall be heard, or that such gesture is seen by such woman, or intrudes upon the privacy of such woman, shall be punished with simple imprisonment for a term which may extend to one year, or with fine, or with both.'

Gendered Dimensions of Fear

'It is not a research but a concern, which is so close to all of us. We all want safety in Northeast. Don't we?'

This quote emerged from one of my enthusiastic respondents, who after filling in the on-line survey e-mailed this quote while forwarding it to her friends and requesting them to fill in the same. The quote itself is a staggering reflection of the dimension of fear that most women live with when out in public, which cannot be answered definitively; but can be stimulated through a useful and rational discussion either possibly through a research of this kind or by negotiating our position in between repudiation and reification.

In her recent article in Open Democracy, Rahila Gupta (2012) points out that there remains no correlation between a woman 'feeling safe' in a public space and the extent to which she is actually safe in that particular place. One of the most common forms of harassment faced especially by young women in public spaces is eve-teasing. Eve-teasing often comprises harassments in the form passing of comments on the physical beauty of women or the way they dress, whistling, starring or singing 'Bollywood songs' or even some form of physical assaults such as fondling, pinching, and rubbing against women (Bhattacharyya, 2009; in press; Ramasubramanian and Oliver, 2003). Although eve-teasing is cognitive, however, it has always been considered as a minor nuisance and often-euphemistic (Nahar, 2008). One possible explanation as to why men eve-teases women is that eve-teasing as a jocular practice is validated both culturally and sub-culturally in all regions of India. This is also evident from the results of the survey conducted by the blank noise project[7] in the cities of Kolkata, Mumbai, Bangalore, Hyderabad, New Delhi, Chennai, Lucknow, Chandigarh and Jaipur. Figures 1 and 2 illustrate a typical situation of a number of men either standing on the road or sitting on their motor bikes. As we in the figures, it is in just this situation that women easily become the victims of harassment. However, evidences shown here and elsewhere demonstrate that it is a pervasive problem, often bigger and crucial than it is ever perceived to be. At times, cases of eve-teasing have turned barbaric, ugly and violent. For instances, on 11 December 2012, Ashwini Malhotra, a journalist by profession was vehemently attacked when he tried to intervene and protect a young woman from three motor cycle riders, who were allegedly harassing a young woman in inebriated condition at the local Milap Chowk area of Jalandhar, Punjab.[8] In a similar incident, on 22 August 2012, Ravi Dangi, a young teenage boy was stabbed to death when he and his friend objected to a woman friend being harassed by eve-teasers at a public space in Bhopal. Other violent cases have also been reported from other parts of the country.[9] Therefore, this research uses the term sexual assault instead of eve-teasing to connote a greater degree of impact of the crime. In fact it is a global phenomenon known by different names in different places: eve-teasing in India, Pakistan, Bangladesh and Nepal, slutwalks in the North America and the UK and sexual assault in Australia. Appalling statistics reveal that one in five women in the USA suffers from sexual assaults;[10] in Delhi, the capital city of India, it is two in every three women[11] and globally, more than 90 per cent of women face public assaults.

In their study, Ramasubramanian and Oliver (2003) suggest that 32 per cent of eve-teasers are university and college goers. Majority of the women in the research (99%) experienced some sort of harassment: verbal (comments, whistling); physical (touching, feeling up); visual (staring, leering); flashing, while using the public spaces in their everyday lives. 48 per cent women received harassment in the roadside; 37 per cent while using public transport; 21 per cent while waiting for public transport and 23 per cent in the market places. However, none of them received any violent physical attack. Nevertheless, it remains unclear whether these harassers are university/college goers.

Figure 1

Common pastime of men (1)

Figure 2

Common pastime of men (2)

The lecherous comments that the sample of women received constitute unsolicited and often offensive remarks such as the shape of a woman's body (Vishnupriya, 45 years), her beauty (Devjaya, 30 years) and sometimes the dress/make-up she wears (Nira, 25 years) or even singing Bollywood songs to attract attention (Dipali, 26 years, a domestic worker).

> Since I am fat and hefty, I often get comments like 'from which shop does she buy her rice?' and also more frequently insolent comments like 'Beware! the elephant is on your way'.
>
> —Vishnupriya

> I wish I could lock and display her in my living room cabinet.
>
> —Devjaya

> Looking good and feeling great with your bright salwar-kamij and red lipstick. Good match!
>
> —Nira

> Although, I come here to work with my two young children (aged 6 and 5), I get teased in a variety of ways. Sometimes they (the men) sing Hindi film songs or whistle at me.
>
> —Dipali

Obviously, the experiences of different women vary with respect to the place where they commute to; the mode of travel and the area where they live in, but all stories reveal fear, fury and disempowerment in public. Yet in a saga of incidents, a new form of harassment against women has emerged in the public spaces of NE India, where the young bike riders target women of all ages to snatch either their necklaces or mobile phones or both. In this research, only 1 per cent of women have been victims of such anti-social behaviour. Gifted to her by her deceased husband on one of her marriage anniversaries, a 73-year-old woman became a victim of two bike riders, when they snatched away her gold chain. She narrates her plight as follows:

> As usual I was out for my morning walk on our main road, when two young motor cyclists snatched away my chain and drove away very fast. I could not even see their faces. They were waving at me and showing me that they have got my chain. I am not very depressed that my chain is gone. But it had emotions attached to it because my late husband had gifted it to me on one of our marriage anniversaries.
>
> —Bhanupriya

Such reprehensible anti-social behaviour[12] can possibly be best explained by growing unemployment and poverty among the youths of Northeast India. According the survey result, 14 per cent of women avoid wearing expensive jewelleries as a measure of precaution when out in public. Anglo-American scholar Rachel Pain comments that women experience some sort of harassment during the course of their life. It is in this context, Pain (1997b: 417) argues, 'amongst all the factors which have been noted to increase fear of crime ... being female has the largest effect' (Starkweather, 2007). Stark evidence suggests that a woman is harassed approximately every 50 minutes in the public spaces of Assam (Bhattacharyya, 2010). Prior study unfolds that the mere presence of a woman in public space could be 'provocative' and might drive some men to harass her (Bhattacharyya, in press). The opinion of Mala (25 years), who is pursuing PhD in Delhi University but hails from Guwahati, further strengthens the finding of Bhattacharyya (in press):

> This time when I visited Guwahati, it was like visiting some other place. Madam, despite my father asking me not to go out for a walk after dinner (which I am used to in Delhi) I went out believing in me that I am old enough to care for myself. But I was wrong. We live in Milanpur, and Chandmari flyover is very near. Guys were throwing bottles and yelling away on bikes. To my utter surprise, a car stopped near me. I was dead scared and came back as fast as I could. It was just 9pm and everyone knows me in that area, despite that I got so scared. Adding to my plight all street lights were off.
>
> —Mala

MacKinnon (1979) argues that such harassment is as an exertion of power to influence the male-dominated and heterosexual nature of public spaces (Bhattacharyya, 2009; Bhattacharyya, in press). That gender remains stratified in the public spaces of Northeast India is clearly reflected from these findings. According to the respondents of the questionnaire survey, the specific places that are unsafe for women are: streets (35%), residential areas (5%), cinema halls (15%), bus and auto stops or taxi stands (25%), parks (8%), market place (bazaars) (12%), shopping malls (5%), local transport (41%), public toilets (3%) and other places (4%). These places are labelled as unsafe because of the lack of street lights (59%), dark lanes and alleys (47%), potholed roads pavements (57%), garbage, debris dumps (3%), any place where someone could be hiding (8%), any entrapment areas-recessed doorways, alleys (4%), harassment from pedestrians, car drivers, attendants (33%), drunk men on the streets (23%), very few people, especially women on the street (67%), lack of effective or visible policing (77%), lack of poor signage or information (2%), poor maintenance of open public spaces (6%), crowded public transport, bus-stops, stations (25%), lack of clean and safe public toilets (16%), lack of vendors or stalls and people in the area (31%), lack of respect for women from men (55%). Michel de Certeau (1984) suggests that walking as a part of everyday practices (in this research, the routine mobility to move about freely in public spaces to fulfil their everyday task), represents an act of power, a sense of belonging and the subversive engagement in and within the public spaces. However, the continuous fear for safety, the vexations and the negotiations attached to the hegemonic gendered public spaces of Northeast India, remains a site of contestation. Therefore, these spaces are deemed to be (re)defined where these women can move about freely to fulfil the mundane practices of daily lives while maintaining their dignity and self-respect in public. In the said context, scholars argue that male-dominated ideologies and societies with history of violence often manifest incidences of sexual assaults in public (Nahar, 2008; Ramasubramanian and Oliver, 2003). Radical feminists label harassment as all 'the process of social control enacted by men over women in which the totality of our lives are available to being policed by them' (Stanley and Wise, 1987: 15). Hence, any form of harassment against women in public imposes some form of restrictions to their everyday routinised mobility (Sharma, 2010, 2012). Most of the women considered under this research use either public transport or travel on foot especially during the day to fulfil their everyday activities. Figures 3 and 4 portray the condition of the public transport (city buses) especially during the morning and evening rush hours. Research evidence suggests that incidences of verbal harassment and stalking are particularly widespread on such crowded buses, where there remains very little room (personal space) for a woman to even stand properly. Ironically, evidence suggests that harassment can also occur in public transport carrying very few people. As Shreya, who is from Manipur shares her pathetic story, where her confidence is brutally shaken but such incidents reflects that women are often seen as objects of molestation. Actions of such harassment would have definitely continued within the bus, had the bus been not boarded by passengers in the next bus stop.

> I was studying in Guwahati at that time. At around 4 pm, I got into a bus from Last Gate to my hostel near Dighali Pukhuri. After I got into the bus, I realised that there were only 9–10 people in the bus. And all of them seemed to be some college goers. I took a seat near the entrance of the bus where the conductor was standing. The group of boys kept passing comments and were whistling at me. One of them came and sat next to me, and put his hand on my knee. I was very scared. Luckily, at the next stop, some more people got into the bus.
>
> —Shreya

This incident bears resonance to the horrific gang-rape of a 23-year-old para-medical student in New Delhi on 16 December 2012 at 21:30 hours, although for Shreya the assault failed to continue.[13] Evidently, women of my sample feel no safer in crowded places than deserted lanes. Majority of the respondents (97%) were concerned that the public spaces of Northeast India did wear a sober look until few years ago, which has now been transformed into violent and dangerous place for women. The sordid examples of harassment against women given here and elsewhere bear witness to this. As one of the respondents (Rina, 35 years) commented:

> I completely miss my old and tolerant Dimapur. In fact, nature of eve-teasing is changing. Before it was songs and funny harmless comments, although disgusting, but now it is too vulgar and violent.
>
> —Rina

Figure 3

Conditions of Public Transport during the Rush Hours (1)

Figure 4

Conditions of Public Transport during the Rush Hours (2)

One of the questions that may arise from these findings as to why men harass women in public? A survey conducted by Trust Law, Thomson Reuters Foundation[14] uncovers that 52 per cent of Indian men feel it is justifiable for a husband to beat his wife. Although, this percentage is marginally above majority, but the underlying attitude holds that the deep-rooted patriarchal mindset remains ingrained in the countless households of India, which consider women as subservient and therefore, be restricted to the private spaces of domestic spheres entailed to household chores, childbearers, carers and (or) other unpaid chores (Bhattacharyya, in press). Such attitudes are of course not startling but can be applied to different corners of India with varying degrees. In the said context, according to the NCRB, in 2011, 97,494 cases of cruelty by husband and relatives, under section 498A of the IPC were reported for an all India total, the rate of crime stands at 8.2 per cent. Echoing on this, in his reality television show *Satyamev Jayate* (Truth Alone Prevails), Episode 7 on 'Domestic Violence: Danger at Home'[15] aired in private channel network STAR and a national broadcaster Doordarshan, the Bollywood actor-cum-anchor, Aamir Khan, divulges that approximately 60 per cent Indian women suffer from domestic violence. Speaking on this issue, the noted feminist activist, Kamla Bhasin, says that the intrinsic problem lies in the word pati, which means 'husband' in general sense of the term but means 'owner' of a woman in its real sense. The word reflects a typical demonstration of 'male power', where most men feel that it is their 'birth right' to batter women. Bhasin goes on to speak that in the whole game of domestic violence, it is the middle class women who suffers the most simply because of the tacit stigma associated with it: fear of losing self-respect and the vicious tongues of the society restrains them from speaking about their abuses in public. In similar context, reflecting on the increasing trend of incidences in rape, cruelty by husband and molestation (Table 1) of all the states of Northeast India, it is more likely that most men, who are violent towards their women in their families, display their 'power' of being men through the possession of their violent attitudes against women in public. The initial episodes of the Indian soap opera, *Mann Kee Awaaz Pratigya* aired on STAR PLUS reinforce such male attitudes. Despite the existence of robust laws on gender, all forms of violence against women in India, including the harassment against women in public (particularly eve teasing), finds a level of social acceptability and suffers greatly from male chauvinism and varied prejudices. One of such prejudice is that scantily dressed women invite rape upon themselves. The following section addresses this issue.

What Constitutes Appropriate Dressing?

One of the growing concerns suggested in the narratives especially among older women[16] is that those women who are scantily clad invite sexual assaults upon themselves. Debates on what constitutes 'appropriate' dressing and 'decency' for a woman continue amongst the feminists of both the global north and south (Beiner, 2007; Chatterji, 2008; Data, 2009; Lahiri and Bandyopadhyay, 2012; Pain, 1991; Valentine, 1989; Wolf, 1991). Anglo-American feminists argue that women can feel out of place in public spaces at night and consequently impose upon themselves a 'curfew'. The sense that women's bodies are 'out of place' in public, at night, is especially apparent if they break the tacit taboo and wear clothing that is considered revealing or provocative, as if it is 'inviting' the would-be attacker (Pain, 1991; Valentine, 1989). In her strident treatise on the feminine experience, *The Beauty Myth,* Wolf (1991) demonstrates that there is a cultural backlash against feminism, which fails to explain women's dress in present day. Wolf's book is a witness to a disturbing message within feminism where she highlights that in 1986, an American woman lost her case of sexual harassment only because she dressed too attractively. Of course, this kind of precedent triggers one to believe that a woman's provocative apparel is a factor of sexual assault, where it is commonly assumed that the intent of such apparel is to 'objectify' a woman (Beiner, 2007). Contrary to these arguments, new studies suggest that there remains no connection between women's sexualised apparels and the resultant victimisation (Abdelhadi, 2008; Moor, 2010). Lahiri and Bandyopadhyay (2012: 21) recently reiterated that 'decency' as a discursive and value-laden concept, which reside radically within the notion of power 'and the hierarchies through which it is instituted' often bear political dimensions and implications (Datta, 2009). Therefore, what constitutes 'decency' with regards to women's dress code is highly apolitical.

Notwithstanding, the values of Indian society consider a woman as the 'honour' of the house. This deep-rooted notion, which resides within the framework of patriarchy, refer to the narratives of 'bodily fear' – fear for loss of shame and honour if a woman is sexually assaulted, more so, if the assault is for a particular dress code, which is considered inappropriate by the society. Since the barriers to global trade were eroded from the 1990s, every aspect of life has been increasingly open to commercial influence – at a speed that is alarming to many Indians (Gupta, 2005; Sinha, 2005). This assault of new commodities, fashions, job opportunities and ideas offer great promise to young people, but it can also be seen as a threat to folk cultural values and ways of living with particular implication on women. Through an array of sumptuous pictures and examples, Tarlo (1996) argues that urban Indian women seeks modern fashions as a marker of joining progressive class, a way to propound power – a symbol of cultural capital (Bourdieu, 1984), which of course remains unevenly distributed among classes.

In her backlash thesis, Susan Faludi (1991) however asserts that media associate 'modern' 'progressive' beauty products with sexual

Table 1

Selected Incidence of Crimes Committed Against Women

States	2011									2005									1999								
	Rape			Cruelty by Husband and Relatives			Molestation			Rape			Cruelty by Husband and Relatives			Molestation			Rape			Cruelty by Husband and Relatives			Molestation		
	I	R	S	I	R	S	I	R	S	I	R	S	I	R	S	I	R	S	I	R	S	I	R	S	I	R	S
Assam	1,700	5.5	7	5,246	16.8	5.3	1,193	3.8	2.8	1,238	4.3	6.7	2,206	7.7	3.8	899	3.1	2.6	703	2.7	4.5	843	3.2	1.9	720	2.8	2.2
Arunachal Pradesh	42	3.0	0.2	18	1.3	00	51	3.7	0.1	35	3.0	0.2	9	0.8	00	67	5.8	0.2	39	0.3	3.3	5	0.4	00	65	5.6	0.2
Meghalaya	130	4.4	0.5	21	0.7	00	74	2.5	0.2	63	2.6	0.3	3	0.1	00	44	1.8	0.1	27	1.1	0.1	0	0	0	17	0.7	0.1
Mizoram	77			9	0.8	00	72	6.6	0.2	37	3.9	0.2	0	0	0	49	5.2	0.1	71	7.6	0.1	0	0	0	74	8.0	0.2
Manipur	53	1.9	0.2	39	1.4	00	38	1.4	0.1	25	1	0.1	20	0.8	00	25	1.0	0.1	12	0.5	0.1	2	0.1	0	13	0.5	00
Nagaland	23	1.2	0.1	1	0.1	00	9	0.5	00	17	0.8	0.1	0	0	0	7	0.3	00	11	0.7	0.1	0	0	0	3	0.2	00
Tripura	205	5.6	0.8	702	19.1	0.7	294	8.0	0.7	162	4.8	0.9	439	12.9	0.8	161	4.7	0.1	72	1.9	0.5	113	3.1	0.3	71	1.9	0.2

I – Incidence R – Rate of Crime P – Percentage share.

Sources: Crime in India, National Crime Records Bureau, Ministry of Home Affairs, Years, 2011, 2005, 1999 available at: http://ncrb.gov.in (accessed 24 October 2012).

liberation and in this way, misrepresent feminism. Hence, the feminist ethic of financial independence is distorted through 'commodification of women' and transformed to a consumer ethic, an ethic bearing purchasing power. In similar context, Bhattacharyya (2009) views the problem as boundaries being transgressed by the appearance of some progressive women, who often dress inappropriately and thereby, become victims of eroticism. Arguably, women's fashions, as with Indian culture in general, teeters on the brink between Indian-style progress and wholesale capitulation to westernisation. That said, a number of high profile Indian professionals have urged Indian women to dress 'appropriately' when out in public, as 'revealing' apparels are considered culturally insensitive and provocative to men (see, Chatterji, 2008).[17] Reverberation of the same tone is evident when the Dimapur chapter of Naga Women's Hoho have urged its women to avoid indecent and skimpy outfits and in this way, keep away from provoking crime. In the said context, many colleges of Northeast India have introduced uniforms for its pupils aimed at maintaining a decorum; mostly *salwar-kameej* for girls but bans 'tight leggings'. Modest dressing remains a marker of Indian cultural ethos but what comprises 'modesty' and 'respectability' for women within the moral economy of Northeast India? Arguably, saris and 'traditional attires' of the states of Northeast India too can sometimes affect the norms of decency if they are worn 'too attractively or too fashionably', which could be perceived as 'provocative' by some and therefore, seductive. As one of the interviewees points out:

> I may want to look attractive and sexy and therefore I dress beautifully. But this does not mean that I want to seduce somebody.
>
> —Rina

Studies, however, unfold that most women maintain a sense of safety and respectability in public by drawing on boundaries to their bodies and personal spaces through the practices of Indian femininity. Such self-accessorised practices constitute a *bindi* (a dot on the forehead), nose rings, *mehendi* and *henna* (painting kits for the hands) and for a married woman, by her *mangalsutra* (long gold chain with black beads) and *sindoor* (vermilion) (Bhattacharyya, 2009; Phadke, 2005; 2007; Phadke et al., 2011). It is apparent from the findings of the research survey that 25 per cent of the women of all ages avoid wearing certain types of clothes when accessing public space. In similar context, Khan (2007) narrates a saga of instances of Muslim women in Mumbai trying to gain self-protectionism while accessing public spaces: through wearing *ridha*,[18] attending women's gymnastic clubs instead of a unisex gym or commuting via segregated women compartment in local trains. These practices have implications of powerful expression of habitus[19] (de Certeau, 1984), capable of deflecting the would-be harassers (Phadke, 2005; 2007; Phadke et al., 2011; Viswanath and Mehrotra, 2007). However, even these cross cutting actions of self-protectionism might fail to prevent a woman from being harassed, which is evident from the Blank Noise Project titled, 'I never ask for it. I have experienced sexual harassment, 'eve-teasing' in the following' (Table 2). This project has been collecting clothes that carry stories of harassment and concludes that it is a myth that women's 'provocative or revealing' apparel invites harassment. The attires and other accessories of beauty and fashion carrying testimonies of harassment range from bikinis, *burquas* (an Islamic outfit covering the body from head to toe, except for the eyes) through to school uniform. Table 2 presents results obtained from the analysis of the attires and accessories the women wore at the time when they were harassed sexually in the streets. Interestingly, 45 per cent young girls in school uniform and 9 per cent women in *burquas* received harassment on the roads when commuting back and forth to attend their daily lessons. That said, one of the participants (Meena, 34) recapitulates that subscription of the fact that scantily clad women provoke crime upon them is barely a fallacy and the root of this misconception is deeply ingrained in the societal values, which demands maintenance of conventional role of women: women ought to hide their sexuality by restraining behaviour that carries unwitting risk of assault in public spaces. Given the current societal scenario, most men have lost respect for women, which drives men to commit a crime against women. As Meena asserts:

> Most heinous crime against women is committed in *Burqua*-clad societies. It is man's inability to properly respect a woman, appreciate her beauty that leads men to commit rapes. One should see the movie *Utsav* by Girish Karnard, which shows how even courtesans were respected in ancient India. The sculptures of *Khajuraho, Konark*, all indicate that women in ancient India were scantily clad but were respected for their beauty and their proficiency in art, be it the art of dance, music or the art of love. But things changed after Mughal invasion and during the Victorian era of British rule. Both men and women have to throw out this idea that scantily clad women are immoral and instead appreciate the beauty of the fair sex. Men who rape have no respect for women; are incapable of actually loving any women; have low self-esteem; are perverts. Men rape only to make the women feel in a very animal manner that women should always serve men. It has nothing to do with dress. So, society should stop dictating women what to wear or not wear.
>
> —Meena

In similar context, research conducted by the Egyptian Centre for Women's Rights, Egypt, suggested that the issue of attire is no deterrent indicator of street assault. The survey unfolds that majority of the women facing harassments on the streets of Egypt were dressed modestly, practicing Islamic femininity and wearing either '*niqab*' (similar to *burquas* but covers mainly the head and the face except for the eyes) or headscarves. In addition, the results of this survey also suggested that 62 per cent of Egyptian men are involved in sexually harassing women (Abdelhadi, 2008). 'In any civilised society the burden of shame of inflicting any kind of violence should lie with the perpetrator, not the victim' (Lahiri and Bandyopadhyay, 2012: 21). However, this is invariably overlooked when it comes to harassment against women and the debates on the norms of 'decency' continue. Nevertheless, women's choices for their attires and their bodies remain controlled by socially sanctioned practices. The complex perception that 'inappropriate attires' contribute to the 'rape culture' are ingrained in the mindsets. The issue of 'appropriate attire' remains a highly contentious and contested issue. Considerably more research on this topic is required to determine the motives of the harassers that might lead to a valid extrapolation.

de Certeau addresses that everyday human actions may stem from emancipatory possibilities to (re)create and (re)imagine social spaces, in this case public spaces of Northeast India. He asserts that the central aim of this (re)imagination is not to fabricate as to how the 'violence of order' is transformed into a controlled behaviour through the introduction of technology but to shed light upon the varied surreptitious ways possessed by planned, dispersed or interim creativity of the groups that remain regulated by the network of controls. However, the public spaces are far more complicated than de Certeau's (re)imagination is. It suffers greatly from the legacies of 'male power' and the new emergent debate as to what constitutes appropriate dress code for women of Northeast India.

The next section discusses the precautionary measures, which has a bearing on women's spatial mobility.

Negotiating Strategies

The preceding sections have well reflected on the narratives of women's fear and the harassment faced by the sample of women in public spaces (jeers, lewd remarks, stalking) irrespective of the time of the day. Most women considered under this study access public space with a purpose: to work, study, shopping, health check-up, pick up children from school, morning walk and so on. The research also demonstrates that fear for safety in public spaces structures and restricts most women's mobility. The findings from the survey suggest that 19 per cent women usually carry sharp objects and pepper sprays when commuting alone; 25 per cent of those surveyed indicates that they avoid going out alone at all times, while

Table 2

I Never Ask for it. I have Experienced Sexual Harassment, 'Eve Teasing' in the following

Attires/Accessories	*Percentage*	*Attires/Accessories*	*Percentage*	*Attires/Accessories*	*Percentage*
School uniform	45	Sleeveless shirt	22	No lipstick	40
Capris	27	Noodle strap tee	18	Open hair	36
Churidar	36	Tube top	13	Oiled hair	13
Salwar	40	Jacket	22	Bald head	4
Trousers	31	Blazer	13	School socks	27
Shorts	22	Ghagra	13	Stockings	13
Jeans	50	long skirt	31	Bare feet	22
Burqua	9	Medium length skirt	22	With bangles	22
Dupatta	22	Short skirt	31	With finger rings	22
Sari	22	Swim suit (one piece)	9	With gloves	22
Long full-sleeve kameez	18	Swim suit (burkhini)	4	With a hat	22
Short full-sleeve kameez	18	Bikini	18	With toe rings	18
Long-sleeve t shirt	27	Red lipstick	18	Work uniform	22
Short-sleeve t shirt	27	Pink lipstick	18	Kaftan	13

Source: Blank Noise project, available at: http://blog.blanknoise.org/2008/03/i-never-ask-for-it-i-repeat-until-we.html (accessed 17 September 2012).

another 46 per cent restrict themselves from going to a certain place or venture alone especially after the dark. These findings echo previous findings conducted by Viswanath and Mehrotra (2007) in the city of Delhi. A very small percentage (5%) of those surveyed suggests that they refrain from using public transport especially during the rush hours. Approximately, 36 per cent of those surveyed avoid accessing crowded/secluded places. These restrictive approaches reflect that these women remain vulnerable when accessing public spaces. Bhanupriya, whose chain has been snatched by anti-social elements, has restricted her 'morning walk' to her own lawn, while Dipali, the domestic worker, is being fetched every day in the evening by her husband, who comes with a torch light.

In response to the question, whether they reported the incident of harassment to the police, majority of the respondents (69%) were simply embarrassed and hesitant to complain of such assaults because of the existent myth that only 'bad women' are harassed sexually (Lahiri and Bandyopadhyay, 2012), 31 per cent were afraid of reporting the crime at a police station for the fear of the social repercussions and vengeance from the perpetrator. It is, therefore, evident that the socio-cultural barriers refuse woman a space to report such crime and, thereby, seek justice (Awasthi, 2006; Viswanath and Mehrotra, 2007). Importantly, majority of the women are very well aware that most police stations are reluctant to register cases related to assaults in public (Awasthi, 2006; Viswanath and Mehrotra, 2007). According to Ramasubramanian and Oliver (2003), only one in 10,000 cases of street assaults against women in India are reported to the police. Evidently, the preconceived perceptions of most police officers unfolds that the complaints lodged by most young women are considered often as 'spurious' because these women turn up at the police stations mostly without their families or sometimes show up in 'revealing outfits' (Lahiri and Bandyopadhyay, 2012; Chatterji, 2008) that are provocative in nature (Awasthi, 2006). This argument is further fortified by the two-weeks-long sting operations conducted by <www.tehelka.com> with 30 senior public servants of the Police Department based in Delhi-National Capital Region. In response to their question whether they could dress for rape, 'a great number of policemen believe that what a woman wears is one of the reasons for rape. A conservatively dressed woman is safe, but if her clothes are 'suggestive', then she is asking for it. This is the norm.'[20] Such staggering revelations of course testify the flagrant chauvinistic attitude of the protectors of our nation against women. At the same time, such findings also unmask an inherent gender gap in the attribution of intent. Similar attitudes were reflected from few high profile officials of Northeast India. Therefore, gender sensitisation remains most essential among these officials. However, these gruesome findings help explain as to why, statistics of NCRB have registered only few cases of eve-teasing (Section 509 IPC) for all the seven states of Northeast India from 2001–2011 (Table 3), despite overwhelming evidence to the contrary (Bhattacharyya, 2009; 2010). Arguably, one does not need to scan NCRB data on sexual harassment (eve-teasing) to agree upon the fact that public spaces of Northeast India remain a hotbed of assaults against women. Even a random scrutiny of the daily newspapers/media reports and the nuanced evidences demonstrated in this research bears strong corroboration to this.

Table 3

Incidences of Sexual Harassment (Eve-teasing) (Section 509 IPC), 2001–2011

States	*2001*	*2002*	*2003*	*2004*	*2005*	*2006*	*2007*	*2008*	*2009*	*2010*	*2011*
Assam	4	7	6	11	19	10	10	2	10	20	8
Arunachal Pradesh	3	2	0	0	0	2	1	1	6	1	0
Manipur	0	0	0	0	0	0	0	0	2	0	0
Meghalaya	0	0	1	0	0	0	1	4	1	0	1
Mizoram	0	0	0	0	4	0	0	0	1	0	1
Nagaland	0	0	2	1	0	2	1	1	0	3	0
Tripura	0	0	0	0	1	0	4	4	5	9	9

Sources: Crime in India, National Crime Records Bureau, Ministry of Home Affairs, Years, 2001, 2002, 2003, 2004, 2005, 2006, 2007, 2008, 2009, 2010, 2011 available at: http://ncrb.gov.in (accessed 24 October 2012).

In summary, the research demonstrates that public spaces of Northeast India are far from salubrious. The evidence from this research unpacks the appalling experiences of women regardless of the attire they wore when accessing the public spaces of Northeast India. The nuanced analysis demonstrates that experience of each woman of my sample remain different and unique but reflects that all remain vulnerable in accessing public spaces, albeit the degree to which they are vulnerable vary from individual to individual. Although, majority of women maintain a sense of self-protectionism when out in public, the subtle narratives intensify fear of bodily assault and humiliation Therefore, the role of the state governments (SGs) remains paramount in tackling this heinous issue. In the next section, attention turns to the action that the SGs might play in redressing inequalities in the gendered public spaces and in this way, build safe and inclusive state for women of Northeast India.

Need for a Safety Audit: Intervention

Access to violence free and safe public space is the basic right of a woman. Yet, from the above analysis, it is seen that the greatest challenge relates to the alarming threat to women's safety and freedom of movement on public transport and in the course of their daily mobility in public spaces. It is in this respect that the 'disconnect' between the official rhetoric of equal opportunities for men and women and the reality of persistent gender inequality becomes clearly visible. Arguably, the state governments play a key part in determining the nature and extent of women's liberation – whether by restricting women's lives through legislation, or failing to intervene in situations of sexual discrimination and harassment. The pandemic prevalence of harassment bears a testimony to the fact that the state governments have yet to tackle this crime with the necessary visibility, available resources and of course, through its political commitment. As discussed above, even the sections 292, 292A, 294, 354, 375, 376 and 509 of the IPC are often toothless and thereby fails to be stringent and powerful enough to penalise the perpetrators with very little or no support for the victims and therefore, needs to be amended. Moreover, it is the failure on the part of the state governments and police departments to build and maintain a social environment in the public spaces of Northeast India, where such sordid acts of assaults against women is not endured. Evidently, the public spaces of Northeast India are abysmally maintained. The research illustrates the whole host of obvious flaws circumscribing the towns and cities of Northeast India. All these flaws bear serious implications not only upon the women's sense of safety but also on other vulnerable: elderly and children. For instance, if a woman is attacked in one of the dimly lit streets/no street-lights, and she hankers to flee from the perpetrator, then it is very likely that she might stumble in one of the uneven pavements or trip on to the open drains. The background of Figure 5 reflects the condition of the streets.

Figure 5

Condition of the roads

Hence, there remains a dire need for state governments to plan and undertake initiatives for gender security and safety audits by taking immediate actions to identify vulnerable spots and then to plug these flaws in public infrastructures. Greater success of such safety audit programmes will depend on partnerships between state governments and other stakeholders-women's organisations and private and civil society sector. The practical guides on *Safer Cities Programme: A Safer and Just City for All,* of the United Nations habitat and *Building Safe and Inclusive Cities for Women,*[21] published by *Jagori*, may be replicated for building a safer cities and towns of Northeast India. The 'Women-Friendly Seoul Project', Korea, which won the 2010 UN Public Service Award, provides detailed guidelines aimed at making Seoul not only safer, but also women-friendly. This project may also be referred to for designing women's needs and safety concerns for towns and cities of Northeast India. In similar lines, North-East Network (NEN) takes a nascent attempt to publish a handbook titled *Assistance for Women and Girls: Make Guwahati Safe –Who can Help? Who to Call? Where to Go? (2011)* for women to seek help(if) and (when) an occasion would arise. The handbook is a guide to a number of helplines, emergency numbers and phone numbers of police departments, police stations and media contacts of Guwahati. The guide is available on-line at the NEN website at <http://www.northeastnetwork.org/resources/handbook-make-guwahati-city-safe-women>. Similar handbooks, perhaps both in English and native languages, for other cities and towns of Northeast India would surely help hundreds and thousands of women in times of distress and need. Importantly, immediate installation of emergency helplines for women for respective states of Northeast India will definitely escalate the safety and security of the public spaces of Northeast India.

One of the small-scale initiatives taken by the police department of Government of Assam (GoA) is training 80 women police officers at Dergaon under the banner *birangana*, who would be first deployed in various locations of Guwahati city for tackling street assaults. However, it remains unclear as to how would they function: as undercover agents acting as decoys or would adopt some other strategies? A related point to reduce harassment on public transport is through the introduction of eco and user friendly women-only buses, where all sections of women including elderly and disabled can gain easy access. In order to intensify women's safety and perception of safety when commuting by public transport, the cities of Toronto and Montreal, Canada have initiated *Between Two Stops* programme for women of all sections and ages aimed at shortening the distance women have to walk at night to reach their final destinations. This women-friendly service obviously enables women of any age commuting during these hours to alight from the bus between stops. Similar programmes where women are allowed to embark/disembark between stops, especially during the odd hours might enhance women's safety to a certain extent.

Technology, such as surveillance cameras (Closed-Circuit Television or CCTV) and speed breakers, might be used to monitor these public spaces. Evidence suggests that GoA has started the process of installation of 91 CCTVs in strategic locations of Guwahati city such as traffic intersections, markets, parking spaces and malls scheduled to be completed by January 2013. Although, this is a very small number but will definitely spur the city's security. Similarly, the city of Agartala installed 20 CCTVs[22] at strategic locations in October 2012 and Shillong is heading towards the installation of CCTVs in and around the city to keep close surveillance.[23] The research fails to gather statistics on this for other towns and cities of Northeast India but more CCTVs must definitely be installed in these and other cities, towns and remote public places of Northeast India including in the public transport. In addition, presence of adequate women police force, building proper pavements with improved lighting in the city's roads and inner lanes are definitely some of the indicators that can boost confidence among women. Moreover, state governments must encourage the growth of petty shops/street vendors in the dimly lit lanes and dark alleys. This, however, does not mean that SGs must allow the growth of liquor, cigarette shops, *dhabas* and auto/taxi stands that are meant largely for and dominated by men, which in turn might make the space more uncomfortable and unsafe for women. Notwithstanding, even all these safety measures may fail to guarantee absolute safety for a woman, however, these measures may definitely play a role in preventing an assault to a large extent.

Importantly, unless and until men's attitude, gaze and their ability to accept women as equals in the public spaces does not change, women fails to access a basic right to violence free life in public (Sharma, 2010): a space where, women and girls can enjoy, express their thoughts and move about freely, while maintaining their self-respect and dignity. Most importantly, safer public spaces must be able to produce sites of camaraderie, where women are treated as individuals, relish a sense of goodwill and belongingness (de Certeau, 1984), without the fear of being assaulted. Only then, women's status will be improved in true sense of the term (Sharma, 2012).

Conclusion

The starting point of this research was an exploration of women's safety or lack of it in the public spaces of Northeast India. Alongside a questionnaire survey, it takes into account the lived experiences of women's fear for safety, which impedes most women in accessing public spaces. The research also demonstrates as to how the geographies of 'male power' is produced and performed through the public spaces of Northeast India (Allen, 2003). It also demonstrates the inability of the men to accept women as equals alongside poor urban design and awful management of public spaces. In so doing, the narratives unfold the understanding of Henri Lefebvre's *spaces of representation*. An assault of women in public space constitutes a violation of human rights and, therefore, remains a hindrance in achieving gender equality and sustainable development. Hence, gender sensitisation among all sections of society (including those responsible for protecting the civil society) remains paramount. Importantly, regular programme on topics such as 'respecting each other irrespective of gender, class, caste and creed; rights of a girl and a woman while accessing public spaces and that any type of assault against a woman is a crime, civic rights and responsibilities of every individuals; all these awareness programmes need to be held in schools, colleges, media and other social clubs'. As noted elsewhere, it is repeated again that safety, security, right to self-respect and dignity is the basic right to every woman. A 'zero tolerance message'. On any type of assaults against women and attempts to justify it must be sent to the harassers.

The research has discussed some of the safety audit measures. If implemented properly, these measures will obviously intensify public consciousness as regards to assaults against women and vulnerable groups and in this way, help users and decision-makers comprehend as to how women (as well as men) of all sections experience the public spaces in different manners. Therefore, a safety audit in Northeast India will not only promote women's right to the public spaces and their basic human right to safety but will also build safe and inclusive state for all women and thereby, gradually promote gender equality.

Notes

1. Manipur: 4 arrested, including 2 soldiers, for gangrape, *IBNlive, CNN IBN* 24 March 2012, available at: http://ibnlive.in.com/news/manipur-2-soldiers-arrested-for-gangrape/242320-3.html (accessed 30 October 2012).
2. However, quick justice has been sought to this young woman by our honourable court. Out of the 16 accused, 11 have been convicted under a number of IPC sections (143, 341, 323 and 354). All the accused have been remanded to 2 years of jail, which is inclusive of the term already served by the accused since July and a fine of INR 3,000 each.

   11 convicted in GS Road molestation case, *The Assam Tribune*, 8 December 2012, available at: http://www.assamtribune.com/epaper/dec0812/at03.html (accessed 08 December 2012).
3. Woman raped in Tripura, *The Telegraph*, Calcutta India, 01 October 2012, available at: www.telegraphindia.com (accessed 30 October 2012).
4. Woman raped in Tripura, *Yahoo! News, India*, http://in.news.yahoo.com/woman-raped-tripura-220121278.html (accessed 30 October 2012).
5. To avoid rape, stop dressing 'indecently': Naga women's body, *The Indian Express*, 7 July 2011, available at: http://www.indianexpress.com/news/to-avoid-rape-stop-dressing—indecently—naga-women-s-body/813786 (accessed 30 October 2012).

6. The survey is available at: http://www.scholarlycommunication.in/survey/index.php/survey/index/sid/821421/newtest/Y/lang/en
7. Started initially in Bangalore in 2003 by Jasmeen Patheja, the then graduate art student at the Srishti School of Art Design and Technology in Bangalore, Karnataka. It is a participatory art project that endeavours to accost and blank out lewd remarks, Bollywood songs and other inappropriate actions such as bottom slapping, stalking against women in public places. The project has now gained a national momentum and has spread to other parts of the country, namely Mumbai, Chennai, Delhi, and Kolkata. Central aim of the project is to collect testimonies from the victims of street harassment and aims to work with the victims as well as the perpetrators of this crime in an effort to transform the public perception of street sexual harassment against women (Nahar, 2008).
8. Journalist injured in attempt to stop molestation, *Hindustan Times*, 11 December 2012, available at: http://www.hindustantimes.com/Punjab/Jalandhar/Journalist-injured-in-attempt-to-stop-molestation-in-Jalandhar/SP-Article1-971086.aspx (accessed 11 December 2012).
9. Eve teasing case: Death for killers, says CM, *The Times of India*, 5 November 2011, and Assaulted by eve-teasers, man dies in Bangalore while protecting niece, *India Today*, 2 May 2012.
10. Nearly 1 in 5 women in US survey say they have been sexually assaulted, *The New York Times*, 14 December 2011, available at: http://www.nytimes.com/2011/12/15/health/nearly-1-in-5-women-in-us-survey-report-sexual-assault.html?_r=1&hp (accessed 15 August 2012).
11. Delhi survey suggests city unsafe for women, BBC News, South Asia, 9 July 2010, available at: http://www.bbc.co.uk/news/10567761 (accessed 15 August 2012).
12. City roads, bylanes still unsafe for women, *The Assam Tribune*, 4 August 2012, available at: http://www.assamtribune.com/scripts/detailsnew.asp?id=aug0412/city07 (accessed 04 August 2012).
13. Gang-raped in moving bus, girl fights for life in Delhi hospital, *The Hindu*, 17 December 2012, available at: http://www.thehindu.com/news/national/gangraped-in-moving-bus-girl-fights-for-life-in-delhi-hospital/article4208833.ece (accessed 17 December 2012).
14. Canada best G20 country to be a woman, India worst – Trust Law poll, 13 June 2012, A Thomson Reuters Foundation Service, available at http://www.trust.org/trustlaw/news/poll-canada-best-g20-country-to-be-a-woman-india-worst/(accessed 05 September 2012).
15. Domestic violence, episode 07: Danger at home, *Satyamev Jayate*, available at: http://www.satyamevjayate.in/issue07/(accessed 06 September 2012).

16. To majority of younger women, dress code is only a symbolic expression for committing an assault against women and blaming the victim for the same.
17. CJ has some 'modest' advice for women, *The Hindu*, 9 February 2008, available at: http://www.hinduonnet.com/2008/02/09/stories/2008020959100600.htm (accessed 19 May 2011)
18. *Ridha* is a kind of attire meant for Muslim women – 'a combination of a coloured loose long skirt, a short frilly cape and a hood covering the hair' (Khan, 2007: 1531).
19. Pierrie Bourdieu's habitus is a socialised norm that dictate way of behaviour and thinking, which is often created and reproduced unconsciously, 'without any deliberate pursuit of coherence... without any conscious concentration' (Bourdieu, 1984: 170)
20. The rapes will go on, available at: http://www.tehelka.com/story_main52.asp?filename=Ne140412Coverstory.asp (accessed 11 November 2012)
21. Available at: http://jagori.org/wp-content/uploads/2006/01/Building-Safe-Inclusive-Cities-for-Women_A-Practical-Guide_2011.pdf (accessed 03 October 2012).
22. Agartala to Install 20 CCTVs for Durga Puja, *North East Today*, 10 October 2012, available at: http://www.northeasttoday.in/our-states/tripura/agartala-to-install-20-cctvs-for-durga-puja/ (accessed 20 December 2012)
23. CCTV surveillance in Shillong soon, *North East Today*, 19 December 2012, available at: http://www.northeasttoday.in/our-states/meghalaya/cctv-surveillance-in-shillong-soon/accessed 20 December 2012).

References

Abdelhadi, M. (2008) 'Egypt's Sexual Harassment 'Cancer'', *BBC News*, 18 July 2008, available at: http://news.bbc.co.uk/1/hi/world/middle_east/7514567. stm, (accessed 18 July 2008)

Allen, J. (2003) *Lost Geographies of Power*. Oxford: Blackwell.

Awasthi, P. 'Crime in City', *India Together*, 30 April 2006, available at: http://www.indiatogether.org/2006/apr/gov-crime.htm (accessed 30 April 2006).

Behal, M. (2002) 'Women's Collectives in Assam: A Short History of their Status and Present Day Realities' in W. Fernandes and S. Barbora (ed.) *Changing Women's Status in India: Focus in the North-East*. Guwahati: North Eastern Social Research Centre. pp. 139–150.

Beiner, T.M. (2007) 'Sexy Dressing Revisited: Does Target Dress Play a Part in Sexual Harassment Cases'. *Duke Journal of Gender Law and Policy*, 14(125). pp. 125–152.

Bhattacharyya, R. (2013) *Are We Empowered As Yet: Lessons from the Lives of University Students of Assam*. Saarbrücken, Germany: Lap Lambert Academic Publishing.

Bhattacharyya, R. (2010) 'Eve Teasing, A Growing Menace: An Analysis of the Social Landscape of Assam'. E-Proceedings of International Geographical Union Commission Seminar, Cotton College, Guwahati, Assam, India, 11–13 December. pp. 1117–1129.

Bhattacharyya, R. (2009) *Examining the Changing Status and Role of Middle Class Assamese Women: Lessons from the Lives of University Students*, PhD thesis, Newcastle University, UK, Available at: https://theses.ncl.ac.uk/dspace/bitstream/10443/303/1/Bhattacharyya09.pdf, (accessed 2 November 2009).

Chandra, B., M. Mukherjee and A. Mukherjee. (2002) *India after Independence 1947–2000*. New Delhi: Viking by Penguin Books. 5th Impression

Chatterji, S. (2008) 'Dress Code Wars Continue'. *India Together*, 28 February, available at: http://www.indiatogether.org/2008/feb/wom-dress.htm (accessed: 28 February 2008).

Datta, A. (2009) *Syncretic Socialism in Post-Colonial West Bengal: Mobilizing and Disciplining Women for a 'Sustha' Nation-State* (PhD thesis). Vancouver: The University of British Columbia.

de Certeau, M. (1984) *The Practice of Everyday Life*, Trans. Steven Rendall. Berkeley: University of CP.

Eyles, J. (1988) 'Interpreting the geographical world: Qualitative approaches in geographical research' in J. Eyles and D.M. Smith (eds.) *Qualitative Methods in Human Geography*. Cambridge: Polity. pp. 1–16.

Faludi, S. (1992) *Backlash: The Undeclared War Against American Women*. London: Virago.

Fennell, H. (1999) 'Power in the Principalship: Four Women's Experiences'. *Journal of Educational Administration*, 37 (1). pp. 23–49.

Gupta, K.R. (2005) 'Liberalisation and Globalisation of Indian Economy' in K.R. Gupta (ed.) *Liberalisation and Globalisation of Indian Economy*. New Delhi: Atlantic. pp. 304–314.

Gupta, R. (2012) 'Sexual violence in Indian Cities'. *Open Democracy*, 4 September 2012, available at: http://www.opendemocracy.net/5050/rahila-gupta/sexual-violence-in-indian-cities (accessed 04 September, 2012).

Hopkins, P.E. (2007) Thinking Critically and Creatively about Focus Groups. *Area*, 39(4). pp. 528–535.

Khan, S. (2007) 'Negotiating the Mohalla – Exclusion, Identity and Muslim Women in Mumbai'. *Economic and Political Weekly*. pp. 1527–1533.

Kvale, S. (1996) *Interviews: An Introduction to Qualitative Research Interviewing*. London: Sage.

Lahiri, C.S. and S. Bandyopadhyay. (2012) 'Dressing the Feminine Body. *Economic and Political Weekly*, XLVII (46). pp. 20–24.

Lefebvre, H. (1991) *The Production of Space*, trans. D. Nicholson-Smith, Oxford: Blackwell.

Lefebvre, H. (2004) *Rhythmanalysis: Space, Time and Everyday Life*, trans. S. Elden and G.Moore, London: Continuum.

Maan ki awaj Pratigya, (Our mind's voice-An unbreakable oath) (mega TV serial since 2010 now finished) *Star Channel, Star Plus*, 22: 30–23:00 hours.

MacKinnon, C. (1979) *The Sexual Harassment of Working Women*. New Haven: Yale UP.

McDowell, L. (1983) 'Towards an Understanding of Gender Division of Urban Space'. *Environment and Planning D: Society and Space*, 1. pp. 59–72.

Nahar, S. (2008) 'Eve-Teasing as sexual harassment in India: Manifestation of the patriarchal Mind-Set'. Paper Presented at the Humanities Conference 08, The Sixth International Conference on New Directions in the Humanities Fatih University, Istanbul, Turkey, 15–18 July.

National Crime Records Bureau (NCRB), Ministry of Home Affairs, Government of India, available at: http://ncrb.nic.in/(accessed 30 October 2012).

Németh, J. (2009) 'Defining a Public: The Management of Privately Owned Public Space'. *Urban Studies* 46(11). pp. 2463–2490.

Oakley, A. (1981) 'Interviewing Women: A Contradiction in Terms' in H. Roberts (ed.) *Doing Feminist Research*. London: Routledge. pp. 30–61.

Pain, R. (1991) 'Space, Sexual Violence and Sexual Control: Integrating Geographical and Feminist Analyses of Women's Fear of Crime'. *Progress in Human Geography*, 15. pp. 415–431.

Pain, R. (1997a) 'Whither Women's Fear? Perceptions of Sexual Violence in Public and Private Space'. *International Review of Victimology*, 4. pp. 297–312.

Pain, R. (1997b) 'Social Geographies of Women's Fear of Crime'. *Transactions of the Institute of British Geographers*, 22(2). pp. 231–244.

Pain, R.H. (1997c) "Old age' and Ageism in Urban Research: The Case of Fear of Crime. *International Journal of Urban and Regional Research*, 21(1), 1997c, pp. 117–128.

Phadke, S. (2005) "You can be Lonely in a Crowd': The Production of Safety in Mumbai. *Indian Journal of Gender Studies*, 12(1). pp. 41–62.

Phadke, S. (2007) 'Dangerous Liaisons—Women and Men: Risk and Reputation in Mumbai'. *Economic and Political Weekly*. pp. 1510–1518.

Phadke, S., S. Khan and S. Ranade (2011) *Why Loiter? Women and Risk on Mumbai Streets*. New Delhi: Viking Penguin.

Pidd, H. (2012) 'Why is India so Bad for Women?' *The Guardian*, 23 July 2012, available at: http://www.guardian.co.uk/world/2012/jul/23/why-india-bad-for- women (accessed 30 October 2012).

Ramasubramanian, S. and M.B. Oliver. (2003) *Portrayals of Sexual Violence in Popular Hindi Films*, 1997–99. *Sex Roles*, 48(7/8). pp. 327–336.

Rose, G. (1993) *Feminism and Geography—The Limits of Geographical Knowledge*. Oxford: Blackwell.

Schwanena, T., M. Kwanband F. Renc. (2008) 'How Fixed is Fixed? Gendered Rigidity of Space–Time Constraints and Geographies of Everyday Activities'. *Geoforum*, 39(6). pp. 2109–2121.

Sharma, K. (2010) 'Fear in the City'. India Together, 22 August 2010, available at: http://www.indiatogether.org/2010/aug/ksh-harass.htm (accessed: 30 October 2010).

Sharma, K. (2012) 'No Space for Women'. India Together, 27 June 2012, available at: http://www.indiatogether.org/2012/jun/ksh-public.htm (accessed: 30 July 2012).

Silverman, D. (1993) *Interpreting Qualitative Data: Methods for Analysing Talk Text and Interaction*. Beverly Hills: Sage.

Sinha, A.K. (2005) 'India: Steps towards Liberalisation and Globalisation' in K.R. Gupta (ed.) *Liberalisation and Globalisation of Indian Economy*. New Delhi: Atlantic. pp. 315–330.

Staeheli, L.A. (1996) 'Publicity, Privacy and Women's Political Action'. *Environment and Planning D: Society and Space*, 14. pp. 601–619.

Stanley, L. and S. Wise. (1987) *George Porgie: Sexual Harassment in Everyday Life*, London: Pandora.

Starkweather, S. (2007) 'Gender, Perceptions of Safety and Strategic Responses among Ohio University Students'. *Gender, Place & Culture*, 14 (3). pp. 355–370.

Tarlo, E. (1996) *Clothing Matters: Dress and Identity in India*. London: Hurst & Company.

Valentine, G. (1989) 'The Geography of Women's Fear'. *Area*, 21. pp. 385–390.

Viswanath, K. and S.T. Mehrotra. (2007) 'Shall We Go Out?' Women's Safety in Public Spaces in Delhi, *Economic and Political Weekly*. pp. 1542–1548.

Wolf, N. (1991) *The Beauty Myth: How the Images of Beauty are Used against Women.* New York: William Marrow.

Women Friendly City Seoul, Seoul Metropolitan Government and Seoul Foundation for Women and Family, 2009.

10

Northeast India in the Era of Globalisation

N. BHUPENDRO SINGH

Ever since the term 'globalisation' appeared for the first time in the second half of the 20th century no other word has meant so many different things to different people and has evoked as much emotions. The forces of globalisation affect virtually every country in the world. It has opened the doors of many new opportunities as well as formidable challenges. All spheres of life - social, political, cultural and economic - have been subjected to both positive and negative elements of globalisation. With all its promises on the overall qualitative improvement of life and social harmony, some see it as the saviour of universal peace and prosperity. On the other hand, with the rising mercury of its negative elements some condemn it as a new kind of chaos. While everyone welcomes the new opportunities that has emerged one cannot simply leave those negative elements unattended. Therefore, the main task now is to analyse, understand and manage globalisation doing our best to harness its benefits and keep those negative consequences at bay.[1]

India joined the club of globalised economy in 1991 when its economy was under the spell of fiscal and balance of payment crisis which compel her to initiate several structural adjustment programme and economic liberalisation. Since then, India's share to the global economy is getting larger. Today, looking at overall health of the economy and growth performance[2], India seems to have struck the right note of the globalisation string. With its vast natural and human resources and ability to synchronise the speed of change taking place in the international market, many have considered India's economy as one of the most resilient economy in the world. Now, the most pertinent question that arises in the recent years is: Has the benefits of globalisation disbursed to all the regions of the Indian union? Certainly the answer is NO.

India's attempt to tackle the problems of income inequalities has been going on since Independence under the centralised planning system. It, however, failed to provide the necessary growth impetus to the poorer states to reduce regional disparities in any meaningful manner. In the post-globalisation era, considering the size and diversity of the country, shrinking role of government would ultimately be a failure to achieve the set objective. With the opening of economy, states with better infrastructure facilities, better skill labour and work culture, investor friendly environment and more importantly states which can reform themselves in accordance to the need of the market oriented economy have attracted much of the private investment – both national as well as foreign. These states have grown much faster than states which are not, leading to widening disparities.[3] This has posed a great challenge to academicians and policy-makers, even though globalisation is an uneven process with unequal distribution of benefits and losses, who needs to ensure the benefits of globalisation be distributed to all the regions/states of Indian union.

Secondly, to what extent the high growth rate achieved so far has been translated into development for the well-being of its people? It is all the more necessary to ascertain the magnitude of development because development shouldn't be seen as mere enhancement of national or personal income as it alone cannot serve the objective of securing the socio-economic equality. High growth rate achieved so far is a big accomplishment as the resources so generated could be utilised for developmental purposes to meet the desired social ends.[4] It would, however, be highly unjustified and misleading to interpret economic growth and economic development synonymously, yet a popular cynicism among the political circle in particular, as development covers much wider range and value. In short, achievement of higher growth rate should be reflected in terms of quality of life of the people.

The failure to realise the value of high growth is the main reason for the rejection of 'shining India/feel good factor' slogan of the ruling party in 2004 General Election. This implies that the higher growth rate achieved so far in the post-globalisation period could not be translated in terms of improvement in the quality of life of the common people. According to Sen, any reform programme should consists of three Rs – reach, range and reason – which every responsible individual should analyse, understand and act accordingly. The values of high growth often depend on what the size, composition and nature of that growth do to the lives and freedoms of the people involved.[5]

With the increasing concern of widening of inter-state disparities and lack of development, it is highly imperative to assess the effects of globalisation on Northeast India – a relatively uncharted region of the country – as 21 years is long enough to give some clear pictures. With this objective, the present study attempts to find the answers of the following quaries: Has the region been able to gain from the benefits of globalisation? What are the major issues and challenges confronting or likely to confront in the coming years? What are the unexplored opportunities that can be harnessed? This would require examining the prevalent scenario of the region in the pre and post globalisation period.

The present study shall cover period from 1980 to 2008, considering 1991 as the dividing year of the two periods. The study has been organised into five sections including introduction. In section II, a brief profile of Northeast states has been sketched. In section III, some of the issues and formidable challenges needed to be addressed sooner than that later has been discussed. Section IV discusses the unexplored opportunities in the region. Finally, the study is concluded in Section V.

Northeast Profile

The Northeast India comprises eight contiguous states[6] of highly undulating hilly terrains, covering 2,63,179 sq km which is about 8 per cent of the total geographical area of the country. The region is one of the landlocked regions of South Asia. About 4,500 km, i.e. 98 per cent of its border is with five different countries of South Asia – Nepal, Bhutan, China, Myanmar and Bangladesh. No other region of the Indian union share common border with so many different countries connecting with the heartland through the tenuous 22 km Siliguri corridor.

The region is the home of extraordinarily diverse mosaic of ethnic groups having distinctive social, cultural and economic identity, more akin to their South Asian neighbours than mainland India. The total population of the region is about 46 million, 3.8 per cent of the country's total population, of which Assam contributes 68.4 per cent of the total population. Assam recorded the highest density of population with 397 per sq km, which is also higher than the national average of 382 per sq km, followed by Tripura with 350 per sq km. Otherwise, the region is sparsely populated with an overall density of population of 174 per sq km.

The decennial growth rate recorded in four states during the decade (2001–11) is higher than the national level of 17.64 per cent. Meghalaya recorded the highest growth rate (27.82%), also third highest among the states of the Indian union, followed by Arunachal Pradesh (25.92%) and Mizoram (22.78%). While Assam (16.93%), Tripura (14.75%) and Sikkim (12.36%) have recorded lower growth rate than all India level. Interestingly, Nagaland, which recorded the highest decennial growth rate of

64.64 per cent in the previous decade, has recorded negative growth rate of 0.47 per cent (Table 1).

Table 1

Area and Population of Northeast India in 2011 Census (Provisional)

State	*Area (sq km)*	*Population*	*Density per sq km*	*Decennial Growth Rate (2001–11)*	*Sex Ratio*	*Literacy Rate*
Arunachal Pradesh	83,743	13,82,611	17	25.92	920	66.95
Assam	78,438	3,11,69,272	397	16.93	954	73.18
Manipur	22,327	27,21,756	122	18.65	987	79.85
Meghalaya	22,429	29,64,007	132	27.82	986	75.48
Mizoram	21,081	10,91,014	52	22.78	975	91.58
Nagaland	16,579	19,80,602	119	-0.47	931	80.11
Sikkim	7,096	6,07,688	86	12.36	889	82.20
Tripura	10,486	36,71,032	350	14.75	961	87.75
India	32,87,240	1,21,01,93,422	382	17.64	940	74.04

Source: http://www.census2011.co.in & http://censusindia.gov.in

The region is richly endowed with bio-diversity, hydro-potential, minerals like oil and natural gas, coal, limestone, dolomite, graphite, quartzite, sillimonite, etc. and forest wealth. Over 10 per cent of forest products requirement in the country are met from this region only. The region has a very high potential to generate hydropower, i.e. about 80 per cent of the total hydropower potential in the country. Arunachal Pradesh alone is expected to generate 2,67,474 MW, i.e. 30 per cent of the total available in the country.

With varied geo-climatic condition, the region is ideally suited for horticulture, floriculture and other plantation crops. A variety of fruits like pineapples, banana, orange, lemon, mango, papaya, etc. grow abundantly in the region. The region is famous for most number of orchid varieties in the country. Tea is the major plantation crop grown in the region and is the largest producer in the country contributing over 95 per cent of the total production. The region is also richly endowed with varieties of medicinal plants having high value in the international market. But, due to the lack of proper infrastructure, transport and communication system and geo-political condition of the region, these resources largely remained untapped.

The region is grossly deficient of infrastructure to tap the available resources and push the economy forward. An examination of the infrastructure index – a composite profile of the availability of physical, social and institutional infrastructure available in the states revealed that all the states of the region are at the lowest rung of the infrastructure index ladder. It shows that the level of infrastructural development in the region is almost negligible.

Table 2

Human Development and Infrastructure Index

Category	*Human Development Index*	*Infrastructure Index*
High	Mizoram	
High Middle	Manipur, Nagaland, Sikkim	
Middle	Arunachal Pradesh, Meghalaya, Tripura	
Lower Middle	Assam	
Low		Arunachal Pradesh, Assam, Manipur, Meghalaya, Mizoram, Nagaland, Sikkim and Tripura

Source: Government of India (2004).

In terms of human development index – a composite index capturing the three dimensions of human development, viz., economic, education and health – the region have done reasonably well than most of the states of Indian union (Table 2). In 2001, among the eight states, Assam ranked the lowest, which has been placed in lower middle category and Mizoram in high category while rest of the states are either in high middle or middle category.[7] According to India Human Development Report 2011, all the states other than Assam have an HDI higher than the national average of 0.467.[8] The success of these states in this regard is mainly induced by the education sector. Apart from Arunachal Pradesh and Assam the literacy rate in the remaining states, as shown in Table 1, are higher than the national average.

The economy of the region primarily depends on agriculture sector contributing over 40 per cent of the income and employ about 70 per cent of the total working population. Although NSDP share of agriculture sector has declined to about 20 per cent, the number of population dependent upon this sector continues to remain high even in the post globalisation period. The decline in the NSDP's share of agriculture sector has been more or less compensated by the increase in the share of service sector. That is, the service sector growth rate during the corresponding period is commendable. Nevertheless, the industrial sector in the region continues to be in pathetic condition. Industrially the region is one of the most backward regions in India. Only Assam, and to some extent Meghalaya, have moved ahead of the rest of the states in terms of industrial development whose industrialisation centred on tea, oil and timber.

An examination of the overall annual compound growth rate of NSDP in the region (Table 3) revealed that there is a slight improvement in post-globalisation period though it varies from state to state.

Table 3

Annual Compound Growth Rate of NSDP and Per Capita Income of Northeast States (at 1999–00 prices)

State	NSDP				Per Capita Income			
	1980–90	1991–00	2001–08	1980–08	1980–90	1991–00	2001–08	1980–08
Arunachal Pradesh	8.37	4.14	6.18	6.85**	5.03	1.68	4.91	4.31**
Assam	3.33	2.04	5.07	3.16	1.14	0.34	3.61	1.28*
Manipur	4.76	4.41	6.25	4.66	2.10	2.12	4.16	2.29*
Meghalaya	4.95*	6.40*	7.34*	5.99*	2.01*	3.69*	6.08*	3.44*
Mizoram	NA	NA	4.59	NA	NA	NA	1.97	NA
Nagaland†	7.55	5.55	5.32	6.89**	3.23	0.62	0.20	2.05**
Sikkim†	NA	6.21	7.98	7.08*	NA	3.14	6.82	4.75*
Tripura†	5.52*	7.88*	6.51	7.10*	2.46*	6.27*	5.13	5.01*
All India	5.25*	6.18	8.14	5.82*	3.03*	4.13	6.54	3.80*

Source: Institute of Applied Manpower Research (2011); NSSO (2011).

Note: † Due to the non availability of data the annual compound growth rate for Nagaland is calculated for the period 1980–2006, Tripura 1980–2007, Sikkim 1993–2008 and Mizoram 2001–08.

* denotes acceleration
** denotes deceleration

During the decade of 1980s, only Arunachal Pradesh and Nagaland experienced higher annual compound growth of NSDP than the national level. In the first decade of post-globalisation period, i.e. 1991–2000, except for Meghalaya and Tripura, the growth rate of all the remaining states drifted below that in the pre-globalisation period. These two states have even performed better than the national level. In the second decade of post-globalisation period, the growth performances in the region have improved significantly. During 2001–08, baring Tripura and Nagaland, all the states of the region have performed better than the previous decade but lower than the national level growth rate. In all the sub-period under study only Meghalaya achieved consistently higher and accelerating growth rate. The accelerating growth rate is also achieved by Tripura during 1980–90 and 1991–2000. The higher growth rate of NSDP in the region is mainly induced by higher and accelerating growth rate of service sector.

The higher growth rate of NSDP experienced in most of the states particularly during 2001–08 is not commensurate with the growth rate of per capita income. The per capita income growth rates of all the states, baring Sikkim, falls below the national level in the corresponding period. While the growth performances of Nagaland have worsened, the performances of all the remaining states have improved considerably compare to the previous decade. The lower growth rate of per capita income experienced may be attributed to high growth rate of population, particularly the poorer section of the society.

Table 4

Current Daily Status (CDS) Unemployment Rates (per 1,000) by Sex in Northeast State

State	*1993–94*				*2009–10*			
	Rural		*Urban*		*Rural*		*Urban*	
	Male	*Female*	*Male*	*Female*	*Male*	*Female*	*Male*	*Female*
Arunachal Pradesh	19	4	18	73	13	11	43	71
Assam	70	124	65	256	56	119	46	109
Manipur	22	11	50	31	40	44	53	44
Meghalaya	6	2	16	41	8	10	33	94
Mizoram	10	5	4	5	18	16	30	43
Nagaland	21	6	69	67	130	227	76	309
Sikkim	6	17	19	49	50	41	2	0
Tripura	34	104	82	215	99	312	109	435
All India	56	56	67	105	64	80	51	91

Sources: NSSO (1997): Employment and Unemployment in India, 1993–94, 50th Round, Report No. 409.
NSSO (2011): Employment and Unemployment Situation in India, 2009–10, 66th Round, Report No. 537.

In the absence of major industrial establishment and other employment opportunities in the region, unemployment rate, particularly urban educated youths, is not only high but also increasing rapidly. According to the Current Daily Status (CDS)[9], as shown in the Table 4, only Assam have experienced considerable decline in unemployment rate in both rural and urban areas for both male and female. The problem of unemployment is more or less wiped out in the urban area of Sikkim but has increased in the rural area. In the remaining states, there is a considerable increase in the unemployment rate in both rural and urban areas for both sexes. In 2009–10, the unemployment rate for both male and female was highest in Tripura followed by Nagaland. The unemployment rate in these two states was even higher than the national level. With the exception of Assam and Sikkim, the problem of unemployment in the region has grown considerably in the post-globalisation period. It is this section of the society which becomes an easy prey to the negative elements like insurgency, drug abusing, human trafficking, etc.

Table 5

Percentage of Population below the Poverty Line and Per Capita Consumption Expenditure

State	Percentage of Population below the Poverty Line				Per Capita Consumption Expenditure (Rupees per month)			
	1983	1993–94	1999–00	2004–05	1983	1993–94	1999–00	2004–05
Arunachal Pradesh	40.9	39.4	33.5	17.6	—	343.75	672.31	798.76
Assam	40.5	40.9	36.1	19.7	117.87	280.42	473.42	613.67
Manipur	37.0	33.8	28.5	17.3	133.25	305.59	596.36	663.50
Meghalaya	38.8	37.9	33.9	18.5	—	390.00	639.13	795.57
Mizoram	36.0	25.7	19.5	12.6	142.73	472.59	935.53	862.78
Nagaland	39.3	37.9	32.7	19.0	—	454.48	1,005.99	1,259.59
Sikkim	39.7	41.4	36.6	20.1	—	321.12	559.97	787.20
Tripura	40.0	39.0	34.4	18.9	—	367.43	589.50	734.79
All India	44.5	36.0	26.1	27.5	125.13	328.18	590.98	700.33

Source: NHDR (2011), pp. 266–267.

Only Mizoram seems to have done exceptionally well in poverty[10] eradication where the percentage has declined from 36 per cent in 1983 to 12.6 per cent in 2004–05. In the remaining states there is only a marginal decline in poverty ratio during the corresponding period. In 1983, the percentage of population living below the poverty line at national level is much higher than that of all the states of the region. It is just the reversal in 1999–2000 – all the states other than Mizoram have higher percentage than national level of 26.1 per cent. However, in 2004–05, the percentage of population living below the poverty line in all the states of the region has gone below the national average of 27.5 per cent. The percentage of population living below the poverty line pegged below 20 per cent. Further, an examination on the per capita per month consumption expenditure revealed that the inequality in the per capita monthly consumption expenditure has also declined with the improvement in growth performance particularly after 2000 onwards.

In 1993–94, Assam has the lowest per capita monthly consumption expenditure followed by Manipur and Sikkim. These three states are even lower than the national level of ₹ 328.18 per month. However, in 1999–2000, only Assam and Sikkim experienced lower per capita per month consumption expenditure than that of national level of ₹ 590.98 per month. The increase in consumption expenditure in the globalisation era is quite impressive. At the same time, inequality in consumption expenditure, as revealed by the Gini coefficient[11], has also increased in most of the states which is an indication of widening disparities among different sections of the society. This implies that the benefits of higher growth rate experienced, though marginally, in the post-reform period have not been tickled down to the poorer sections of the society in the desired pace and the problem of income inequality within the state has worsened.

An overall scenario of the region in the post-globalisation period is not very impressive as in the case of other region of the Indian union. This may be attributed to the prevailing geo-political condition in the region and attitude of the Central Government in tackling the issues of the region. In the following section, we shall examine some of the challenges which required an immediate attention and opportunities that can be harness.

Challenges

Being one of the most neglected regions of the Indian Union, overall state of affairs in the region is quite alarming. The unattended issues and problems of the past are being accumulated, multi-layered and have become multifarious. Over and above, the mounting pressures of emerging challenges of rapid transformation need to be countered. The clock is ticking fast and situation in the region is very delicate which may explode anytime from now if not tackled carefully. At this juncture, the old habit of alibis and hinting would only aggravate the maladies of the past and swell negative elements of the globalisation. Instead, it is the time to think and act collectively.

The region has more issues to be addressed and challenges to face than any other parts of the country. Of which, the three most important areas which require immediate attention are insurgency, infrastructure and governance. All the other issues are derivatives which would dry up once these three are addressed.

Insurgency

The problem of insurgency in the region has a long history. The insular politics and Delhi centric approach of the Indian Government is at the core of much of the discontents, widespread criticism, feelings of subjugation and notion of being colonised. There is a constant fear in the minds of the people that their identity is being eroded due to the submergence into the vast ocean of Indian humanity.[12] The people of the region started alienating themselves and the feeling of self-determination started to germinate. With the aim of preserving their own identity, various ethnic groups inhabiting in the region, undisturbed for centuries, began to differentiate among each other severing the local ties and affinities and started to struggle with arms.[13] Thus, insurgency which has mushroomed in the region, and the secessionist movements, either for sovereignty or for separate homeland, began to lock horns leading to a vertical division among various ethnic groups.

Therefore, prior to any policy programme to resolve the problem of insurgency in the region, the political processes that has been framed and pursued to convert a breeding ground of insurgencies must be reversed first. Simultaneously, the attitude and security obsess mindsets of the Central Government should also change and embrace the region with open arms so as to restore the lost confidence of the common people.

Insurgency is the major problem inflicting the region. With the passage of time, it has increasingly become more complex and difficult to understand as their objectives, role and activities varied widely.[14] In the name of nationalist movement they were involved and interfered in every state's affairs including household chores, like a moral police, of their people. Each insurgent group runs parallel government. In a way, apart from Sikkim and Arunachal Pradesh, all the remaining states have multiple governments.

The problem of insurgency has become the stumbling block in the course of development. It foundered every development strategy and hampered all the developmental works. Kidnapping, extortion, killing, *bandh*, strikes and curfews have become the order of the day. At the same time, the numbers and activities of the plain criminals masquerading as insurgents have also increased alarmingly. Today, the region has become the killing field and specialised in the export to death bodies, if not the manufacturing products. In short, the region has reached the pinnacle of the industrialisation of insurgency and criminalisation process.

It would not be easy to find the solution. However, keeping in mind the rising global terrorism, it would be wise to work on a holistic approach for amicable solution sooner than later. At the same time, what every insurgent group, operating in the region, should realise that the formation of separate homeland or attainment of more autonomy or sovereignty is not the solution because within itself formation of new group with new demand can not be ruled out.

Infrastructure

The rich natural and human resources available in the region could not be utilised to the full extent mainly due to the geo-political condition, including ever-deteriorating law and order, which has a lot of implication on the development of must needed infrastructure. The negligence of the Central Government in the past and due to the problems of insurgency at present resulted into the gross deficiency of infrastructure in the region. This has crippled the free flow of factors as well as products. In such a situation, it would be hard for the region to accrue the benefits of globalisation. It is also not surprising to find the lack of FDI inflow in the region. During April 2000 to May 2012, the region received only 73 million US dollar, i.e. 0.04 per cent of the total FDI inflow in the country.

The lack of infrastructure, as revealed by the infrastructure index given in Table 2, has not only spoiled the prospect of economic development but has also created a horizontal division among various ethnic groups affecting the fabrics of social harmony in the region. All the 'constituent states of the region are internally locked–themselves locked and locking out others, unable to connect with each other physically in terms of poor transport links, and more seriously, unable to make connections intellectually and emotionally with their closest neighbours, or even with and among their own people.'[15] It has displaced the common understanding and linkages for peaceful coexistence and regional cooperation.

In order to reconnect the lost connectivity, trade and commerce and more importantly to foster emotional attachment among various ethnic groups inhabiting in the region, infrastructures like roads, transports, communications electricity, banking, etc. must be developed adequately. Such exercise would not only enlarge the base for the growth of the economy in the region but also enhance the regional cooperation – an engine of growth in this era of globalisation.

Underdevelopment breeds insurgency and insurgency retards development. These two are mutually reinforcing. This is a classic case of vicious cycle of underdevelopment-insurgency-underdevelopment. Therefore, any policy programmes either to resolve the problems of insurgency or development of much needed infrastructure should go concurrently and not sequentially as it hampered the progress of one another.

Further, as it has been asserted in the Planning Commission report on Transforming the North-East, the approach of the Central Government should change from 'planning for the Northeast to planning with the Northeast'.[16] This implies that under the prevailing circumstances mere allocation of funds or implementation of new policy would not suffice to tackle the problems in the region. Considering the emotional sentiments of the inhabitants and sensitivity of the issues, the region must be handled with care. Every developmental programme for the region should have the consent of the inhabitants and needs to be executed with sincerity without delay.

Governance

'The state is responsible for the creation of conducive political, legal and economic environment for building individual capabilities and encouraging private initiatives.'[17] It would, however, depend on the quality of the governance–mechanism, processes, systems, structures and institutions that guide the social, economic and political relationship. Good governance exercises its legitimate political power in a manner that is perceived as equitable, non-discriminatory, socially sensitive, participatory, transparent and accountable to the people at large. This includes not only the process of transformation of human and natural endowments to a socially desired ends but also reveals the long term vision and commitment of the state to secure human well-being and sustained development of the people.[18]

The state of governance in the region is in pathetic condition. Government machinery is on the brink of collapse. Corruption, squandering of public funds, deteriorating law and order, lack of transparency and accountability, bureaucratic rigmarole, insensitivity and so forth are quite rampant in the region. There is widespread allegation of insurgency-government officials-bureaucrats-politician nexus, including law enforcing agencies, and siphoning off public funds. All this has eroded the individual capabilities and institutional capacities to meet the social objectives.

Until and unless the quality of governance has been improved, no matter how much is the fund earmarked for whatever the policy programme initiated would not be successful and only the common people have to bear the brunt. Taking into consideration of the paradigm shift in the development strategy and the amount of funds allocated[19] in recent time, we may no longer be able to blame the Central Government in the near future. The present state of affairs in the region is past deed of the Central Government and what the future generation will face would be decided by what our government has done today.

Opportunities

The economy of the region has been disrupted by the forces discussed in the preceding section in spite of her rich natural resources. Besides the natural resources, many new opportunities have also emerged with the changing contour of world economy that can boost the economy of the region. But, the need of the hour is to focus on those areas which would lead to growth of the economy, develop the sense of participation and can extinguish the social and political chasm. The two main areas that can boost the economy are as follows:

Tourism

Tourism is one sector where the region has comparative advantage. This industry is highly competitive where the tourists have a wide range of choices and look for good value of their money. With bountiful nature's breathtaking scenic beauty, salubrious climatic conditions, extraordinarily diverse rich art and cultural heritage of the people, this region can become a hotspot for eco and adventure tourism.

Tourism industry involves a vast network of business activities relating to attracting, receiving, accommodating, managing and servicing of tourists. These include hotels, restaurants, transport agency and several other related activities. The development of this industry would promote national integration and international understanding, generate employment and revenue and provide prospective buyers for local manufactured products especially handloom and handicraft products – a dying industry due to lack of access to market.

Tourism can generate more employment per million of rupees spent than any other activities. It can generate jobs in the remotest corners for unskilled to highly specialised skilled workers which would help in the realisation of plan objectives. It would also enlarge the base of locally manufactured products. All this, however, would be possible only when there is well-developed infrastructure like transport and communication and sense of participation of the people of the region.

Border Trade

The lack of connectivity and access to market, the main causes for under utilisation of resources and weak resource-industry linkages, have set the economy of the region by half a century behind. The region has lost the markets in her neighbourhood, particularly in Bangladesh, due to partition, insurgency and diplomatic strains and tensions.

Due to the peripheral location and stiff competition from mainland industries having better access to critical inputs like finance, technology and management, the base of traditional manufacturing in the region has been eroded leading to deindustrialisation. While resource base can support a variety of industries at all scales, the existing industrial structure, dominated by small-scale demand based industries has not been developed proportionately. This has widened the gap between resource base and industrial structure in the region. Further, due to the restriction of free movement of men and material across the border, the notion of isolation has developed in the minds of the people. It is in this context, that there is a strong argument to develop border trade.

In this increasingly borderless world, establishment of border trade would not only provide an opportunity to revive the local manufactured units but also serve as a transit corridor for the mainland big industrial units to explore the vast Asian market. This would also bring the centrality and visibility of the otherwise peripheral Northeastern region.[20] It is with this vision that 'look east policy' was initiated in 1991. Unfortunately, as old habits die hard; the Central Government still continues to live in the shadow of security obsessed mindset and prefers inward looking approach. As a result, even after 15 years of implementation of border trade agreement, it has failed to invigorate the region's trade with their neighbouring countries. As a result, India's look east policy has, by and large, bypassed the region.

The percentage of trade with neighbouring countries have zoomed up to 10 per cent of the country's total volume of trade in 2010–11 from a mere 1.7 per cent in 1987–88. However, over two-third of the total volume of trade with these countries flow via Bay of Bengal while the land borders of the region have been left for transit corridors for illegal trade. The tepidity of the Central Government in implementation of the policy has only led to rise in the porosity of these borderlands. An impressionistic assessment reveals that there is a rise in negative activities like cross-border insurgency, gunrunning, smuggling drugs, narcotics and AIDS, money laundering, trafficking women, illegal immigration, etc. which further add to the existing multifarious problems in the region.

Sport

The rich human resource available in the region can be utilised for developing sport as an industry, as in any advanced country of the world, if we cultured them in a systematic manner. The sporting temperament is very much present in the tradition and cultural nerves of the region. The inborn physical dexterity and latent talent of the people is also highly suited to sport. With very little resources and proper infrastructure, the sport persons of the region have proved their sporting talent in various sporting arena every now and then.

The lack of employment opportunities in the absence of big industrial establishment, many educated youths fall prey to needle and gun culture – a major problem, with which the government is trying to find an entry point to tackle. The utilisation of available human resources in the development of sport can prevent youths of the region from indulging into anti-social activities, to some extent if not all, as the disciplined life and strict dietary habit of a sportsmanship would divert their mindsets. Sport provides young people to learn core skills such as discipline, confidence, leadership, tolerance, cooperation and respect. It also teaches the value of effort and how to manage victory as well as defeat. Further, the development of sport can reduce the ever growing ethnic conflict and communal tension boiling in the region as sport is all about participation and inclusion, bringing individual and communities together. The development of sport can provide responsible citizens required for building a strong nation. Besides, it would also generate employment as well as revenue resulting from manufacturing sporting goods, holding sports events, providing sport related services and the media. Over and above, sport is one of the most cost effective measures for cutting healthcare cost.[21] The region can be a major tourist destination if various traditional sport and game are properly developed. Thus, development of sport in the region can assist in realising the socio-economic objectives of the plans.

Unfortunately, despite the achievement of numerous sporting laurels both at the national and international arena by the sport persons of the region, the government, both at the Centre and States has failed to realise the benefits of developing sport in the country. The performance of our athletes in every Olympic Game bears testimony to the development of sport in the country. All this can be attributed to lack of incentive, infrastructure and excessive political interference. The country's obsession with cricket must change. What one should not forget is that other sport can also win prestige, fame and commercial value, like cricket. If so, with an adequate incentive and development of sport's infrastructure, the region could become the powerhouse of the Indian sports.

Conclusion

Globalisation has become the most potent force that emerged in recent time. It virtually affects every walk of life – positive or negative. Unlike other regions of the Indian union, Northeast India is more likely to be swamped by its negative effects. The region is at the throes of discernible crisis. Since 1991, there has been increase in inequality and unemployment, decline in the quality of the governance, rise in smuggling, trafficking, illegal immigration, corruption, squandering of public funds, escalation in insurgency related activities, etc. These have led to underdevelopment and erosion of the capacity of the individual and quality of life. A sense of deprivation has developed particularly among the educated youths of the region. The clock is ticking fast and fuse is not long. It is time to work on a holistic approach to resolve the problems in the region.

Notes

1. Chanda, Nayan, 2003, 'What is Globalization? Coming Together: Globalization Means Reconnecting the Human Community', YaleGlobal Online, http://www.globalenvision.org/library/8/567.
2. Recently it has been argued that the turning point of higher growth rate in India was 1980 but not 1991 as perceived by many. For more details see Nayyar, Deepak. 2006. 'Economic Growth in Independence India: Lumbering Elephant or Running Tiger?', *Economic and Political Weekly*, Vol. 41, No. 15, pp. 1451–1458.
3. Some authors even argued that coastal states with open port facility have outperformed non-coastal states in the post globalization era. For more detail see Kishore, Adharsh. 2002. *Towards an Indian Approach to Globalization*,http://www.rba.gov.au/PublicationsAndResearch/Conferences /2002/kishore.pdf.
4. Sen, Amartya, 2005, 'The Three R's of Reforms', *Economic and Political Weekly*, Vol. 40, No. 19, p. 1.
5. ibid., p. 1.

6. Sikkim becomes the member of North-East Council on December 2002 after an amendment of the NEC Act 1971. Since then all development purposes of the state has been treated at per with the other seven states of the region. However, the addition of Sikkim in the Northeastern Region is yet to be reflected in the literature of NER.
7. GOI. 2004. *Report of the Twelve Finance Commission*, Ministry of Finance, Government of Rajasthan. http://finance.rajasthan.gov.in/doc/12fcreng.pdf, p. 61.
8. India Human Development Report 2011 have given only this statement and did not provide the neither the state ranking according to HDI nor the index value of all the states of the region other than Assam. See IAMR. 2011. *India Human Development Report: Towards Social Inclusion*, New Delhi: Oxford University Press, p. 22.
9. The Report of the Special Group on Targeting Ten Million Employment Opportunities per Year over the Tenth Plan Period has viewed that Current Daily Status (CDS) is the better measure to capture unemployment than Usual Principal and Subsidiary Status (UPSS).
10. The expert committee report on the methodology for estimation of poverty have given the statewise percentage of population below the poverty line for 2004–05 and 2009–10 and have shown completely different picture. For more detail see GOI (2009): *Report of the Expert Group to Review the Methodology for Estimation of Poverty*, Planning Commission and GOI (2012): *Press Note on Poverty Estimates, 2009–10*, Planning Commission.
11. The National Human Development Report 2001 provides the estimate of Gini Coefficient for rural and urban area only. It does not provide the combine estimate of the two. However, looking into the estimate for rural and urban area one can easily conclude that there an increase in the inequality of per capita consumption expenditure. For 2004–05, see the state-wise Lorenz Ratio given in NSSO. 2006. *Level and Pattern of Consumer Expenditure 2004–05*, 61st Round, Report No. 508, p. 45.
12. Verghese, B.G. *Unfinished Business in the North East: Pointers Towards Restructuring, Reform, Reconciliation and Resurgence*, Seventh Kamal Kumari Memorial Lecture, http://www.freeindiamidia.com/economy/19_june_economy.htm.
13. ibid.
14. Roy, Sanjay K. 2005. 'Conflicting Nations in North-East India', *Economic and Political Weekly*, Vol. 40, No. 21, pp. 2176–2182.
15. Prabhakra, M.S. 2004. 'Is North-East India Landlocked?', *Economic and Political Weekly*, Vol. 39, No. 42, p. 4608.

16. GOI. 1997. *Transforming the North East: Tackling Backlogs in Basic Minimum Services and Infrastructure Needs*, High Level Commission Report to the Prime Minister, Planning Commission, http://planning commission.nic.in/reports/genrep/ne_exe.pdf, p. 2.
17. GOI. 2001. *National Human Development Report*, Planning Commission, http://planningcommission.nic.in/reports/genrep/nhdrep/nhdreportf. htm, p. 114.
18. ibid., p. 114.
19. Apart from all the constituent states being classified as Special Category States, establishment of NEC and induction of DoNER speaks the volume of fund allocated to this region.
20. Verghese, B.G., op. cit.
21. UN. 2003. Sport for Development and Peace: Towards Achieving the Millennium Development Goals, http://www.un.org/wcm/webdav/ site/sport/shared/sport/pdfs/Reports/2003_inter-gency_report_ENGL ISH.pdf.

Reference

Ahluwalia, Montek S. (2000) 'Economic Performance of States in Post-Reforms Period'. *Economic and Political Weekly*, Vol. 35, No. 19. pp. 1637–1648.

Bajpai, M. (2002) 'A Decade of Economic Reforms in India: The Unfinished Agenda', Working Paper no. 89, Center for International Development, Harvard University, http://www.ksg.harvard.edu/CID/cidwp/089.pdf.

Barbora, Sanjay. (2006) 'Rethinking India's Counter-insurgency Campaign in North-East'. *Economic and Political Weekly*, Vol. 41, No. 35. pp. 3805–3812.

Baruah, Sanjib. 'The Problem', http://www.manipuronline.com/North-East/ November2005/theproblem23_2.htm.

Bhattacharya, B.B. and S. Sakthivel. (2004) 'Regional Growth and Disparity in India: A Comparison of Pre and Post-Reform Decades', http://iegindia.org/worksakthi244.pdf.

Chanda, Nayan. (2003) 'What is Globalization? Coming Together: Globalization means reconnecting the human community', http://www. globalenvision.org/library/8/567.

Ghosh, Madhusudan. (2006) 'Economic Growth and Human Development in Indian States'. *Economic and Political Weekly*, Vol. 41, No. 30. pp. 3321–3329.

Government of India. (1997) 'Transforming the North East: Tackling Backlogs in Basic Minimum Services and Infrastructure Needs', High Level

Commission Report to the Prime Minister, Planning Commission, http://planningcommission. nic.in/reports/genrep/ne_exe.pdf.

Government of India. (2001) 'National Human Development Report', Planning Commission, http://planningcommission.nic.in/reports/genrep/nhdrep/nhdreportf.htm.

Government of India. (2002) 'Report of the Committee on India Vision 2020', Planning Commission, http://planningcommission.nic.in/reports/genrep/pl_vsn 2020.pdf.

Government of India. (2004) 'Report of the Twelfth Finance Commission (2005–10)', Ministry of Finance, http://finance.rajasthan.gov.in/doc/12fcreng.pdf.

Government of India. (2009) *Report of the Expert Group to Review the Methodology for Estimation of Poverty*, Planning Commission, http://planning commission.nic.in/reports/genrep/rep_pov.pdf.

Government of India. (2012) *Press Note on Poverty Estimates, 2009–10*, Planning Commission, http://planningcommission.nic.in/news/press_pov1903.pdf.

Grare, Frederic and Amitabh Mattoo. (2003) *Beyond the Rhetoric: The Economics of India's Look East Policy*. New Delhi: Manohar Publishers & Distributors.

Gupta, K.R. (2005) 'Liberalization and Globalization of Indian Economy' in K.R. Gupta (ed.) *Liberalization and Globalization of Indian Economy*, Vol. VI. New Delhi: Atlantic Publishers and Distributors. pp. 304–315.

Humanshu. (2007) 'Recent Trends in Poverty and Inequality: Some Preliminary Results'. *Economic and Political Weekly*, Vol. 42, No. 6. pp. 497–508.

Institute of Applied Manpower Research. (2011) *India Human Development Report 2011: Towards Social Inclusion*. New Delhi: Oxford University Press.

Khanna, Sushil. (2005) 'Economic Opportunities or Continuing Stagnation', http://www.manipuronline.com/Economy/November2005/stagnation oropportuny18_1.htm.

Kishore, Adharsh. (2002) 'Towards an Indian Approach to Globalization', http://www.rba.gov.au/PublicationsAndResearch/Conferences/2002/kishore.pdf.

Kurian, N.J. (2000) 'Widening Regional Disparities in India: Some Indicators'. *Economic and Political Weekly*, Vol. 35. No. 7. pp. 538–550.

Nayyar, Deepak. (2006) 'Economic Growth in Independent India. Lumbering Elephant or Running Tiger?' *Economic and Political Weekly*, Vol. 41, No. 15. pp. 1451–1458.

NSSO. (1997) *Employment and Unemployment in India, 1993–94*, 50th Round, Report No. 409.

NSSO. (2006) *Level and Pattern of Consumer Expenditure, 2004–05*, 61st Round, Report No. 508.

NSSO. (2006) *Employment and Unemployment Situation in India, 2004–05*, 61st Round, Report No. 515.

NSSO. (2011) *Employment and Unemployment Situation in India, 2009–10*, 66th Round, Report No. 537.

Prabhakra, M.S. (2004) 'Is North-East India Landlocked'. *Economic and Political Weekly*, Vol. 39, No. 42. pp. 4606–4608.

Ramachandran, H. 'Governance and People's Participation', 15 Background Paper: Vision 2020, http://planningcommission.nic.in/reports/genrep/reportsf.htm.

Roy, Sanjay K. (2005) 'Conflicting Nations in North-East India'. *Economic and Political Weekly*, Vol. 40, No. 21. pp. 2176–2182.

Sen, Amartya. (2005) 'The Three R's of Reforms'. *Economic and Political Weekly*, Vol. 40, No. 19. pp. 1971–1974.

Sinha, A.K. (2005) 'India: Steps Towards Liberalization and Globalization' in K.R. Gupta (ed.) *Liberalization and Globalization of Indian Economy*, Vol. VI. New Delhi: Atlantic Publishers and Distributors. pp. 315–330.

Sinha, Aseema. 'Globalization, Rising Inequality, and New Insecurities in India', http://209.235.207.197/imgtest/TaskForceDiffIneqDevSinha.pdf.

UN. (2003) *Sport for Development and Peace: Towards Achieving the Millennium Development Goals*, http://www.un.org/wcm/webdav/site/sport/shared/sport/pdfs/Reports/2003_intergency_report_ENGLISH.pdf.

Upadhyay, Archana. (2006) 'Terrorism in the North-East: Linkages and Implications'. *Economic and Political Weekly*, Vol. 41, No. 48. pp. 4993–4999.

Verghese, B.G. 'Unfinished Business in the North East: Pointers Towards Restructuring, Reform, Reconciliation and Resurgence', Seventh Kamal Kumari Memorial Lecture, http://www.freeindiamidia.com/economy/19_june_economy.htm.

Index